Scientific Models
for Religious Knowledge

Scientific Models for Religious Knowledge

Are the Scientific Study of Religion
and a Religious Epistemology Compatible?

ANDREW RALLS WOODWARD

☙PICKWICK *Publications* · Eugene, Oregon

SCIENTIFIC MODELS FOR RELIGIOUS KNOWLEDGE
Are the Scientific Study of Religion and a Religious Epistemology Compatible?

Copyright © 2018 Andrew Ralls Woodward. All rights reserved. Except for brief quotations in critical publications or reviews, no part of this book may be reproduced in any manner without prior written permission from the publisher. Write: Permissions, Wipf and Stock Publishers, 199 W. 8th Ave., Suite 3, Eugene, OR 97401.

Pickwick Publications
An Imprint of Wipf and Stock Publishers
199 W. 8th Ave., Suite 3
Eugene, OR 97401

www.wipfandstock.com

PAPERBACK ISBN: 978-1-5326-6018-4
HARDCOVER ISBN: 978-1-5326-609-1
EBOOK ISBN: 978-1-5326-6020-7

Cataloging-in-Publication data:

Names: Woodward, Andrew Ralls, author.

Title: Scientific models for religious knowledge : are the scientific study of religion and a religious epistemology compatible? / Andrew Ralls Woodward.

Description: Eugene, OR: Pickwick Publications, 2018. | Includes bibliographical references and index.

Identifiers: ISBN: 978-1-5326-6018-4 (paperback). | ISBN: 978-1-5326-609-1 (hardcover). | ISBN: 978-1-5326-6020-7 (epub).

Subjects: LCSH: Religion and science. | Knowledge, Theory of.

Classification: BL240.3 W661 2018 (print). | BL240.3 (epub).

Manufactured in the U.S.A.   10/01/24

For R.
With whom I found my river
2024

Contents

Prologue and Note to Readers | ix
Acknowledgements | xi

Part 1: Systems of Human Beliefs— Knowledge Claims and Belief Claims

1 Background Information and Assumptions | 3
2 Knowledge Claims and Belief Claims | 35
3 Attitudes of Mind toward Testing Beliefs | 57

Part 2: Science and Religion Compatibility Systems

4 What Is a Compatibility System? Who Is It For? | 77
5 Presentation of Potential Compatibility Systems | 106
6 Philosophical Models in Scientific Life | 122
7 Philosophical Models in Religious Life | 136

Part 3: A Scientific Study of Religious Activity and a Religious Epistemology

8 A Scientific Study of Religious Activity | 149
9 Designing a New Religious Epistemology for a Scientific Study of Religion | 162
10 What about the "Beyond"? Two Pathways Moving Ahead: Ultimism and an Inductive Faith | 183

Bibliography | 223
Index | 231

Prologue and Note to Readers

WHEN A HUMAN WRITES or types the word "G-o-d" (a series of three characters typed on a computer screen or a series of lines and curls created using ink), or when a human says the word "God" (a physical vibration of the vocal cords, producing "g," "ah," and "d" sounds), all sorts of different *ideas* about what this *God* is or isn't generally get brought to mind for that person. And, for other people, *other* ideas about what this *God* is or isn't get brought to mind as well. No wonder, then, that there is such a lack of consensus about religious ideas and concepts, such as *God*—or about, say, *Myth*—among religious devotees . . . a lack of consensus about what exactly a suitable religious epistemology *is* within the academic context of a modern research university.

A religious epistemology includes the methodological form of nontested yet faith-imbued beliefs—but in modern universities what could that elusive methodological form be? On the other hand, it is generally argued by philosophers of science that there *is a consensus*—among scientific practitioners and engineers—about what a scientific epistemology is and what the modern scientific method amounts to. A scientific epistemology includes the methodological form of tested beliefs—a distinguishing feature of the stored-up, human knowledge, which is taught in modern universities. In short, there is no confusion about what science is, but "confusion" seems to abound concerning what "religion" is . . .

Adding to this "confusion" is the fact that most comparisons and contrasts of science and religion are really comparisons and contrasts of science and Christianity, or science and Islam, etc. In *Scientific Models for Religious Knowledge*, we aim to get outside of typical, polarized debates between traditional, *a priori* theism and radical, scientistic naturalism. Instead, a new science and religion compatibility system—between *a scientific study of religion* and *a religious epistemology*—is our new, elusive problem. Moreover, we shall look at a comparison and contrast of "science and religiosity *simpliciter*"—a comparison and contrast of modern science with what is (by many accounts) the simple deference of the human mind to the actions of culturally postulated superhuman agents.

To foster the exploration of our new science and religion compatibility system (between a scientific study of religion and a religious epistemology), we shall develop and apply a new concept which I call *igmythicism*—in fact, an extension of philosopher Paul Kurtz's *igtheism*. In this book, the novel igmythicism will aim to "open our minds" to a *new* science and religion discourse, one centred on a *new* conception of *myth*. As in *igtheism*, the prefix *ig*, from *ig-mythicism*, is derived from the word *ignorant*, although *ignorant* does not imply a negative attitude *per se* toward *myth*. Rather, the "ignorance" of igmythicism will refer to our realization that the statement "*myths are descriptions of physical reality*" is in fact a nonsensical statement! Yet, in a creative, practical move, igmythicism will provide us with an opportunity to clarify—to eliminate—the "ignorance" of traditional myths by suggesting a new, alternative conception of *myths*—*myths* as *symbolic, human-sourced representations of physical reality*.

To that end, *Scientific Models for Religious Knowledge* presents its own thesis, yet, in a "religiously neutral" fashion (as it were), keeps itself *open* to the personal motivations of *atheists*, *theists*, *agnostics*, and *igtheists* alike. It is my hope that graduate students, scholars, upper-year undergraduates, and general non-fiction readers—*who are looking for more open-ended, dispassionate approaches to the philosophies of science and religion*—will be drawn to the igmythicism explored here as well as to its unique constructive theology, contextualized in a modern scientific cosmos. Creatively, readers who identify as atheist, theist, agnostic, *or* igtheist, and especially those readers least able to understand *myths* in a literal sense, will be interested in the argument set forward in this book. From start to finish, this book will pay critical attention to the contributions of scholars in the philosophy of religion, the philosophy of science, and the scientific study of religion. Authors covered include Paul Kurtz, Donald Wiebe, Peter L. Berger, Susan Haack, J. L. Schellenberg, Karl R. Popper, and William Warren Bartley. Expositions will show that igmythicism is not entirely new—that, as a framework for resolving science and religion debates, igmythicism is not just being "pulled out of thin air." In this sense, *Scientific Models for Religious Knowledge* is also a helpful, pedagogical resource—useful for readers and students who are looking to expand and tweak their learning in the philosophies of science and religion . . . as these subjects are taught, analyzed, and evaluated, in our modern research universities.

Acknowledgements

THIS BOOK AROSE FROM my Doctor of Theology (ThD) research thesis, defended in 2016, at the University of Toronto. Around that time, I was a graduate student and adjunct professor in the philosophy of science and religion at the University of Trinity College, located in the University of Toronto. Prior to the ThD, I completed degrees in engineering chemistry (undergraduate) and theological studies (master's). As I began to get my bearings with more philosophy-centred work, in philosophical theology and the philosophy of science and religion, some very kind scholars mentored me throughout that process: Particular thanks go to my fantastic thesis director and friend, Professor Donald Wiebe, and to my external thesis examiner, Professor John L. Schellenberg—whose thoughtful comments and unique ideas were very important to me. Even though at times Don and John might disagree with one another's arguments, and although they might have some scruples about my conclusions in this book, I feel very privileged to have learned from their respective philosophical designs and/or nonsectarian philosophies of religion!

Also, although I never knew him, I count Professor Ninian Smart (who died in 2001) as one of my mentors, too—by way of my teacher, Don Wiebe, who was one of Ninian's students. If there is such a thing as an "academic genealogy," then I am glad to trace the evolution of my learning through my own teachers as well as through the teachers who taught them. On that note, thanks also to the following teachers, who I crossed paths with during my doctorate: Professors David Neelands, Marsha Aileen Hewitt, Thomas E. Reynolds, Abraham H. Khan, and James Robert Brown—who all provided me with useful ideas, or asked me incisive questions, which always helped me to clarify my own thoughts and to move forward with my writing.

Throughout my studies in engineering, theology, and philosophy, I also benefited greatly from conversations with mentors outside university, or close friends, whose thoughtful guidance I am so grateful for: Whether it was discussing philosophical or religious ideas with them, or relying on them for some advice or direction, thank you to Don McLean Aitchison, Stephen Vail, Malcolm J. A. Horsnell, Don Workman, Margaret M. Evans, and Anne Alexander.

Andrew Ralls Woodward
Toronto, 2018

PART 1

Systems of Human Beliefs
Knowledge Claims and Belief Claims

Ah, that he could pass again into his neutrality! Who can thus avoid all pledges and, having observed, observe again from the same unaffected, unbiased, unbribable, unaffrighted innocence—must always be formidable.

—RALPH WALDO EMERSON, *SELF-RELIANCE* (1841)

1

Background Information and Assumptions

INTRODUCTION, PURPOSE, AND DEFINITIONS OF TERMS

Epistemology is a central area of analytic philosophy. Epistemology includes our look into the methodological forms (or structures) of propositional beliefs.[1] The methodological forms of propositional beliefs are those special methodologies and philosophical thinking strategies through which humans justify how it is that they can acquire beliefs about the physical world. For example, in a modern university, the epistemic structure of an empirical theory is the methodological form of scientific beliefs. In contrast, in a modern university, what a suitable methodological form is for religious beliefs seems less clear or understood. About epistemology, both the philosophy of science and philosophical theology (philosophy of religion) raise epistemological questions. For instance, questions about *knowledge claims* and *belief claims*: (i) What kinds of knowledge claims are legitimate and

---

1. At the start of the book, in this initial paragraph, I identify *beliefs* as *propositional beliefs*, which refer, most generally, to various systems of human beliefs, whether *scientific beliefs, religious beliefs*, or *beliefs arising from any other kinds of human inquiry*. In this same paragraph, I then go on to distinguish between (a) *tested beliefs* in scientific practice and (b) *non-tested yet faith-imbued beliefs* in religious life. In the remainder of the book, I deal with the general concept of *propositional beliefs* by following and maintaining this useful, epistemic distinction between (a) *tested beliefs* in scientific practice and (b) *non-tested yet faith-imbued beliefs* in religious life.

what kinds are not? (ii) How do we adjudicate the acceptability of a knowledge claim; the acceptability of a belief claim?

Epistemology is relevant to both science and religion, because both scientific and religious exercises involve the making of conjectures about states of affairs in the physical world. As human beings, we might mentally possess or utilize various propositional beliefs about states of affairs in the physical world. When demarcating, then, between scientific beliefs and religious beliefs, we can make an epistemic distinction between (a) *tested beliefs* in scientific practice and (b) *non-tested yet faith-imbued beliefs* in religious life. For the sake of a typology, in this book I shall connect the *tested beliefs* of science to what are called *knowledge claims*, and connect the *non-tested yet faith-imbued beliefs* of religion to what are called *belief claims*.[2] A knowledge claim in scientific practice might entail the chemist's proposition: "an atom is the smallest physical piece of a chemical substance." A belief claim in religious life might entail the theist's testimony: "a superhuman agent called 'God' intervenes in the physical world." From the outset, my typology, however useful as a heuristic, may appear to some to favour the modern scientific enterprise: I do connect what seems to be the intellectually robust phrase *knowledge claims* with the tested beliefs of science, leaving the more skeptically evocative phrase *belief claims* to be connected with the scientifically non-tested beliefs of religion. I acknowledge this possible "distinguishing" of the modern scientific enterprise; it will be addressed in my arguments. Without delay, let us begin.

The preceding terminology of *claim(s)*—applied in the phrases *knowledge claim(s)* and *belief claim(s)*—is quite deliberate on my part. I will now take a few paragraphs to unpack this terminology, also hopefully alleviating any concerns for those who might find this terminology a bit peculiar. First to *knowledge claims*: In various instances, some of the professors of science and religion, whose projects I shall analyze in this book, utilize the terminology of *knowledge claim(s)*. For example, postmodernist philosopher, Mikael Stenmark, suggests that, among other things, "belief in God is typically a direct *knowledge claim*."[3] In a different context, the postfoundationalist philosopher, J. Wentzel van Huyssteen, speaks of the "provisional and fallibilist nature of all of our *knowledge claims*."[4] Humanist philosopher, Paul Kurtz, argues that "a meaningful *knowledge claim* may be mistaken; but at

---

2. To be developed further, my typology is based, in part, on the Thomistic distinction between (i) a claim *known*—the intellect is compelled to assent by the proposition itself, and (ii) a claim *believed*—the intellect is compelled to assent by a faith-imbued belief about the proposition.

3. Stenmark, *How to Relate Science and Religion*, 80; emphasis added.

4. Van Huyssteen, *The Shaping of Rationality*, 86; emphasis added.

least in principle it can be disconfirmed."[5] And, finally, longtime advocate for the scientific study of religion, Donald Wiebe, writes that "*knowledge claims* alone provide an 'entry permit' to our world."[6]

My choice, then, of the terminology of *knowledge claim(s)*, is at least shared by other writers; however, unpacking my conception of *knowledge claims* is helpful to clear up any confusion, especially where my use of this terminology might differ from what others have in mind. For our purposes, in this book, consider that a *knowledge claim*—made by a knowledge claimant—involves four conceptual components:

1. A *cognitive state*, encompassing the knowledge claimant's attempt to know the physical world.

2. A *specially certified proposition*—i.e., a *tested belief*—which is the *object* of the preceding cognitive state.

3. A *verbal statement* made by the knowledge claimant that he or she mentally possesses (in this case) a *tested* belief. Moreover, that this tested belief is *open* to external analysis by outside parties.

4. Most importantly, some *reasons*, provided by the knowledge claimant, which are used to attempt to convince (and ideally assure) outside parties that the knowledge claimant's tested belief in fact constitutes justified, human knowledge. The claimant's *reasons* may be thought of as *epistemic standards* used to adjudicate the claim's proposition. Here, I suggest that we think of the analogy of an *insurance claim*: When making an insurance claim, the insurance claimant attempts to convince an outside party—in this case, the insurance company—that his or her account of events is accurate. This requires providing *reasons* for why the insurance company should accept the insurance claim as legitimate.

Next, about *belief claims*:[7] Belief claims, made by belief claimants, share two of the four components of knowledge claims, but *probably* not all four.

---

5. Kurtz, *The New Skepticism*, 94–95; emphasis added.
6. Wiebe, *The Irony of Theology*, 220; emphasis added.
7. Like the terminology of *knowledge claims*, the terminology of *belief claims* is also used by other science and religion writers. For example, Don Wiebe, in his essay *Is Religious Belief Problematic?* (1994) in *Beyond Legitimation: Essays on the Problem of Religious Knowledge*, writes, "Religion is, to be sure, more than intellectual assent to *belief claims* (propositions, statements, etc.), since it involves the adoption of a particular style of life and a commitment to a peculiar set of moral ideals" (1994, 17–18; emphasis added). Then, in the same essay, Wiebe argues, "Whether . . . a particular religious *belief claim* is acceptable or not is not easily settled for such claims are often 'peculiar'—not straightforward as are most empirical or theoretical scientific claims"

I say *probably*, because, at this stage, my analysis is still too premature to argue convincingly that belief claims differ, epistemically, from knowledge claims. (Similar to our characterization of a knowledge claimant, as your author, I, too, must provide *reasons* for my arguments, which I shall develop throughout this book.) However, at first glance, consider that a *belief claim*—made by a belief claimant—involves two conceptual components:

1. A *cognitive state*, encompassing the belief claimant's attempt to know the physical world.

2. A *verbal statement* made by the belief claimant that he or she mentally possesses (in this case) a *non-tested* belief.

So, in my preceding scheme, belief claims do not include specially certified propositions (component (ii) for knowledge claims), nor do they include reasons (epistemic standards), which would be used to attempt to convince outside parties that the belief claimant's non-tested belief constitutes justified, human knowledge (component (iv) for knowledge claims). Belief claims do not include specially certified propositions, precisely because the objects of the cognitive states of belief claims are *non-tested beliefs* instead of tested beliefs. I should mention that belief claims might include *propositions of some kind*—i.e., *scientifically non-tested beliefs*—but the point is that the propositions of belief claims are not specially certified propositions. Moreover, the non-tested beliefs of belief claims do *not* appear to be open to external analysis by outside parties. (In the spirit of open-mindedness, I will accept that *some* non-tested beliefs of *some* belief claims might be open to *some* external analysis by outside parties, but, as we shall see later, this is not the norm in practice.) Finally, belief claims do not include reasons, which would be used to adjudicate their non-tested beliefs, because, as mentioned, belief claims in general do not appear to be open to external analysis by outside parties. Put simply, belief claimants do not seem to require reasons to support their non-tested beliefs. (Hence, the insurance claim analogy is irrelevant when discussing belief claims.)

Returning now to the purpose of this book, the question of whether—and in what fashion—a belief claim (religion) is epistemically different from

---

(1994, 28; emphasis added). Note, however, that my account of *belief claims* is slightly broader than Wiebe's account of *belief claims* when Wiebe states that "religion is, to be sure, more than intellectual *assent to belief claims (propositions, statements, etc.)*" (1994, 17; emphasis added). Whereas Wiebe speaks of *assent to* belief claims (propositions, statements, etc.), I already include the activity of assent *within* my conception of belief claims—as the *verbal statement* (in a belief claim) made by the belief claimant that he or she mentally possesses a non-tested belief (or a non-tested proposition, a non-tested statement, etc.).

a knowledge claim (science) is central to this book's concern with the possible compatibility of science and religion. However, providing an answer to that question, where the intents and purposes of both knowledge claims *and* belief claims are respected, will be difficult. Nevertheless the distinction between these two types of claims, at least in so far as any distinction is applied in one's life or in one's academic work, seems not always clear or understood. Thus, throughout this book, we shall often consider the question: *under what circumstances (if any) might science and religion be compatible*? Furthermore, which individuals, academic disciplines, or professional groups, may possess the interest to design and build a compatibility system between science and religion? Phrasing the question in more candid but not unreasonable terms, as twenty-first-century scholars situated in the context of Western intellectual life, should we even care about potential science and religion compatibility?

As mentioned, this book will explore the implications of both knowledge claims in scientific practice and belief claims in religious life. I shall argue that one can achieve some compatibility between knowledge claims in science and belief claims in religion by designing and implementing a *philosophical theory of rationality* in one's life and in one's academic work. This theory of rationality will allow us to *test* the propositional beliefs of knowledge claims, and, if at all possible, to test the propositional beliefs of belief claims. In both instances, *propositional beliefs* refer to *beliefs about states of affairs in the physical world*. The goal of this book, then, is to defend the two-fold thesis statement outlined as follows:

1. A *theory of rationality* refers to a philosophical system for *testing* the propositional beliefs of knowledge claims, and, if possible, testing the propositional beliefs of belief claims. In both instances, *propositional beliefs* refer to *beliefs about states of affairs in the physical world*.

2. If a philosopher or theologian is successful in designing a *compatibility system between science and religion*, the compatibility system will be based on a theory of rationality which *consistently* tests the propositional beliefs of knowledge claims, and, if possible, the propositional beliefs of belief claims. Looking ahead, our goal will be to attempt to design a compatibility system (of some kind) specifically between *a scientific study of religion* and *a religious epistemology*—for special application in a modern university setting.

Any nonsectarian, academic project includes substantive assumptions which any writer brings to his or her project. For the sake of clarity and to avoid the unintended formulation of circularities, it seems reasonable that, in philosophy of science and philosophical theology, as few substantive assumptions as possible be utilized in a project. (For similar reasons, in scientific research, as few experimental variables as possible to carry a scientific project through to completion is desirable.) This philosophical project includes two substantive assumptions. Both assumptions carry high degrees of initial plausibility in modern research universities. The two substantive assumptions are outlined as follows:

1. *Phenomenal reality provides a standard of observed experiences used for testing beliefs about states of affairs in the physical world.* It is important to note that, in this first assumption, observed experiences used for testing beliefs are *intersubjectively available*, observed experiences of phenomenal reality.

2. *Religious people's testimonies inform us that religious people possess beliefs about superhuman agents and/or beliefs about trans-empirical worlds.* It is important to note that, in this second assumption, beliefs about which religious people testify are beliefs interpreted *phenomenologically*—that is, the religious individual's *mindset* as that mindset *is understood by* the individual who is testifying about (reporting) the belief experience. In this assumption, the *relevances* of beliefs about superhuman agents and/or trans-empirical worlds are the *implications* that perceived superhuman agents and/or trans-empirical worlds have *for the physical world* and for states of affairs in the physical world.

This leads me to point out that, by placing this book within an academic context where the scientific enterprise is acknowledged as "distinguished," but not infallible, my motivation is to provide this project with a reasonable foundation, academically, to approach the intellectual problem of constructing a religious epistemology. A religious epistemology includes the methodological form (or structure) of non-tested yet faith-imbued beliefs. The problem of constructing a religious epistemology—especially in the context of a modern university—exists because any *theory of rationality*,[8] which allows intellectual space for the presence of belief claims, at the same time begins to sacrifice the cognitive values characteristic of a scientific

---

8. Also implicit here is the question: what, really, *is* a theory of rationality anyway? As we shall see, given the diversity of philosophical theories of rationality that are proposed (and available for consideration) in science and religion literature—including foundationalist, postmodernist, and postfoundationalist versions—whatever a theory of rationality really *is* will not be easily determined. Nor will there be a simple answer either to the question: what *should* a theory of rationality be? Rather, various answers to these questions will be proposed by various science and religion scholars. These facts are important to keep in mind, especially because I shall also be arguing for and sketching my own particular philosophical theory of rationality before the end of the book.

epistemology. A scientific epistemology includes the methodological form (or structure) of tested beliefs. As cognitive values characteristic of a scientific epistemology are lost, the question arises of whether we still in fact possess an "epistemology"? Or have we moved into some "lawless" epistemic world where no clear benchmark for testing the propositional beliefs of either knowledge claims or belief claims is maintained? Alternatively, if we remove belief claims from our religious epistemology, but consequently preserve the cognitive values of science, have we in fact missed the point of what a religious epistemology was supposed to accomplish in the first place? What a religious epistemology "was supposed to accomplish in the first place" is the mental recognition, *for the religious devotee*, that traditional religious life does include non-tested beliefs, *which are supposed to differ* epistemically from tested beliefs in science. Moreover, the *a priori* recognition (again, for the religious devotee) that these non-tested beliefs will not diminish the existential value or faith-based aims of a religious epistemology.

Keep in mind, too, that a *religious epistemology* itself is a kind of *belief claim* in religious life, even if only an attempted belief claim.[9] (This fact is important later when I shift from analyzing belief claims and knowledge claims generally to an analysis centred specifically on a religious epistemology and a scientific study of religion.) In short, these are the issues and themes to be developed and considered throughout this book. Finally, although the particular theory of rationality I shall argue for may not, on a practical level, provide a consistent benchmark for *all* possible knowledge claims or belief claims, it will be a theory of rationality which at the very least is *honest* about its philosophical and theological benefits and limitations. (Unfortunately, I rarely find honesty about such epistemic matters in contemporary science and religion literature.)

Some definitions for important terms and concepts, utilized throughout this book, are outlined as follows (and are elaborated further in later chapters):

---

9. A *religious epistemology* itself is a kind of *belief claim* in religious life, because to claim that one possesses a religious epistemology involves the two conceptual components of belief claims, outlined previously: (i) A cognitive state, encompassing this belief claimant's attempt to know the physical world—in this case, this belief claimant's attempt to possess a religious epistemology which includes non-tested beliefs about the physical world. (ii) A verbal statement made by this belief claimant that he or she mentally possesses (in this case) a religious epistemology—which itself is a non-tested belief, likely including a collection of other, corresponding non-tested beliefs, all of which are assented to by this belief claimant.

- *Culturally postulated superhuman agents,*[10] hereafter referred to as *CPS-agents*, are utilized in religiosity to explain causes for states of affairs in the physical world.

- The *hypersensitive agency detection device,*[11] hereafter referred to as the *HADD*—an evolutionary-based, cognitive device—is utilized in cognitive science of religion literature to attempt to "explain" religious activity.

- *Science* and *modern scientific thought*, which comprise modes of investigation and inquiry, occur when propositional claims are made about states of affairs in the physical world. Modern scientific thought includes tested beliefs about chemical reactions, cells, genes, electrical current, or curved spacetime. Scientific exercises utilize the substantive content of scientific theories as causes for states of affairs in the physical world. I refer to the propositional claims of scientific thought as *knowledge claims*. Scientific exercises and the cognitive values of a scientific epistemology provide an intellectual benchmark for testing many beliefs in modern research universities.

- *Theology* and *theological thought*, which, like science, comprise modes of investigation and inquiry, occur when religious exercises *attempt* to utilize the critical method of the sciences.[12] Thus theological thought occurs when propositional claims are made about concepts characteristic of religious thought. Theological thought and religious thought include non-tested (yet faith-imbued) beliefs about the gods, God, Allah, brahman, or nirvāna. Unlike scientific exercises, however, rarely do theological exercises utilize the substantive content of scientific theories as causes for states of affairs in the physical world. Instead, theological exercises utilize the actions of CPS-agents as causes for states of affairs in the physical world. I refer to the propositional claims of theological thought and religious thought as *belief claims*.

- *Religiosity,*[13] or *religious activity*, occur when the human mind defers to the actions of CPS-agents—intentional agents which possess be-

---

10. McCauley and Lawson, "Cognitive Constraints on Religious Ritual Form," 8.

11. Barrett, *Why Would Anyone Believe in God*, 31–32. The phrase *hypersensitive agency detection device* (HADD) was coined by Justin L. Barrett.

12. Wiebe, *The Irony of Theology*, 13.

13. The term *religiosity* refers to the quality or state of being religious—e.g., the simple deference of the human mind to the actions of CPS-agents to make sense of the physical world and/or one's existence in the world. It must be noted that the use of the term *religiosity* in this book is different from uses of *religiosity* implied by many desktop dictionary definitions of *religiosity*: e.g., the *Oxford Dictionary of English* defines

liefs and desires—rendering the human mind a *religious mind*. Thus religiosity is embedded and transmitted in the cultural constructs of modern *religions*: religions, functioning as social institutions, allow metaphysical meaning-making (e.g., mythical projection toward an afterlife) to be socioculturally imprinted over humans' ordinary cognitive capacities for religiosity. Religiosity is also ubiquitous: unlike scientific thought, religiosity is found in all human groups, having existed since at least the cultural explosion of our human species *H. sapiens sapiens*[14] (60,000 to 30,000 years ago), and, in terms of ritual activity only, possibly before (70,000 years ago).[15] Modern scientific thought, in contrast, has existed in a few human societies for about 400 years only. Also, some forms of ancient science, similar in method to modern science, existed among the Presocratics in Milesia (sixth c. BCE).[16]

---

religiosity as the noun derived from the adjective *religiose*, indicating a behaviour which is "excessively religious." In this book, religiosity is not meant to imply that a human behaviour or activity is excessively religious. Rather, in this book, religiosity indicates any activity typical of a religious mind, whether the activity is enacted within a social religious institution, or not. Furthermore, religiosity may involve testimonies about some reality "out there" or "in here," allowing humans to project their human thoughts and emotions, their greatest hopes and fears, beyond a finite human existence. Along this vein, Ninian Smart (2015, 9) observes that people "behave and react religiously, and this is something that the study of religion picks out; just as economics picks out the economic behaviour of people." In addition, regarding the classification of data as "religious," Steven Engler and Michael Stausberg note how the term *religious* is used to delimit a set of phenomena of interest, yet "there are no *essentially religious* facts, the religiosity of which is independent of our scholarly operations" (Engler and Stausberg 2011, 10). Thus, according to Engler and Stausberg, data classified as "religious" (or "economic" or "political") are brute facts which have been interpreted within a conceptual/theoretical platform and then classified as "religious" (or "economic" or "political"). Interpretation is, of course, part and parcel of any scholarly operation involving application of a theoretical system.

14. Steven Mithen, in his *The Prehistory of the Mind: The Cognitive Origins of Art, Religion and Science*, points out that, in the *Homo* lineage, the modern human species *H. sapiens sapiens* is distinguished, anatomically, from the ancient human species *H. sapiens*. Mithen (1996, 25) explains that, when compared to the ancient *H. sapiens*, the modern *H. sapiens sapiens* possesses a less robust physique, reduced and generally absent brow ridges, a more rounded skull, and smaller teeth. Anatomically modern *H. sapiens sapiens* emerges in the fossil record 100,000 years ago; however, at that time it remains behaviourally similar to ancient *H. sapiens* and *H. neanderthalensis*. It is not until 60,000 to 30,000 years ago, Mithen argues, that modern *H. sapiens sapiens* undergoes a "cultural explosion," a change in the cognitive nature of the human mind, producing evidence of art, religiosity, and technology, and resulting in a *H. sapiens sapiens* which is behaviourally similar to human beings today (1996, 15).

15. McCauley, *Why Religion Is Natural and Science Is Not*, 148.

16. Popper, "Back to the Presocratics," 189.

- Finally, to wrap up our definitions, a comment, too, on *faith*: I take the overused, sometimes controversial, but for my analysis unavoidable concept of *faith* to be a *life stance*—a life stance centred on one's own sociocultural environment, including one's subjective background experiences and/or future life goals. In this sense, *faith* and *worldview* are similar concepts (although *worldview* does not necessarily presuppose *faith*). In this book, when I speak about a physical or social reality as *faith-imbued*,[17] I am speaking about a physical or social reality which is conceived and interpreted under the auspices of one's sociocultural environment, including one's subjective background experiences and/or future life goals. For some, this will amount to the auspices of a typically religious worldview (including whatever background experiences and/or future life goals contribute to and perpetuate that religious worldview). For others, interpreting a physical or social reality as *faith-imbued* might amount to interpreting those realities through the lens of an alternative, postmetaphysical mode of thought—one that is not traditionally religious, but nevertheless one that is *interpretive*, often drawing on one's private emotional and psychological constitutions. Thus, I do not intend to reserve the concept of *faith* to describe typically religious worldviews only, but, more generally, *faith* refers to any life stance which, in a non-scientific fashion, contributes to and buttresses one's conceptions of physical and social realities.

INITIAL PLAUSIBILITY OF ASSUMPTIONS

In the late nineteenth and early twentieth centuries, a field of academic study called the scientific study of religion was developed. Importantly, a *scientific study of religion* itself—by virtue of its intrinsic critical methodology and corresponding tested beliefs—is a kind of *knowledge claim* in modern science, even if only an attempted knowledge claim.[18] (This fact

---

17. At times, I will also speak about belief claims as *faith-imbued*: belief claims are made under the auspices of one's own sociocultural environment, including one's subjective background experiences and/or future life goals.

18. A *scientific study of religion* itself—by virtue of its intrinsic critical methodology and corresponding tested beliefs—is a kind of *knowledge claim* in modern science, because to claim that one possesses a critical methodology suited to a scientific study of religion (and to advocate for such a study) involves the four conceptual components of knowledge claims, outlined previously: (i) A cognitive state, encompassing this knowledge claimant's attempt to know the physical world—in this case, this knowledge claimant's attempt to possess a critical methodology suited to a scientific study of religion, which epistemically includes tested beliefs about the physical world. (ii) A specially certified proposition—in this case, the critical methodology intrinsic to a scientific

is important later when I shift from analyzing knowledge claims and belief claims generally to an analysis centred specifically on a scientific study of religion and a religious epistemology.) In various forms, the scientific study of religion continues in the twenty-first century, drawing primarily on resources from analytic philosophy, scientific historiography, evolutionary psychology, anthropology, and cognitive science of religion. Most scholars of religious studies who work in the scientific study of religion have decided the dogmatic premise of *religious truth* is best not assumed or utilized as an explanatory force in one's academic work. One commentator, Don Wiebe, began to outline this methodological situation in his *Religion and Truth: Towards an Alternative Paradigm for the Study of Religion*.[19] Put simply, in traditional faith-imbued theology, the meaning of *religious truth* referred to the fact that beliefs about CPS-agents were presupposed in one's method. Indeed, in Judaeo-Christian thought (as one example), it seems the concept of *religious truth* is equated with ideas of religious revelation or assumptions that biblical agents—El, Satan, the archangel Michael, *et al.*—are ontological realities as opposed to culturally postulated psychological and/or psychoanalytic realities. However, the removal of religious truth as an underlying assumption in one's method is motivated by the fact that, from an etic perspective, we do not possess any observed experience—*open to intersubjective testing*—which can account for the existence of an ontological (metaphysical) reality for religious truth or for substantive existences for the biblical agents mentioned in this paragraph.

This methodological problem, concerning substantive assumptions about religious truth, has received considerable attention. In *The Sacred Canopy: Elements of a Sociological Theory of Religion*, sociologist of religion, Peter L. Berger, pointed out how any scientific theorizing about religious concepts must be completed without any affirmations, positive or negative, about the ontological statuses of religious concepts.[20] Religious concepts, of course, include CPS-agents and trans-empirical worlds. Bracketing out the question of whether religious concepts possess independent, metaphysical realities, Berger and his colleagues were drawn to study the phenomenon

study of religion—which is the object of the preceding cognitive state. (iii) A verbal statement made by this knowledge claimant that he or she mentally possesses (in this case) a methodology suited to a scientific study of religion. Moreover, that this methodology is open to external analysis by outside parties. (iv) Some reasons, provided by this knowledge claimant, which are used to attempt to convince (and ideally assure) outside parties that this claimant's methodology suited to a scientific study of religion in fact constitutes and provides access to justified, human knowledge.

19. Wiebe, *Religion and Truth*, 4.
20. Berger, *The Sacred Canopy*, 100.

of religion as a human enterprise, one that originates from the products of collective human activity and human consciousness.[21] Berger refined his position later in *A Rumor of Angels: Modern Society and the Rediscovery of the Supernatural*, clarifying that, when independent realities for religious concepts are bracketed, this amounts to a methodological imperative only.[22] Understanding religion as a human enterprise, within the framework of a methodological perspective, does not preclude theological reflection (within a faith-imbued perspective) about the existence of an independent, superhuman reality. In fact, Berger wonders if religious concepts thought to originate in the human imagination can be interpreted as reflections of an independent, superhuman reality?[23] Still, however, even while acknowledging the possibility of such theological reflection, Berger is careful to keep any affirmations about a superhuman reality separate from methods of theorizing in modern academic disciplines. Thus, in the academy, religion ought to be studied scientifically; theological reflection kept private.[24]

The most useful aspect for us from *The Sacred Canopy* is that Berger brings to our attention the "empirically available"[25] phenomenon of contemporary religious life—the source material, as it were, for an academic study of religious ideas and practices, found in the *observable* and *researchable* social world of everyday religious institutions.[26] This observable social world of everyday religious institutions contrasts with the reported "other worlds"[27] of religions, which are neither empirically observable nor researchable for the purposes of a scientific study of religion.[28] Under Berger's guidance, then, our scientifically oriented conception of the modern religious

---

21. Such an approach brings to mind the Feuerbachian "God" as a human, psychological projection and "religion" as a human monologue. Regarding Feuerbach, the Hegelian dialectic is reversed, becoming, as Berger (1970, 46) puts it, "a 'conversation' between man and man's own productions."

22. Berger, *A Rumor of Angels*, 46.

23. In this sense, Berger (1967, 180) is thinking along the lines that, although *qua* sociology, the Hegelian dialectic is inverted—so as to allow an empirical study of human affairs—such a construction does not preclude *qua* theology a re-inversion of that dialectic such that religious concepts (although human productions) are seen to be reflections of an independent, superhuman reality.

24. The notion that theological reflection be kept private in the academy describes an *ideal*, academic situation, which is not readily practiced: e.g., see Martin and Wiebe, "Religious Studies as a Scientific Discipline: The Persistence of a Delusion," 587–97.

25. Berger, *The Sacred Canopy*, 128.

26. Berger, *The Sacred Canopy*, 128.

27. Berger, *The Sacred Canopy*, 88.

28. Berger, *The Sacred Canopy*, 88.

situation refers to our look at the empirically observable and researchable phenomenon of contemporary religious life.

Along a similar but not identical vein, Don Wiebe encourages the application of "talk about God" theology—or, "academic theology"—in the scientific study of religion. *Academic theology* is described by Wiebe as a mode of thought comprising our *attempt* to place religious aspects of a social world, where the actions of CPS-agents were the primary mode of causality, into a methodological framework which is more similar to the epistemology of modern science.[29] *Prima facie* such an attempt suggests the adoption of a critical attitude toward religious modes of thought. Indeed, critical "talk about God" theology is contrasted with acritical "God-talk" theology, which suggests a study of religious modes of thought guided by the agentic presuppositions of a mythopoeic worldview.[30] For obvious reasons, "God-talk" theology is not tolerated in the scientific study of religion, because it depends on a mythopoeic worldview and the use of CPS-agents—elements which not all researchers can agree on. In practice, the precise epistemic nature of theology as a mode of thought is tendentious: In their *attempts* to utilize "science," religious exercises develop a systematic and polemical method—centred on the propositional character of the scientific method—which is understood to constitute theology. It appears, however, this is where the *attempted* use of "science" ends, for rarely do religious exercises utilize the substantive content of scientific theories as their primary mode of causality. This complicated mixing of sources and methods renders theology a hybrid mode of thought, including substantive contributions from mythopoeic worldviews and the application of a systematic, "rational" method. Thus, when the epistemology of theology is unpacked, theology is seen to be neither a religious activity nor a scientific one, but in its own curious way theology attempts to be both religious *and* scientific.

Theologian Oliver D. Crisp, in contrast to approaches adopted in the scientific study of religion, contextualizes the substantive nature of religious and theological truth differently. Crisp assumes there must be some innate religious truth in the physical world; the task of theological exercises is to uncover this truth. In *Analytic Theology: New Essays in the Philosophy of Theology* (2009), discussing substantive assumptions that play into analytic theology, Crisp states, "The substantive element includes several features that are interrelated: the presumption that there is some theological truth [religious truth] of the matter and that this truth of the matter can be

---

29. Wiebe, *The Irony of Theology*, 12.
30. Wiebe, *The Irony of Theology*, 15.

ascertained and understood by human beings."[31] Analytic theology (faith-imbued analytic theology), like analytic philosophy, prioritizes precision, clarity, and logical coherence when assessing theological claims. However, analytic theology, Crisp argues, cannot avoid the substantive assumption about religious and theological truth mentioned in the preceding quotation. Crisp, I suggest, does not consider the epistemic implications of the inclusion of such a substantive assumption in one's method. Philosopher of religion, Michael C. Rea, is right to point out that analytic theologians will find it natural to utilize God as an explanatory force in their academic arguments.[32] Furthermore Crisp's substantive assumption, that there is some innate religious and theological truth in the physical world, would especially encourage the use of God as an explanatory force in analytic theology. However, to utilize the action of a CPS-agent (God) as the explanation for a state of affairs in the physical world is not to explain, mechanically, *how* the state of affairs did in fact occur.

The situation outlined in the preceding paragraph, where the activity of theologizing using CPS-agents is contrasted with the activity of explaining using scientific theories, is perhaps the methodological dividing line between a faith-imbued study of religion and a scientific study of religion.[33] Such a distinction is important in this book, which leads me to say it is at this juncture where I part company with faith-imbued theologians. For now, my own position, and that of most of the scholars whose arguments I shall utilize in the following chapters, is best contextualized within the framework of methodological atheism.[34] As will be pointed out, the radically

---

31. Crisp, "On Analytic Theology," 35.

32. Rea, "Introduction," 9.

33. When scientific and faith-imbued studies of religion are compared and contrasted, initial concerns may arise as to whether a scientific study of religion tends toward a reduction of religious phenomena to social, cognitive, or philosophical explanatory forces. Likewise, concerns about constitutive reductionism of religious concepts toward a naturalistic ontology may arise. Many of the authors whose arguments I shall utilize in the following chapters address these factors. As this point, to help to alleviate any potential concerns that reductionism eliminates "religion," I note Jeppe Sinding Jensen's comment in his chapter *Epistemology* in *The Routledge Handbook of Research Methods in the Study of Religion*: Jensen (2011, 43) notes that, if a study of religion were to avoid reduction completely, the only task remaining would be to repeat and state the activities of religious devotees. It is the case that, in a faith-imbued study of religion, repeating and stating the activities of religion may be desirable, especially when apologetic aims are included in one's project. However, as this book is not faith-imbued, Jensen's comment is helpful in pointing out the relevance and usefulness of reductionism as applied in a *scientific* study of religion.

34. The phrase *methodological atheism*, describing an empirical study of religious concepts where the ontological statuses of religious concepts are bracketed, is outlined

counterintuitive cognitive capacity required to function as a methodological atheist—and to function as any *neutral*, dispassionate, or disengaged observer—is difficult to master: Similar to Lot's wife,[35] I have been tempted to look back to an "easier" time—for me, back to an easier time of simply "crying to the gods," but doing so within the confines of mythopoeic thought patterns which are triggered cognitively by a maturationally natural cognitive system.[36] However, throwing away whatever faith-imbued intellectual ground I might have stood on liberates me from the confines of whatever is thought to be intellectually "safe." In addition, neither an unjustifiable first principle of foundationalism nor an epistemological tribe in a relativistic framework will provide an intellectual escape hatch for me.

Thus, functioning as a writer in the scientific study of religion, in this book I exclude from my analysis the assumption that *religious truth* possesses an ontological reality. *However,* what I also exclude is the assumption that *scientific truth* possesses an ontological reality.[37] (The phrases *religious truth* and *scientific truth* refer to propositionally oriented truth statements about states of affairs in the physical world.) To that end, as I outlined in my *Adventure in Human Knowledges and Beliefs*, finding a common ground, ontologically, in scientific work is often difficult. I argued that in contemporary philosophy of science there exists a common misunderstanding that scientific beliefs provide us with foolproof (infallible) knowledge of

---

by Peter L. Berger in *The Sacred Canopy* (100). Berger credits the coining of the phrase itself to his colleague Anton C. Zijderveld.

35. From the famous narrative in Genesis 19, Lot's wife looks back on her home city of Sodom as she flees to Zoar with her husband and daughters. In a contemporary Jewish interpretation of this myth, Sol Scharfstein (2008, 71) maintains that Lot's wife looked back because she possessed a secret longing for her previous life.

36. McCauley, *Why Religion Is Natural and Science Is Not*, 224.

37. The phrases *religious truth* and *scientific truth* refer to propositionally oriented truth statements about states of affairs in the physical world. That is, *hypothetically speaking*, should a knowledge claim or a belief claim provide a foolproof description of physical reality *as* reality is, then the knowledge claim or belief claim in question would entail a propositionally oriented scientific truth or religious truth. In this sense, I follow the tradition of the correspondence theory of truth. In the correspondence theory of truth, *truth* is thought to be a description of physical reality that consistently describes reality independent from subjective human thought about reality. Coherentist and pragmatist theories of truth complement the correspondence theory of truth: Coherentist and pragmatist theories provide criteria for how truth statements might be adjudicated, although the correspondence theory outlines the primary nature of *truth* (Wiebe 1981, 178–79). In the coherentist theory, truth statements are compared to previous bodies of knowledge claims or belief claims. In the pragmatist theory, truth is assessed by how well the knowledge claim or belief claim in question accomplishes a task or presents a useful model to depict states of affairs in the physical world.

the external, physical world[38]—knowledge which exists independent of our own conceptualizations of the physical world and exists whether or not our conceptualizations of the physical world are accurate. However, through experimental work, the scientific enterprise does not provide us with infallible knowledge about states of affairs in the physical world, but rather science provides us with *tested* beliefs about states of affairs in the physical world. Tested beliefs—i.e., objects of the cognitive states of knowledge claims—are expressed epistemically in the methodological form of scientific theories. In the philosophy of science and religion, the epistemic distinction between phenomenological and substantive statements about the observed world is important—for one, that distinction marks a difference between phenomenal appearances of objects and substantive realities[39] of objects thought to exist "behind" appearances.[40] The phrases *scientific truth* and *religious truth* are thought to depict substantive realities for physical objects, e.g., *electron*, and metaphysical objects, e.g., *God*, respectively. However, it is precisely those assumptions—about the existences of substantive realities *behind* the appearances of objects—which I discard from my analysis. To be explained in the following pages as I unpack the two assumptions which I do make in this book, the notion of phenomenal reality is important in my assessment of science and religion, yet affirmations about substantive realities for either religious objects *or* scientific objects remain methodologically bracketed.

The philosophy of science I suggest, then, is perhaps best described as a *neutral*, disengaged philosophy of science: a philosophy which analyzes the products and method of the sciences without affirming anything, positive or negative, about the ontological status of the external, physical world.[41] (The converse approach would be a philosophy of science which

---

38. Woodward, *Adventure*, 8.

39. In recognizing an epistemic distinction between *phenomenological* and *substantive* statements, *substantive* statements in philosophy are also referred to as *theoretical* statements. In *How the Laws of Physics Lie*, Nancy Cartwright (2002, 1) notes, "Normally for philosophers, 'phenomenological' and 'theoretical' ['substantive'] mark the distinction between the observable and the unobservable." Realists maintain this distinction between phenomenological and theoretical statements: if theoretical statements are false, corresponding phenomenological statements must also be false (Cartwright 2002, 3). However, Cartwright, an instrumentalist, rejects this distinction.

40. Cartwright, *How the Laws of Physics Lie*, 19.

41. As in philosophy of religion, I suggest that Wiebe's objective genitive versus subjective genitive distinction (Wiebe 1994, 112) can also be applied to explicate the precise nature of the relationship between the enterprises of *philosophy* and *science* in the discipline *philosophy of science*: (i) Is philosophy of science to be performed as a neutral, dispassionate account of scientific products and method—a philosophy *of* scientific practice (objective genitive)? Or (ii) is philosophy of science to be performed as an insider's account of the scientific enterprise—"science's philosophy"—i.e., philosophy

is performed *by* science—where the truth of the external, physical world is affirmed to correspond with the statements of science. In the converse approach, statements of science would also be affirmed to be infallible.) Thus, similar to the methodological atheism adopted in the academic study of religion, the particular philosophy of science I advocate for is a "methodological atheism" about the truth of scientific statements (as with religious statements)—a "methodological atheism" about the ability of scientific statements to correspond in a foolproof manner with the truth of the external, physical world.[42] In summary, it would not be inaccurate to classify my philosophy of science as a philosophy of science which brackets the ontological status of the external, physical world. For the purpose of a more complete literature review of twentieth-century philosophy of science, various perspectives on the ontological and epistemological statuses of scientific theories will be considered in later chapters.[43] For now, some

---

done *by* science (subjective genitive)? In philosophy of religion, Wiebe's characterizations are similarly described as follows: (i) Is philosophy of religion to be performed as a neutral, dispassionate account of religious products and discourse—a philosophy *of* religious life (objective genitive)? Or (ii) is philosophy of religion to be performed as an apologetic, insider's account of the religious enterprise—"religion's philosophy"—i.e., philosophy done *by* religion (subjective genitive)? As explained, in the assumptions of this book, the objective genitive options in (i) are utilized for the methods of both philosophy of science and philosophy of religion and, to that end, the method of the academic study of science and religion.

42. The assumptions underlying my philosophy of science are similar to the assumptions employed in Nancy Cartwright's instrumentalism: Cartwright remarks, "The fundamental laws of the theory are true of the objects in the model [constructed model to fit observed phenomenon into a theory], and they are used to derive a specific account of how these objects behave. But the objects of the model have only *'the form or appearance of things'* and, in a very strong sense, not their *'substance or proper qualities'*" (Cartwright 2002, 17; emphasis added).

43. At this point, it will suffice to mention that opinions concerning the ontological status of *scientific truth* in modern scientific practice are likely varied, although the specific question of whether scientific beliefs provide foolproof knowledge of the external, physical world seems either taken for granted or overlooked entirely. For some twentieth-century philosophers of science, however, the question of the truth of scientific beliefs is a question worthy of consideration: e.g., Thomas Kuhn characterizes truth as dependent on the scientific paradigm under which a researcher works. Kuhn (2012, 170) wonders if it is even helpful to imagine an objective world, independent from paradigm-dependent conceptualizations of the external world? In Karl Popper's thought, a scientific community of researchers decides, by way of critical discussion, if a scientific theory will be falsified and which theory, among competing theories, is more *nearer* to the truth or an *approximation* of truth. For Popper, a knowledge claim cannot be demonstrated to be true, but could be demonstrated to possess a high degree of certitude (an *approximation* of truth) or be demonstrated to be false. As an undergraduate engineering student, I experienced how chemistry, physics, and other technical subjects, are taught in universities as if the knowledge claims passed on in those disciplines,

methodological *neutrality*—about the ontological statuses of the external, physical world and religious concepts—is the order of the day. Left without substantive realities for *religious truth* or *scientific truth* to hold on to, I will now assess the cogency of the two substantive assumptions which I do make in this book. (Having thrown away religious and scientific truths—"all that I had," the story of the woman in the Temple who readily gave away her two coins[44]—all that she had—oddly comes to mind; however, please excuse this idiosyncratic use of a religious narrative.)

As mentioned previously, the two substantive assumptions which I do utilize in this book carry high degrees of initial plausibility in modern research universities—i.e., it is widely accepted in modern research universities that the claims of both assumptions possess firm bases in physical reality. The first substantive assumption—*(i) phenomenal reality provides a standard of observed experiences used for testing beliefs about states of affairs in the physical world*—speaks to a fundamental principle of scientific methodology. The causal theory of knowledge requires we possess a quantitative perception of the state of affairs under study, demonstrating how information contained in a knowledge claim is less surprising (more believable) than was previously thought. Subjecting the propositional belief of a knowledge claim repeatedly to tests of ruthless criticism requires the standard of *intersubjectively observed experiences of phenomenal reality*—for only in this way, it is rightly argued, can intersubjective reckoning about a knowledge claim within a community of scholars be maintained. Pragmatist philosopher, Susan Haack, captures the situation in her *Evidence and Inquiry: A Pragmatist Reconstruction of Epistemology* when she describes the intersubjective method of a modestly naturalistic epistemology: "It depends on the assumptions both that sensory and introspective experience is a source of empirical information for us, and that there are *no other* ultimate sources of empirical information."[45]

Haack, a defender of modern science "within reason"[46] (i.e., within the limitations of human cognition and acknowledging that all knowledge

---

from teacher to student, are statements of truths (some natural sciences or engineering students may disagree, but I think most would agree that the concept of a *theory* is rarely used in university courses). In actuality, it would be helpful if the clarification was made in undergraduate courses that knowledge claims in the natural sciences and engineering disciplines are not truth claims, but are the most well-corroborated scientific theories that we possess (Woodward, *Adventure*, 11–12).

44. See the biblical narrative in Mark 12:41–44.

45. Haack, *Evidence and Inquiry*, 17; emphasis added.

46. The pun "within reason" is noted from the title of Haack's *Defending Science—Within Reason*. In *Defending Science*, 9, Haack notes her choice of language "within reason" is intentional: (i) the scientific enterprise informs us how the physical world is,

claims are corrigible), is careful to distance her work from scientism, a pejorative term, describing an unabashed confidence in the scientific enterprise. Interestingly Haack prefers the term *distinguished* when describing the scientific enterprise: she believes uncriticized distinction has to be earned—something the sciences have not done—but she argues the sciences do comprise a "distinguished" enterprise.[47] At first glance, Haack's position, that there are no sources for empirical information except the source of sensory (and introspective) experience, could be misinterpreted as an example of what Mikael Stenmark calls ontological scientism.[48] In such a view, philosophers argue the only ontological reality which exists is the reality made known to us by the knowledge claims of scientific theories (or that if there is any other kind of reality it most certainly is subordinate to the reality made known by science). This view, however, is not what Haack espouses and I believe the distinction is worth making: In clarifying the method of a modestly naturalistic epistemology what Haack is essentially doing is making a case for the high initial plausibility of the assumption that a phenomenal, physical world exists and that the constitution of this physical world is naturalistic. Formulating an assumption with a high initial plausibility—even if the assumption assumes the existence of a physical world only—is a different matter from making an absolutist claim (a claim thought to be infallible) that the only world which exists is a physical world.[49] Put simply, there might be "other" realities; religious devotees testify to religious

---

although the enterprise is fallible ("within reason" colloquially), and (ii) the scientific enterprise is limited by our human cognitive capacity and the fact that we bring our own imperfect perceptions of the physical world to our scientific work ("within reason" philosophically).

47. Haack, *Defending Science—Within Reason*, 23.

48. Stenmark, *Scientism*, 7.

49. A similar assumption is made by Willem B. Drees in his *Religion, Science and Naturalism*. Distinguishing between *existence* and *access*, Drees (140) notes that, although human cognitive capacities limit *access*, this need not exclude the possibility that metaphysical objects have *existence* outside of sense perceptions. Drees (12) summarizes his position as follows: "The natural world is the whole of reality *that we know of* [italics mine] and interact with; no supernatural or spiritual realm distinct from the natural world shows up *within* our natural world, not even in the mental life of humans." Drees (13) explains that in the preceding quotation he italicizes *within* to point out that, in applying this assumption, we are concerned with tested beliefs within the natural world only. In contrast, questions which exist at the ontological boundaries of natural science (e.g., boundaries of particle physics, cosmology) may require concepts or explanatory accounts which do in fact transcend the natural world (18). Note also that Drees's formulation of this assumption could be mistaken to be an example of Stenmark's ontological scientism. Drees's formulation is most certainly an example of Stenmark's epistemic scientism. In this book I argue Stenmark's epistemic scientism should not be classified as a type of scientism.

experiences originating from "other," trans-empirical worlds. However, as will be discussed further, the methodological problem is that reported religious experiences are not repeatable experiences. Even if some religious experiences were repeatable, their claims cannot be measured numerically and most especially their causal connections cannot be reproduced inside the parameters of an experiment. The non-availability of a method to generate intersubjective scrutiny about the ability of religious experiences to accurately describe or predict states of affairs in the physical world, means religious experience (at least in academic work) is not a legitimate source of empirical information. Thus, here we have another reason that the first assumption—*phenomenal reality provides a standard of observed experiences used for testing beliefs about states of affairs in the physical world*—is an assumption with a high initial plausibility.

Another type of scientism proposed by Stenmark is epistemic scientism:[50] in this view it is not irrational to hold religious beliefs in one's personal life; however, we cannot test religious beliefs as we can test scientific beliefs. Therefore, we cannot *know* if our non-tested, religious beliefs are accurate descriptions of physical reality. Unlike Stenmark, I shall be suggesting this particular view, about tested beliefs being epistemically different from non-tested beliefs, should not be classified as a type of scientism *per se*. Rather, what I see this particular view amounting to is a researcher making clear an epistemic distinction between origins and uses of tested beliefs (objects of cognitive states of knowledge claims) in scientific work and origins and uses of non-tested beliefs (objects of cognitive states of belief claims) in religious life. Also, in Stenmark's classification system of six distinct types of scientism,[51] outlined in his *Scientism: Science, Ethics and Religion*, so-called epistemic scientism is the most "belief-friendly" type of scientism he proposes. Haack's perspective outlined previously, concerning sensory and introspective experience as the only source material for empirical information, would still allow the presence of belief claims within the philosophical constitution of one's own thought patterns and worldview (i.e., it is not irrational to hold religious beliefs or other non-tested beliefs in one's personal life). What Haack's view does not allow is the presence of belief claims in the source material for empirical information (i.e., the propositional beliefs of belief claims cannot be tested as the propositional beliefs of knowledge claims can be tested).

50. Stenmark, *Scientism*, 4.

51. The six types of scientism proposed by Stenmark will be revisited in chapter 3. For now, the six types are as follows: (i) epistemic scientism, (ii) rationalistic scientism, (iii) ontological scientism, (iv) axiological scientism, (v) existential scientism, and (vi) comprehensive scientism.

The second substantive assumption of this book—*(ii) religious people's testimonies inform us that religious people possess beliefs about superhuman agents and/or beliefs about trans-empirical worlds*—speaks to religious experiences as those experiences are reported by religious devotees. In outlining the rationale for this assumption, I use the language of *testimonies* because, as mentioned already, I exclude from my analysis the assumption that religious truth possesses an ontological reality. Thus, in this second assumption, I am not assuming that the superhuman agents or trans-empirical worlds, about which religious people express beliefs, are metaphysical realities. What I am assuming, though, is that, given a population of people (I speak generally here), some of those people, when asked about their religious commitments, will provide testimonies about superhuman agents and/or trans-empirical worlds.[52] In this second assumption, then, the beliefs about which religious people testify are best interpreted in a phenomenological sense—the religious individual's *mindset* as that mindset *is understood by* the individual who is testifying about (reporting) the belief experience. So, in this second assumption, we are not concerned with how the physical world really is; rather, we are concerned with *how religious individuals perceive the physical world to be*—which religious individuals tell us about by way of their public testimonies about reported religious phenomena such as superhuman agents and trans-empirical worlds. In this fashion, superhuman agents and trans-empirical worlds, about which religious people testify, amount to kinds of *cultural postulations*—types of propositional claims—which more precisely are *belief claims* arising from within the cultural construct of religion and, physiologically, from the predilections of a maturationally natural cognitive system.

In a maturationally natural cognitive system, an important feature of religiosity is the apparent detection of CPS-agents in the physical world through the biological activity of the HADD.[53] Experimental psychologist, Justin L. Barrett, describes agents as "thinking, feeling, intentional beings . . . people, animals . . . ghosts, goblins, and gods."[54] In cognitive science of religion, an experimental component of the scientific study of religion

52. Drees (1998, 166) points out that various categories of religious experiences are reported: (i) *interpreted* (e.g., experiences contextualized vis-à-vis a pre-existing framework), (ii) *quasi-sensory* (e.g., visions, dreams), (iii) *revelatory* (e.g., insight, inspiration, immediate changes in perception), (iv) *regenerative* (e.g., feelings of renewal), (v) *numinous* (e.g., enhanced consciousness), and (vi) *mystical* (e.g., union with a perceived divine reality).

53. The HADD (*hypersensitive agency detection device*)—an evolutionary-based, cognitive device—is utilized in cognitive science of religion literature to attempt to "explain" religious activity (Barrett 2004, 33; McCauley 2011, 82).

54. Barrett, *Why Would Anyone Believe in God*, viii.

which has developed especially in the last few decades, religiosity is understood as embedded in the cultural construct of religion: social institutions allow meaning to be socioculturally imprinted over the quotidian capacities of a natural cognitive system. For example, the cultural constructs of *God* and *Allah*—sources of metaphysical meaning in religion—are imprinted over the natural cognitive capacity which causes humans to desire to detect agency in the physical world. It could be suggested, then, that contemporary religious institutions capitalize on humans' cognitive inference systems. Religious institutions (and religious texts) market the "God-concept" as a "person-like agent"—such person-like agents are cognitively appealing to the human mind. Counter-ontological representations of a person-like agent include an ontological category (the category of *person*) and a violation of that category within a catalogue of possible supernatural templates for religious concepts. As the argument goes, for cognitive reasons pertaining to outcomes from our evolutionary heritage, the human mind is predisposed to be prepared to acquire counter-ontological variations of certain mental concepts. Variations of these mental concepts seem to coalesce well with the nature of religious thought. Scientific testing in the area of experimental theology seems to provide an empirical basis for the claims of cognitive science of religion. (This work will be assessed in chapter 8.)

OUTLINE OF THESIS STATEMENT AND ARGUMENT

The following is a detailed outline of the two-fold thesis statement characterizing the aims of this book: As stated, I am arguing (i) that a theory of rationality refers to a philosophical system for testing the propositional beliefs of knowledge claims, and, if possible, testing the propositional beliefs of belief claims; (ii) that if a philosopher or theologian is successful in designing a compatibility system between science and religion, the compatibility system will consistently test the propositional beliefs of knowledge claims, and, if possible, the propositional beliefs of belief claims. Moreover, then, a compatibility system (of some kind) specifically between a scientific study of religion and a religious epistemology should consistently test all of its propositional beliefs.

Debates surrounding compatibility systems between science and religion (generally) often take place without a clear method for adjudicating which side has won. Wiebe, in his essay "*Science and Religion: Is Compatibility Possible?*," explains a *compatibility system*,[55] a concept developed by

---

55. In the context of the academic study of science and religion, the concept of a *compatibility system* is taken from Ninian Smart's work and is outlined in his *The*

religious studies teacher, Ninian Smart, as follows: "A 'compatibility system' is essentially a justification of accepting two apparently conflicting systems of thought. If no *prima facie* conflict existed, there would be no impetus to construct such a system."[56] It seems that for many, upon first impression, science and religion exist in some kind of conflict, encompassing different methodologies with distinct goals and aims—with distinct intentionalities.[57] In addition, the building of a potential compatibility system between science and religion (or a compatibility system between science and other metaphysical belief systems) tends toward the question of whether the human (yet metaphysical) activity of "thinking about the gods" is an activity to be accomplished with or without an assumption about the nature of the gods—i.e., whether the gods are an ontological or a socially constructed reality? It is my sense that any student of science and religion is wise to keep an awareness of these concerns in mind; these concerns will influence my analyses in following chapters.

In terms of religious revelation, a type of "religious knowledge" thought to present a metaphysical reality independent from personal human preference,[58] historian of medieval philosophy, Étienne Gilson, outlines options to contextualize revelation[59] in relation to rational speculation about states of affairs in the physical world. To begin with, in its most ambitious sense, revelation is thought to provide a substitute for all other sources of propositional claims, including sources of science, ethics, and metaphys-

---

Science of Religion and the Sociology of Knowledge: Some Methodological Questions, 82–83. Wiebe discusses and assesses compatibility systems in his *Beyond Legitimation: Essays on the Problem of Religious Knowledge* (1994)—for example, in *Beyond Legitimation*, see Wiebe's *Science and Religion: Is Compatibility Possible?* (58) or his *Is Science Really an Implicit Religion?* (87). In 2014 I utilized the concept of a compatibility system in my *Adventure in Human Knowledges and Beliefs*, presenting a post-Kuhnian-type relationship between knowledge communities and belief communities (Woodward, *Adventure*, 58).

56. Wiebe, "Science and Religion," 58.

57. See chapter 4 for an analysis of the distinct intentionalities of science and religion.

58. Gilson, *Reason and Revelation*, 32.

59. That revelation is thought to present a metaphysical reality independent from personal human preference will be important as we consider how scientific and religious modes of thought differ: If revelation indicates a substantive and final physical-world-transcending reality, then religious modes of thought, which rely on revelation as a source of knowledge, must be radically different from scientific modes of thought. Modern science is open to change and modification, the impetus for change being new information uncovered from new learning about the world; furthermore, new information obtained from science impacts evolving human preferences about human behaviours and attitudes.

ics.[60] In more modest terms, attempts are made to epistemically blend claims arising from revelation with claims arising from rational speculation.[61] Gilson goes on to characterize individual relationships between revelation and rational speculation as various schools of thought founded by Augustine of Hippo, Averroës, and Thomas Aquinas. Firstly, in the school of Augustine, the certitude of religious faith is taken as the beginning point of all rational knowledge. In such a scenario, all speculation moves in a direction from revelation toward reason.[62] However, Gilson argues that even for the Augustinian an application of natural reason is initially required. Revelation is accepted only if religious devotees possess "good reasons"[63] to think that such revelation has occurred. Thus Gilson contends that the action of the Augustinian *believing* that revelation has occurred—e.g., believing that God has spoken—is a different matter from providing a *rational* account of the reality of revelation which is held by faith.

Secondly, Averroism—the school of Averroës—provides another possibility to characterize revelation in relation to rational speculation. The goal of Averroism was to respond to the attempted reconciliation between philosophical knowledge and the content of Islamic faith. Creating an opposition between faith and reason, Averroës contended that absolute truth is located within the claims of Aristotelian philosophy only—i.e., reason speaks once and for all.[64] According to Averroës, however, to indicate the exact place and function of religious faith relative to philosophy is to consider the possibility that revelation may prescribe the use of philosophical speculation. As the argument goes, as part of one's philosophical inquiry into creation, one's mind is thought to be raised to knowledge of a creator god.[65] (In this view, philosophy need not be inimical to faith after all.) In a curious twist, the question is then raised as to whether a supernaturalistic ontology is even required to provide an account of revelation? Indeed, in a rhetorical sense, revelation is already rendered an absolute truth, cognitively acceptable so long as human imagination remains stronger than natural reason.[66] However, as Gilson points out, for the dialectically minded, appeals to human imagination and emotion are *not* justifiable reasons to believe. In response to this accusation, that the appeal to imagination is not enough, the task

---

60. Gilson, *Reason and Revelation*, 5.
61. Gilson, *Reason and Revelation*, 15.
62. Gilson, *Reason and Revelation*, 16–17.
63. Gilson, *Reason and Revelation*, 18.
64. Gilson, *Reason and Revelation*, 39.
65. Gilson, *Reason and Revelation*, 40–41.
66. Gilson, *Reason and Revelation*, 43.

of faith-imbued theology would become one of formulating a dialectical justification for revelation or a justification which demonstrates that claims arising from revelation are just as probable as claims arising from natural reason.

Thirdly, Thomism—the school of Thomas Aquinas—is helpful in making a distinction between claims that can be *known* and claims that are *believed*. Regarding the origins of Thomism, Gilson remarks, "Despite their radical opposition, the Theologism and the Rationalism of the thirteenth century had at least one common feature; their onesidedness. Theologism would maintain that every part of Revelation should be understood, while Rationalism would uphold the view that no part of Revelation can be understood."[67] According to Gilson, Aquinas sees the problem of the opposition between faith and reason as a problem of differing degrees of intellectual assent: In the case of faith, assent to a claim is possible because the substantive content of the claim is part and parcel of revelation—e.g., testimonies that "God has said it" or "made it so."[68] Thus, in faith, assent is determined by the act of *believing* that the proposition is an accurate description of physical reality. In contrast, in the case of science, assent to a claim is possible because the tested, substantive content of the claim is part and parcel of observed nature.[69] Thus, in science, assent is determined by the act of *knowing* that the proposition is an accurate *and tested* description of physical reality. Aquinas's distinction between claims *known* and claims *believed* need not be a complete separation nor an Averroistic opposition between faith and reason.[70] For the Thomist, the dichotomy of faith and reason is thought to grow into a single "organic unity."[71] However, it would be an error to neglect Gilson's thesis that Thomistic thought is still grounded in the difference between degrees of assent resulting in either *knowledge* or *belief*. Also, in considering the dialectical probabilities of faith, arguments held by faith convince no one unless one already believes arguments based on faith. As such, in Gilson's view, the typical Thomist never pretends to know what is actually to be believed and likewise does not claim to believe

---

67. Gilson, *Reason and Revelation*, 69.

68. In this case, intellectual assent is determined by the perceived authority of revelation (an object of a faith-imbued cognition)—by the *belief* that the proposition (which is thought to be made possible through perceived revelation) provides an accurate description of physical reality.

69. In this case, intellectual assent is determined by the object of science (object of cognition)—by the *tested contents* of the proposition itself, which indicate that the proposition provides an accurate description of physical reality.

70. Gilson, *Reason and Revelation*, 78.

71. Gilson, *Reason and Revelation*, 84.

what can in fact be known.[72] Thus, in such a system, *knowledge* and *belief* are psychologically distinguished by their proper places and functions, but nevertheless both *knowledge* and *belief* remain important in the life of the Thomist.

I apply Aquinas's distinction, between claims *known* and claims *believed* (as explained by Gilson and outlined in the preceding paragraph), to help formulate the typology in this book of *knowledge claims* (with their corresponding tested beliefs) and *belief claims* (with their corresponding non-tested yet faith-imbued beliefs). Indeed the Thomist *believing* a non-tested proposition is a different matter, psychologically, from the Thomist *knowing* a self-evident proposition. Similar to Gilson's analysis, theologian B. A. Gerrish describes the psychological aspect of Thomistic faith as located in the human intellect.[73] The intellect of faith, however, although amounting to a high degree of certitude for the religious believer, is an intellect not compelled to assent by the proposition, but compelled to assent by a choice of will to believe the proposition. Hence, Gerrish dichotomizes Thomistic faith from Thomistic knowledge (*scientia*) at least when knowledge is taken in the scientific sense—i.e., knowledge as self-evident propositions.[74] The intellect of scientific knowledge, then, is an intellect compelled to assent by the self-evident character of the proposition itself. In a creative move, Gerrish imagines the intellect of Thomistic faith as landing on a cognitive scale, halfway between the intellect of self-evident knowledge and the intellect of mere opinion (although, as mentioned, faith still amounts to a certainty for the religious believer).[75]

Where am I going with all of this? Well, Étienne Gilson's presentation of Thomistic thought, and its corresponding psychological separation between *knowledge* and *belief*, is useful to us—in supporting my motivation for employing the knowledge claim and belief claim typology adopted in this book. However, it is also important for us to take a look at current, twenty-first-century ideas about the nature (and role) of the *experience of believing* in religious life as well as in scientific practice. That analysis will help to fortify our already growing conceptions of tested beliefs[76] and non-tested yet faith-imbued beliefs[77]—which continue to reappear now and throughout

72. Gilson, *Reason and Revelation*, 83–84.
73. Gerrish, "'Assent' in Thomas Aquinas," 6.
74. Gerrish, "'Assent' in Thomas Aquinas," 6.
75. Gerrish, "'Assent' in Thomas Aquinas," 6.
76. Recall that, in this book, tested beliefs are the objects of the cognitive states of knowledge claims.
77. Recall that, in this book, non-tested yet faith-imbued beliefs are the objects of the cognitive states of belief claims.

Background Information and Assumptions   29

the book. About the cognitive nature of believing, in his recent *Evolutionary Religion* (2013), philosopher of religion, J. L. Schellenberg, argues that all instances of believing are *involuntary*,[78] "involving a feeling or sense."[79] In this conception of believing, experiences of beliefs are thought to occur under circumstances beyond one's direct control, instead of the believer's own actions directly causing him or her to experience beliefs. Schellenberg even applies the analogy of an involuntary depression coming over a person,[80] which the person seemingly cannot control, to describe his notion of the experience of believing as an involuntary mental activity. Important to note is that involuntary beliefs, although passively felt or sensed, still involve the believer *thinking about* the world—kinds of "world-thoughts,"[81] as Schellenberg puts them, which involuntarily manifest beliefs. Most important for us to recognize is that, to experience an involuntary belief by way of these "world-thoughts," is to say *how* the physical world is *for* the believer (or disbeliever) in question.[82]

Firstly, I agree that, prior to one's active participation in any project of human inquiry, one already experiences some *involuntary background beliefs*, whether sensory or introspective, which are not consciously apprehended. Secondly, however, my epistemic separation in this book—between *tested beliefs* and *non-tested beliefs*—raises the question here of whether some acts of believing include both involuntary *and* voluntary mental states? If initially this sounds odd, then hear me out: On the one hand, it could be argued that intersubjectively available evidence, which supports tested beliefs, causes one to experience *no choice but to believe* that tested beliefs are accurate descriptions of the physical world—in effect, to experience an involuntary believing state. Expressed in more blunt terms, the relevant point is: so long as intersubjectively tested evidence is available, what other choice could one really have *but to believe tested beliefs*? Yet also, on the other hand, it seems the intersubjectively available evidence, which supports tested beliefs, mentally *pushes* one, as it were, toward a deliberate, *conscious* assent to tested beliefs—as it were, toward a voluntary believing state. In this alternative sense, tested evidence can be seen to encourage and even help promote one's conscious (voluntary) assent to a particular tested belief, which corresponds to the tested evidence available.

---

78. Schellenberg, *Evolutionary Religion*, 40.
79. Schellenberg, *Evolutionary Religion*, 80.
80. Schellenberg, *Evolutionary Religion*, 40.
81. Schellenberg, *The Wisdom to Doubt*, 1, Kindle.
82. Schellenberg, *The Wisdom to Doubt*, 1–2, Kindle.

Furthermore, my own characterization of *knowledge claims* (in this book) outlines how knowledge claims are situated, in part, by a conscious, voluntarily expressed desire to make known their tested beliefs to others—to ensure that their tested beliefs are open to external analysis by outside parties. It seems, then, that both involuntary and voluntary mental states are at play when tested beliefs are the objects of one's cognitive, believing experiences. About involuntary (passive) beliefs generally, Schellenberg raises the point that, in this case, the believer is thought to be passively *represented to* by the world rather than the believer *actively representing the world to* himself or herself.[83] But, again, to my preceding point that assenting to tested beliefs also includes a voluntary mental act: (a) *to actively represent the physical world to oneself* is the same as (b) *to consciously attempt to describe (represent) the physical world—the goal of intersubjectively testing beliefs and then assenting to those tested beliefs; what knowledge claims aim to accomplish.* Thus, intrinsic to the human experience of assenting to *tested beliefs* (objects of knowledge claims) are the following *two* mental activities:

1. A voluntary mental activity to consciously describe the physical world, or at least to attempt to do this.
2. An involuntary mental activity of passively feeling or sensing tested beliefs about the physical world—where, because of the evidence available, there really is no choice but to believe these tested beliefs.

Thus, in the preceding believing process, the believer works to consciously (voluntarily) describe the physical world and, at the same time, the physical world seems to (as it were) make itself known to the believer by way of seemingly uncontrollable (involuntary) beliefs which are intersubjectively tested.

About the suggestion that both involuntary and voluntary mental states are involved in the experience of assenting to tested beliefs, Susan Haack, too, comments that trusting our senses seems to be an involuntary mental activity—that is, *prima facie* trusting or believing our senses just seems a natural way to go.[84] However, the involuntary trusting of our senses is just one aspect of the believing experience where tested beliefs are concerned. As Haack also puts it, about the external *analysis* of beliefs, "It is sentences or propositions, not states of a person, which can support or undermine each other, probabilify or disconfirm each other, be consistent or inconsistent with each other, cohere or fail to cohere as an explanatory

---

83. Schellenberg, *The Will to Imagine*, 2, Kindle.
84. Haack, *Evidence and Inquiry*, 270.

story."[85] In other words, (i) *involuntary mental states* might cause us to trust our senses or to experience a passive feeling that a tested belief is accurate, but these involuntary mental states are still different from (ii) *deliberate, voluntary mental states*, which are the mental states which allow beliefs to be consciously apprehended in verbal sentences. Once expressed in verbal sentences, one's beliefs are open to external analysis by outside parties . . . are open to comparison with other, competing beliefs—all in all, are open to the epistemic processes involved in the adjudication of beliefs by way of a hypothetico-deductive method.

Therefore, to wrap up this discussion: While it is the case that what Schellenberg describes as the "voluntary acceptance"[86] of a proposition might not require any involuntary belief, involuntary belief might, and can, co-exist alongside some element of a voluntary believing state—even if just a voluntary believing state actualized as the *voluntarily expressed desire* (included in knowledge claims) to consciously ensure that the tested beliefs of knowledge claims are open to external analysis by outside parties. In contrast, the non-tested beliefs of belief claims, appearing to be not open to external analysis by outside parties, do not include any deliberate, voluntary believing state. Although, since according to Schellenberg, all instances of believing must be involuntary, assenting to non-tested beliefs would have to at least include the involuntary mental activity of passively feeling or sensing non-tested beliefs about the physical world. However, in this case, non-tested beliefs would be passively felt, not because natural reason leaves one with no choice but to believe them (they are non-tested beliefs, so there is in fact a choice to not believe them), but passively felt just because they are part and parcel of one's reported religious inclinations. Thus, intrinsic to the human experience of assenting to *non-tested beliefs* (objects of belief claims) is the following *single* reported mental activity:

1. A reported, involuntary mental activity of passively *feeling* or *sensing* non-tested beliefs about the physical world—where these non-tested beliefs are faith-imbued; for the religious devotee, these non-tested beliefs are reported to be part and parcel of his or her *felt/sensed* religious inclinations.

So, having now unpacked my rationale for adopting the *knowledge claim* and *belief claim* typology,[87] and, moreover, having fortified our growing conceptions of *tested beliefs* and *non-tested beliefs*, in the remainder of this

---

85. Haack, *Evidence and Inquiry*, 124.

86. Schellenberg, *Evolutionary Religion*, 80–81.

87. As mentioned, this typology serves (i) as a useful heuristic and (ii) possesses a psychological Thomistic flavour.

section I contrast knowledge claims from science with belief claims from religion, pointing out how, curiously, both types of claims attempt to describe shared states of affairs in one, physical world. Without meaning to sound too melodramatic, let the epistemic trouble begin.

In contrast to quantitative perceptions and our fairly basic assumption that a physical world does exist, reported phenomena of mythic perceptions, or, say, Platonic universes, and overall speculation about trans-empirical worlds, all lack the standard of observed experiences necessary for an intersubjective study. Both scientific exercises and religious exercises making claims about states of affairs in the *same* physical world creates *epistemic tension* in the academic study of science and religion. While it may be the case that some religious testimonies refer to objects of belief residing in a trans-empirical world—a "world" thought to exist outside the limits of sensory experience—it is also the case that many religious testimonies involve claims made about an interplay between this so-called non-physical, trans-empirical world and the *physical*, empirical world. For example, claims of religious miracles are often claims concerning events which are thought to occur as violations of the *physical* laws of nature in the observed world.[88] In Christianity (one example), there exists the claim that an invisible CPS-agent, through an inexplicable divine mystery, is made visible in *physical*, human form[89]—a claim seemingly made by liberal and conservative Christian groups alike. Among an Islamic group in Pakistan during the Zia regime (another example), there existed the claim that jinns, creatures depicted in Arabian mythology, are comprised of a *physical*, chemical composition, capable of being extracted as energy.[90] In Buddhist thought, rather than being a metaphysical component of the illusion of saṃsāra only, the claim was made by nineteenth-century Buddhist monks that Mount Meru does in fact exist in the *physical* world and that demigods inhabit its summit and slopes.[91]

Secondly, in more technical matters, regarding the origin and constitution of physical reality, Hebraic creation narratives in Genesis, Arabic creation narratives in Surah Al-A'raf,[92] and ancient Near Eastern geocentric cosmology in Joshua,[93] are used by religious devotees to make claims about

---

88. Hoodbhoy, *Islam and Science*, 14.
89. For example, see biblical passages such as John 1:14 or Philippians 2:8.
90. Hoodbhoy, *Islam and Science*, xiii.
91. Lopez, *Buddhism and Science*, 55.
92. For example, see biblical passages Genesis 1:1–30 and 2:4–22, or, in the Qur'an, see Surah Al-A'raf 7:11–25.
93. See the biblical passage Joshua 10:13.

Background Information and Assumptions   33

states of affairs concerning the origin of human life and the structure of the solar system. At the same time, the substantive contents of the scientific theories of natural selection, common descent, and heliocentrism,[94] are used by scientific practitioners to make claims about states of affairs concerning the origin of human life and the structure of the solar system. Finally, to consider two timely examples at the interface of science and religion: (i) CPS-agent-based, revelatory information in Leviticus and Romans is used by religious devotees to make claims about states of affairs concerning the proposed *unnaturalness* of same-sex attraction.[95] At the same time, scientific theories describing sexual orientation as inborn, determined biologically by the modification of gene expression,[96] or determined by biopsychosocial factors,[97] are used by scientific practitioners to make claims about states of affairs concerning the proposed *naturalness* of same-sex attraction.[98] (ii) In questioning the right for aid in dying for terminally ill patients, biblical texts are used by religious devotees to make claims about states of affairs concerning the future course of one's life as fixed,[99] predetermined by the activity of a CPS-agent. At the same time, scientific theories about human physiology are used by scientific practitioners to make claims about states of affairs concerning the future course of one's life as in flux, determined by the chemical reactions of an unpredictable biological organism. In all examples mentioned, information about states of affairs provided by claims of religious devotees is different from—and, in terms of causality, conflicts with—information about the very same states of affairs provided by claims of scientific practitioners.

The epistemic problem outlined in the examples in the preceding paragraphs, where religious exercises make claims about states of affairs in a physical world which is also the territory of the claims of science, cannot

94. Riexinger, "Islamic Opposition to the Darwinian Theory of Evolution," 483.

95. For example, see biblical passages such as Leviticus 18:22; 20:13; and Romans 1:26–27.

96. Friberg *et al.*, "Homosexuality as a Consequence of Epigenetically Canalized Sexual Development," 343–68.

97. Downey and Friedman, "Neurobiology and Sexual Orientation," 131–53.

98. I should clarify that, like many in the modern world, I hold the view that all sexual orientations and gender identities, including non-heterosexual orientations and non-cisgender identities (all those included in the LGBTI initialism), are inborn and natural, determined biologically. In this example, however, about non-heterosexual orientations, I deliberately contrast the term *naturalness* with the term *unnaturalness* to recognize the sociocultural observation that some religious institutions seem to consider same-sex attraction to be unnatural—that is, in those institutions' plausibility structures, to be a violation of societal norms.

99. For example, see biblical passages such as Psalm 31:15 or 1 Corinthians 6:19.

be ignored. To disregard this epistemic problem would amount to an intellectually bankrupt book. I will not accept that knowledge claims in science and belief claims in religion innocently co-exist in epistemic harmony when in fact both types of claims blatantly attempt to describe the same states of affairs in the same physical world—and in doing so conflict epistemically with one another. Furthermore, to accept that knowledge claims and belief claims can simply co-exist without any epistemic problems arising, is to deny that any kind of theory of rationality is even necessary in one's life or academic work. However, when this epistemic conundrum, concerning knowledge claims versus belief claims and their shared use of the same states of affairs in one physical world, is acknowledged, initial complications for potential compatibility between science and religion inevitably begin to arise. Also relevant now is the question: *are knowledge claims an epistemic benchmark for belief claims*? I begin to address this question in chapter 3; however, before doing so I must present in chapter 2 a survey of various belief claims arising from diverse religious, philosophical, and psychical traditions.

2

Knowledge Claims and Belief Claims

A SURVEY OF RELIGIOUS, PHILOSOPHICAL, AND PSYCHICAL BELIEF CLAIMS

THE PLETHORA OF BELIEF claims made and attested to in modern human societies are not limited to a single religious or philosophical tradition, but encompass many traditions. To that end, notoriously problematic in religious studies and academic theology is the task of defining the term *religion*, if such a task is even possible. A large part of the difficulty in defining the term *religion* arises from the multiplicity of popular religious and philosophical belief systems, which are often characterized as types of "religion," but nevertheless remain mutually exclusive in their substantive content and aims. In *The Sacred Is the Profane: The Political Nature of "Religion"* (2013), religious studies teachers, William E. Arnal and Russell T. McCutcheon, point out that providing a definition for *religion*—to say what religion *is* within some fixed limits—is difficult to achieve without also theorizing about the nature of religion.[1] In this case, a circularity among the activities of defining and theorizing becomes unavoidable.

However, it may be this apparent interest to develop a suitable definition *per se* for *religion* is misguided; that perhaps the task is not so important after all. As cognitive anthropologist, Pascal Boyer, observes, anthropological findings in the study of religious behaviour present the (somewhat unexpected) conclusions that religious activity, i.e., religiosity, can exist without

---

1. Arnal and McCutcheon, *The Sacred Is the Profane*, 18.

having a "religion"—that religiosity can exist without having the concept *religion* at all.² Although the idea of a universal religion—which any person could adopt regardless of one's previous religious background—is not a universal idea, Boyer claims the label *religion*, applied to various modes of thought involving CPS-agents, is merely a label. In societies where multiple institutional religions exist, the label *religion* is a convenient way to distinguish these various institutions; however, relying on and testifying to the activities of CPS-agents in one's life does not require that one have a "religion," as examples from various cultures illustrate.³ With this in mind, within the scientific study of religion, the concept of *religiosity* seems preferred over the concept of *religion*—in fact, it may be more accurate to describe this book as a *scientific study of religiosity* rather than a study of religion. (Although in literature the academic field is formally known as the *scientific study of religion*, the phrase *scientific study of religiosity* is perhaps more accurate in describing the field's purpose.)

Nevertheless, in attempting briefly to offer a definition for the term *religion* (as a heuristic, if anything), what is the case is that modern religions are grounded in and maintain their existences through the frameworks of socially constructed institutions. To the social reality of *religion*, then, a modern religious institution provides such elements as (i) a religious epistemological framework through which a community adjudicates its belief claims and (ii) a group of religious devotees who, through their shared goals, submit belief claims to test in a consensus theory of truth. (Whether a religious institution realizes it possesses these features, or not, is another matter.) To be argued in greater detail later, *religiosity*, in contrast, is a much more open-ended concept: in a cognitive fashion, religiosity exists, is developed, and is transmitted between individuals *without* the aid of any social institution and *without* any consensus on the truth of belief claims. *Religion*, though, may be thought of as a mythopoeic mode of thought—one centred on mythological texts, CPS-agents, and testimonies of religious devotees. In an anthropological fashion, connecting religion specifically to the activities of CPS-agents, Melford E. Spiro famously describes *religion* as "an institution consisting of culturally patterned interaction [relationship] with culturally postulated superhuman beings [agents]."⁴ Indeed, *superhuman agency*, *causality*, and *relationship* are key elements in many current world (and

---

2. Boyer, *Religion Explained*, 9.

3. See examples referenced in chapter 8, including examples from Boyer's fieldwork.

4. Spiro, "Religion: Problems of Definition and Explanation," 96.

primitive) religions.⁵ In a different but similar sense, religion amounts to an *eros* to knowledge, closing "a gap" or making "a jump" between empirical and trans-empirical worlds, and meaning-making in the context of a finite human existence. Indeed, the construction of meaning, especially, as Berger puts it, in face of the seemingly "empty vastness of the universe,"⁶ is a common theme in many religions—not to mention the desire to find sources of meaning in human life is often urgent and intense. More specifically, Wiebe, in his seminal book *The Irony of Theology and the Nature of Religious Thought* (1991), suggests the following definition for *religion*: "Religion, that is, will be taken to consist of the stories of transcendence [a trans-empirical world]; of another realm of reality; of superhuman/supernatural being(s) that have the power to help (or to harm) humankind."⁷ Wiebe's definition is useful, because it points out common themes in *religion* regardless of any one particular religious institution or tradition.

Religion defined as *belief about a trans-empirical world* seems particularly helpful. It is difficult to contemplate a religion that would not involve reflection about (or reported testimony about) some reality "out there" or "in here," especially one which allows humans to project their human thoughts and emotions, their greatest hopes and fears, beyond their finite human existence. Concerning this, Wiebe rightly observes, "The recognition of human limitation—of finitude—in face of the inexorable processes of nature that eventuate in death, and the transcending of those limitations by postulating (recognizing/assuming) the existence of a superhuman source of power on which humans can draw, is what religion is essentially all about."⁸ The propositional character of religion, where the substantive beliefs of religion are "housed," if you will, in the epistemic form of *belief claims* means science and religion are well-suited for epistemic comparison and contrasting. As outlined in chapter 1, both scientific and religious exercises involve the making of propositional claims about states of affairs in the physical world.

Socially and institutionally, however, religion is perhaps best conceptualized as the corporate expression of faith, displayed in a community of people who share the same beliefs and, more or less, adhere to shared religious testimonies expressed propositionally in the form of belief claims. In *The Social Construction of Reality: A Treatise in the Sociology of Knowledge* (1966), sociologists, Peter Berger and Thomas Luckmann, present their

---

5. Wiebe, *Religion and Truth*, 16.
6. Berger, *The Sacred Canopy*, 100.
7. Wiebe, *The Irony of Theology*, 33.
8. Wiebe, *The Irony of Theology*, 33.

thesis of *social construction* whereby humans are thought to act as the producers of their own social worlds. Put simply, Berger and Luckmann propose that the social world of a community was created by the community. (The type of community in question might be what I call a *knowledge community* composed of scientists or engineers, or a *belief community* composed of religious devotees or members of, say, a theosophic society.) The crux, however, of Berger's and Luckmann's thesis is that members of a given community do not realize they have created their own social world. Instead they believe (assume) their social world maintains an existence, *a priori*, independent from their own human actions. Nevertheless the social world was in fact created by the community.[9] Berger and Luckmann present mechanisms through which a social world is thought to be created, unknowingly, by a community:[10] From birth, humans are subject to various influences determined by the community in which they live. For one, languages help to create social worlds, providing humans with the ability to separate their everyday experiences into various knowledge and belief categories. In a community, different roles are carried out by different individuals; over time, those roles become routine, providing the community with an institutional framework. Also, the sharing of history between community members produces a body of knowledge passed between generations.

Speaking about social construction generally, philosopher of science, Ian Hacking, is careful to point out that, when the social construction of any X is proposed, the first question to resolve is *what is X*?[11] For example, for our concerns in science and religion, is X a physical or metaphysical object, an idea in one's imagination, or a human institution? Or, more ambiguously, is X a philosophy-laden (or theology-laden) concept such as *truth*, *fact*, or *reality*? Suppose, then, that X is taken as the human institution known as *religion*: About religion as a human institution specifically, Berger suggests that "religion is the human enterprise by which a sacred cosmos is established,"[12] where *sacred* is "a quality of mysterious and awesome power, other than man [people] and yet related to him [them], which is believed to reside in certain objects of experience."[13] Here is, yet again, another possible definition for *religion* and a definition perhaps well suited to the uses of all who identify as theist, atheist, agnostic, or igtheist.[14] From sociological,

9. Berger and Luckmann, *The Social Construction of Reality*, 61.
10. Berger and Luckmann, *The Social Construction of Reality*, 37, 53–55.
11. Hacking, *The Social Construction of What*, 68.
12. Berger, *The Sacred Canopy*, 25.
13. Berger, *The Sacred Canopy*, 25.
14. Semantic differences between these four terms—*theist*, *atheist*, *agnostic*, and

psychological, and psychoanalytic viewpoints, it is widely accepted that gods have a place in the lives of many humans: in that sense, there is some "reality" for the existence of gods, even though the nature of that reality and its objects of experience may in fact be socially constructed. Characterizing the study of belief claims as a study of worldviews and analyzing the place for beliefs about gods in the lives of humans, Smart observes, "The modern study of worldviews helps illuminate worldviews, of course, both traditional and secular, which are such an engine of both continuity and change, and therefore it explores feelings and ideas and tries to understand what exists inside the heads of people. *What people believe is an important aspect of reality whether or not what they believe is true.*"[15] My use of the term *worldview* deserves a brief disambiguation, as this term carries various meanings. Characterizing the study of belief claims as a study of worldviews, the sense in which Smart applies the notion of worldviews, means that a worldview must include a conceptual framework for theorizing about the physical world and one's existence in the world. Given the role religions play in creating a meaningful human existence for the religious devotee—especially in face of what is a physically unpredictable, finite human existence—religious beliefs are naturally included in the substantive content of one's worldview.

James W. Underhill, in his recent study (2013) of the thought of linguist Wilhelm von Humboldt, notes that both *Weltanschauung* and *Weltansicht* are used to describe the English *worldview*, although each German term, *Weltanschauung* and *Weltansicht*, brings a different meaning to the English realization of *worldview*. Humboldt's contribution to the concept of a worldview is that of the less common *Weltansicht*, the element of language

---

igtheist—are described as follows: *Theist* is often used to label a person who says he or she believes in God. In contrast *atheist* is often used to label a person who says he or she does not believe in God. (Here I am using the term *God*, but *Allah* or the name of another CPS-agent—*Zeus, Attis, Adonis*, etc.—could be substituted here.) However, as I noted from my internship work during university as an interim school chaplain and interim church minister: "The problem with the terms *atheist* and *theist* is that these terms, however useful they may be to categorize groups of people, are only labels. . . . Some people's beliefs change throughout their lives (we eliminate some beliefs and/or add other beliefs to our conscious minds), but people retain the meaning or purpose in life that arose from previous beliefs even if those beliefs are based on religious stories now understood to be historically irrelevant" (Woodward 2014, 47). Another term, commonly used, is Thomas Huxley's term *agnostic*, describing a person who says there is no way to know whether or not God exists. Finally, another term, less commonly used, is Paul Kurtz's term *igtheist*, a person who says that the statement "*God exists*," a proposition with no existential import, is a meaningless statement. In *The New Skepticism: Inquiry and Reliable Knowledge*, Kurtz explains the life of an igtheist as follows: "I cannot say whether or not such a being [God] exists since *I do not comprehend what is being asserted*" (197; emphasis added).

15. Smart, *Worldviews*, 1–2; emphasis added.

itself in shaping one's conception of the physical world. Humboldt argued that *Weltansicht* is for the most part an unconscious affair, except for a few "exceptional individuals"[16] who analyze language itself as a mode of conceptualization.[17] In contrast, the more common *Weltanschauung*, an intuitive mode of thought expressing one's innate need to conceptualize the physical world, depends on the more fundamental *Weltansicht*. The distinction between the two German terms is perhaps best articulated as *Weltansicht* being one's first sensory contact with the physical world, in which language itself contextualizes contact, and *Weltanschauung* being the secondary formulation of belief claims and application of beliefs to interpret the world.[18]

Julian Huxley appears to understand *worldview* as *Weltanschauung*: Huxley used the metaphor of a human skeleton to describe the nature of religious beliefs as "idea systems" in one's life.[19] As types of worldviews and paradigms of rationality, idea systems comprise frameworks for life similar to the physical framework of a human skeleton. An evolutionary skeleton provides shape and structure to a human body which is then "clothed" by a biological body. Belief claims treated as worldviews provide intellectual structuring to ideas in the mind and, in doing so, cause one to make commitments toward following various paradigms of rationality. Finally, this intellectual structuring of ideas in the mind is "clothed" by the everyday outcomes of human experience, learning, and critical encounters with the world. Interestingly, an interlocutor as different as Sigmund Freud, whose psychoanalytic theory of mind is utilized as a critical theory of religion,[20] explains *Weltanschauung* as "an intellectual construction which solves all the problems of our existence . . . which, accordingly, leaves no question unanswered and in which everything that interests us finds its fixed place."[21] Thus, for Freud, the goals of possessing a *Weltanschauung* are that, within this intellectual construction, one can feel secure, know what to strive for, and deal expediently with one's emotions—tasks which belief claims in many religions are readily seen to accomplish.

In recognizing the semantic distinction between *Weltansicht* and *Weltanschauung* (but a distinction which Underhill points out has not been well understood in the English context of *worldview*), it seems the use of *worldview* in this book is best correlated with *Weltanschauung*, the substantive

16. Underhill, *Humboldt, Worldview and Language*, 17.
17. Underhill, *Humboldt, Worldview and Language*, 17.
18. Underhill, *Humboldt, Worldview and Language*, 18.
19. Hoodbhoy, *Islam and Science*, 119.
20. Hewitt, *Freud on Religion*, 17–18.
21. Freud, "The Question of a Weltanschauung," 158.

element of one's conception of the physical world and the intellectual foothold in the mind where belief claims are formulated and maintained. Indeed, it is these components of *Weltanschauung* which appear to situate Smart's understanding of *worldview*. At the same time, however, it is worth noting the contribution of *Weltansicht* to *worldview*: belief claims of *Weltanschauung*—themselves types of metaphysical constraints placed around one's conception of the physical world—are constrained previously by the particular language system of *Weltansicht*, which precedes the formulation of beliefs. Therefore, in this book, exploration of belief claims as exploration of worldviews presupposes (i) the existence of a language system which contextualizes sensory contact with the physical world (*Weltansicht*) and (ii) the seemingly intuitive need of humans to interpret the physical world and their existence in the world (*Weltanschauung*).

Regarding the seemingly intuitive need of humans to interpret the physical world and their existence in the world, Jonathan Evans points out that, for some, the cognitive foundations of science and religion are thought to share a common goal—to "explain" states of affairs in the physical world.[22] However, to be discussed, the epistemic nature of an *explanation* in scientific causation is radically different from the agentic "explanations" of religious claims. To that end, perhaps unsettling for some, but intriguing for others, is Boyer's thesis presented in his *Religion Explained: The Evolutionary Origins of Religious Thought* (2001). Boyer wonders, given such a varied human phenomenon as religiosity, how can religiosity originate from and be explained by a human physiology (brain) which is not varied, but the same for all humans?[23] Furthermore, humans can be quite gullible, but they are not gullible in such a way that just *any* claims are acceptable to them. About this, Boyer remarks: "Religious claims are indeed beyond verification; people do like sensational supernatural tales better than banal stories and generally spend little time rethinking every bit of cultural information they acquire. But this cannot be a sufficient explanation of why people have the concepts they have, the beliefs they have, the emotions they have."[24] To illustrate the diversity of religiosity as a human phenomenon—and the diverse range of metaphysical claims ("supernatural tales") reported by various human groups—I provide in the following paragraphs a brief survey of substantive belief claims in some world religions and philosophical and psychical traditions. Also surveyed are examples of *legitimation strategies*[25]—rhetorical

22. Evans, *Thinking Twice*, 37.
23. Boyer, *Religion Explained*, 3.
24. Boyer, *Religion Explained*, 29.
25. Lewis, "How Religions Appeal to the Authority of Science," 24.

techniques used by some religious, philosophical, or psychical groups to attempt to "justify" their claims relative to the epistemology and method of modern science. The worldviews surveyed in the following paragraphs are as follows: (i) Judaism, Christianity, and Islam (Abrahamic Traditions), (ii) Buddhism (East Asian Tradition), (iii) Hinduism (South Asian Tradition), (iv) Spiritualism and Parapsychology, and (v) New Age and Occult.

Judaism, Christianity, and Islam (Abrahamic Traditions)

In the substantive belief claims of Judaism and Christianity, the creation of the physical world *ex nihilo*, the covenant between God and Israel, and the liberation of God's people from bondage in Egypt are key themes. In a typological fashion, Christianity adds to these themes additional claims about the relationship between Jesus Christ and God's chosen people from all races and backgrounds. Similarly, in the belief claims of Islam, Allah's messenger, Mohammed, receives supernatural information from Allah and delivers that information to Allah's followers. In all cases, beliefs are held in an axiomatic fashion. Also common to the monotheistic religions is the notion of direct, self-revelation, vouchsafed from a CPS-agent—an anthropomorphic god referred to (generally) as El, Allah, or God—to religious messengers, prophets, and followers. John Hick remarks how the Christian mind employs various degrees of self-consciousness and self-critical reflection, resulting in various Christian worldviews and hermeneutics.[26] Differing accounts about inclusive or pluralistic modes of salvation, beliefs about the resurrection of Jesus as a physical or mythological event, and the lifestyle of the supposed historical Jesus, contribute toward various Christianities. Similarly, as Dorothee Sölle puts it, "There is no one theology, but extremely different theologies, even in one and the same historical situation."[27] Sölle is speaking from a Christian context, but no doubt her comment applies to Judaism and Islam also. Indeed, post-Enlightenment religiosity involves the splitting of all monotheistic religions into various groups.

In Judaism, the *Haskalah*, the Jewish Enlightenment, from the eighteenth to nineteenth centuries, resulted in the orthodox, conservative, and liberal groups of contemporary Judaism,[28] differing in their interpretations of Mosaic Law and in the cultural trappings they possess. There are also non-religious Jews, living in Tel Aviv, who cease from work on Saturday to observe a religious law (*Shabbat*), suggesting some substantive faith

---

26. Hick, "The Non-Absoluteness of Christianity," 16.
27. Sölle, *Thinking about God*, 7.
28. Hammer, *Claiming Knowledge*, 4.

expression also for secular Jews. Islam, too, has experienced phases of modernization. In *Islam and Science: Religious Orthodoxy and the Battle for Rationality* (1991), physicist Pervez Hoodbhoy argues that the epistemic values of Islamic society and modern science are incompatible; however, he is careful to note there also exist modernized interpretations of Islam (e.g., Islam practiced in Turkey) which allow a separation between the worldly and other-worldly.[29]

As a legitimation strategy for monotheistic religions, whose substantive beliefs include beliefs about a creator god, Ian G. Barbour (speaking from a Christian context) describes the *anthropic principle*.[30] As the assertion goes, fine-tuned, natural phenomena, including physical constants, the rate of expansion of the universe seconds after the Big Bang, the strength of the strong nuclear force in forming chemical elements, and various particle-antiparticle ratios, exist in such a way that any slight (even infinitesimal) deviations from the values of these parameters would mean that human life could not have evolved.[31] Darwinism of course repudiates any suggestion that cosmic teleology has a place when explaining the origin of life—a major obstacle to theism.[32] (Darwinism, then, is also an obstacle to "creation science"[33]—although different from general theism, "creation science" also includes a cosmic teleology.) Some advocates of theism utilize the anthropic principle to argue it could only have been the work of a creator god which brought into existence the very specific values of these physical parameters

---

29. Hoodbhoy, *Islam and Science*, 138.

30. The development of the concept *anthropic principle* (*anthrōpos* is Greek for *human*) is attributed (in different instances) to physicists Robert H. Dicke and Brandon Carter in the mid-1960s and 1970s. Two versions of the anthropic principle are reported: (i) The *weak* anthropic principle affirms that, for a universe to be "observed," it requires the potential for living observers to exist. (ii) The *strong* anthropic principle is that described by Barbour (*Religion and Science*, 204–5) which affirms that specific values for physical parameters are required for the potential for life.

31. Barbour, *Religion and Science*, 204–5.

32. Riexinger, "Islamic Opposition to the Darwinian Theory of Evolution," 483.

33. Various types of "creation science" or "creationism" are reported: (i) Young-earth creationists claim the creation narratives in Genesis are literally true—that the earth was created in six, 24-hour days, sometime around 4004 BCE. (ii) Old-earth creationists claim the creation narratives in Genesis are compatible with modern geological chronology. There exist two branches of "theory" for old-earth creationists: (a) Day-age theory proposes each of the six "days" in Genesis is actually a long period of time, accommodating the ages of geological dating. (b) Gap theory proposes the six days in Genesis are literal; however, the creation of the physical world in six days occurs *after* a previous period (gap) of geological formation (Haack, "Point of Honor: On Science and Religion," 273).

that are necessary for human life to exist.[34] To put it bluntly, this amounts to a kind of legitimation strategy which argues that scientific accounts describing the origin of human life in fact support the faith-imbued assumption of an enchanted, physical world. It is my observation that, when analyzing the merit of the anthropic principle, one is wise to consider whether the assumption of an enchanted, physical world itself contributes toward the apparent attractiveness of the anthropic principle as a legitimation strategy.

Buddhism (East Asian Tradition)

David L. McMahan points out that Buddhism possesses a unique reputation in the West as being a religion which is, in fact, very much compatible with modern science[35]—this reputation alone lends itself well toward a legitimation strategy for Buddhism.[36] There exists speculation as to whether Buddhism is better classified a world religion or a philosophical belief system: as there is no CPS-agent utilized in the metaphysics of Buddhism, the label *religion*, to some, seems inappropriate. As Buddhist studies teacher, Donald S. Lopez, notes in his *Buddhism and Science: A Guide for the Perplexed*: "His [the Buddha's] was a religion, if it was a religion at all, that required no dogma, no faith, no divinely inspired scriptures, no ritual, no worship of images, no God. This view of the Buddha seemed to have enjoyed particular popularity among the more anticlerical of the European scholars."[37] However, like other world religions, what Buddhism does possess is the notion of closing "a gap," or making "a jump," between empirical and trans-empirical worlds—in Buddhism's case, the ultimate metaphysical reality of nirvāna. Also, like the CPS-agents of other religions, nirvāna is a culturally postulated reality which is interacted with (culturally) by followers of Buddhism.[38]

34. Haack, "Point of Honor: On Science and Religion," 279–80.

35. To be discussed in chapter 4, the precise nature of what it means for science and religion to be "compatible" is far more complex than mere "reputed" compatibility: that Buddhism enjoys a reputation in the West for being compatible with modern science is not enough to conclude that Buddhism and science are, without doubt, compatible. Also, in the popular sense that Buddhism and modern science enjoy a reputation for being "compatible," there is no indication there as to whether this apparent compatibility is epistemic, substantive, institutional, or personal. Such factors will also be dealt with in chapter 4.

36. McMahan, "Buddhism as the 'Religion of Science,'" 117.

37. Lopez, *Buddhism and Science*, 6.

38. About the objection that Buddhism not be classified a world religion *per se*, Wiebe notes how this objection often arises from the accusation that one's definition for *religion* is ethnocentric, assuming the truth of one particular *type* of religion over another. However, as Wiebe (1981, 16) points out, such an objection can be overcome

In Buddhist cosmology, metaphysical and physical beings, including gods, humans, animals, ghosts, and demons, wander through samsāra—the realm of rebirth. The flat earth cosmography of Buddhism includes the mythological Mount Meru which floats in a large body of water also containing several islands.[39] In addition, above and below the surface of the water are various realms of rebirth. "Gods" are distinguished into three types: (i) gods of the Realm of Desire, inhabiting different heavens and celestial realms, (ii) gods of the Realm of Form, inhabiting states of deep concentration in various heavens, and (iii) gods of the Formless Realm, inhabiting a non-physical state of rebirth.[40] Finally, just as there are various Christianities or various Judaisms, various Buddhisms are reported. For example, for Victorian Buddhist scholar Thomas W. Rhys Davids, it was the southern Buddhism of Sri Lanka which is closest to the Buddhism of the supposed historical Buddha.[41] (Southern Buddhism contrasts with the northern Buddhism of Tibet and Nepal.)

Hinduism (South Asian Tradition)

Swami Vivekananda, the nineteenth-century Bengali teacher who brought Vedantic philosophies to the West, attempted to describe the belief claims of Advaita Vedānta—a branch of Hinduism—as claims that are scientific in nature.[42] Stressing that, not only do spiritual laws of the Vedas parallel physical laws of nature, but also that the Vedas proclaim truths about the physical world which modern science is only now just confirming, Hinduism has sought a legitimation strategy through the distancing of itself from other religions and the aligning of itself, or so it claims, with scientific theories. According to C. Mackenzie Brown, Vivekananda attempted to legitimate Advaita Vedānta specifically by separating it from other world religions via the claim that Advaita Vedānta is, in fact, a scientifically verified worldview.[43] To accomplish this task, Vivekananda presented propositions such that the law of the conservation of energy conflicts with a Judaeo-Christian understanding of creation *ex nihilo*: since the total cosmic energy of the physical

---

by the simple clarification that, in a scientific study of religion, the truth of religion is bracketed anyway—religion proper is assumed to be no more "true" than any other human enterprises, including secular ones.

39. McMahan, "Buddhism as the 'Religion of Science,'" 125.
40. Lopez, *Buddhism and Science*, 43–44.
41. Lopez, *Buddhism and Science*, 5.
42. Brown, "Vivekananda," 209.
43. Brown, "Vivekananda," 209.

world has always been constant, there never could have existed a time, or so went his argument, when matter did not exist. In addition, Meera Nanda points out that in present-day India it is not uncommon to find a cultural milieu where Hindu metaphysical claims, about karma, Ātman, or prana, are repositioned to be aligned parallel with scientific theories of evolution and quantum mechanics. The precise nature of this repositioning seems difficult to contemplate; however, it involves the general belief that Hindu religious thought (or, for some, Hindu *philosophical* thought) presents answers to questions about states of affairs in the physical world which are currently asked by modern science or will be asked in the future.[44]

The modern Hindu worldview, concerning in particular its use of both scientific and religious claims to describe the physical world, includes a hierarchy of truths, but also a blurring of the precise nature of causality. Nanda explains how the evolutionism invoked in the belief claims of Hinduism is not always a strictly Darwinian account of the origin of life. While Darwinian theories of natural selection and common descent are permitted, these claims are often relegated to a "lower" level truth, describing the merely physical components utilized in providing an account of the origin of life. Modern Vedic Evolutionism,[45] on the other hand, expresses a "higher" level truth about the existence of human beings. In terms of causality, then, Darwinism loses, contributing no explanatory function toward the mechanism(s) responsible for the origin of life.[46] Instead, "higher" level truths—spiritual forces—are said to co-exist with physical reality, the result being that the causation claimed to actually occur in Modern Vedic Evolutionism is that of the reincarnation of a karma-bearing soul.

Spiritualism and Parapsychology

Spiritualism (or Spiritism) refers to claims about the sources and meanings of alternative states of consciousness—e.g., mesmerism, trances, manifestation of foreign personalities, and mediumship. Spiritualism is an example of both an esoteric tradition and a "medical" one (a pseudo-medical one in modern terms). The ability of Spiritualism to attract medical-based and psychoanalytic practitioners to study its claims (and to take those claims seriously) has been a legitimating force for Spiritualism. Cathy Gutierrez dates the origin of Spiritualism to 1848 when two sisters in New York State reported to have attempted communicating with a poltergeist, resulting in a

44. Nanda, "Madame Blavatsky's Children," 280.
45. Nanda, "Madame Blavatsky's Children," 281.
46. Nanda, "Madame Blavatsky's Children," 283.

trans-Atlantic interest in séances and paranormal phenomena.[47] Key tenets of Spiritualism evolved to include claims that (i) members of all religions and races go to heaven, (ii) the dead—being culturally superior to the living—exist on an advanced plane, providing guidance to the living, and (iii) when allied with science, the communicative techniques of Spiritualism, between the living and the dead, are perfected.[48] In *Claiming Knowledge: Strategies of Epistemology From Theosophy to the New Age* (2004), Olav Hammer explains how, for the members of any esoteric tradition, such as Spiritualism, the adoption of a pragmatic, emic epistemology is helpful in legitimating the claims in question—i.e., the creed, "if it works, it is true," becomes favoured.[49] As a kind of naive realism, then, Spiritualism may be thought to capitalize on the "fact" that Enlightenment values of critical rationalism have gone astray; reports of alternative states of consciousness are suddenly taken at face value. As Hammer puts it, in such a scenario, the epistemic step from professed belief to established fact is very small.[50]

Nevertheless, despite the apparent naive realism of Spiritualism, the field of parapsychology, established through the efforts of the Society for Psychical Research in 1882, seeks to organize a scientific discipline centred on claims about the supernatural.[51] As a legitimation strategy, naturalizing the supernatural context of Spiritualism is problematic. On the one hand, parapsychology is careful to avoid explicit reference to supernatural causation; however, parapsychology also wishes to avoid the tendency toward describing its claims as illusions or epiphenomena. According to Egil Asprem, in looking toward the *as of yet unexplained*, parapsychology presents a residual category for "scientific" research—i.e., theorizing about claims which fall outside the established epistemic boundaries of science.[52] Concepts common to parapsychology such as *supernormal* and *telepathy* also aid in the attempted legitimation of Spiritualism and other psychical phenomena. For example, Frederic W. H. Myers's concept of the *supernormal* contends that some phenomena deviate from "normality"—that *a priori* these phenomena are not fixed by the physical laws of nature. In utilizing such a concept, parapsychology attempts to avoid the problematic contention that it does in fact make claims about invisible, supernatural phenomena (thereby avoiding the contention that it makes claims which violate the laws of nature), but

47. Gutierrez, "Spiritualism and Psychical Research," 591.
48. Gutierrez, "Spiritualism and Psychical Research," 591–92.
49. Hammer, *Claiming Knowledge*, 507.
50. Hammer, *Claiming Knowledge*, 507.
51. Asprem, "Parapsychology," 633.
52. Asprem, "Parapsychology," 639.

keeps itself open to the fact that it does (unashamedly) make claims about phenomena which are residually separate from the "normal," natural world. Similarly, when no natural cause can be discerned, Jeffrey J. Kripal points out that, in psychical research, telepathy is posited as a causal mechanism to explain seemingly coincidental relationships between internal, subjective visions and external, physical events.[53] In all cases, the empirical concept of *causality* is mixed with the supernormal aims of parapsychology in attempts to legitimate claims about reported psychical realities.

New Age and Occult

Jochen Scherer explains how the concept of *synchronicity*—that is, meaningful coincidences—permeates New Age thought.[54] C. G. Jung coined the term *synchronicity* to describe a situation where an event in one's life in the physical world appears to coincide in an extraordinary way with a psychological breakthrough in the same person's life.[55] Indeed, for "New Agers," as Scherer calls them, coincidences are by no means random accidents but are thought to be scenarios (synchronicities) which connect different events in one's life into a purposeful and unified whole. Notions of a "thread of continuity" in one's life or that one has been "guided" are common to New Age; the popular notions of "that's a miracle," serendipity, or that an event was "lucky" may also be interpreted as examples of synchronicity.

In her *Freud on Religion*, psychoanalyst Marsha Aileen Hewitt describes the "kernel of truth,"[56] which Freud thought telepathy—the claim that thoughts can be transferred between individuals without the aid of the senses—might provide to the study of the occult.[57] Interestingly, according to Hewitt, Freud was unable to completely resolve his view on telepathy, fluctuating between attitudes of accepting telepathy as a reported phenomenon to be taken seriously and rejecting telepathy as charlatanism. At any rate, what is the case is that, unlike the occult generally speaking, Freud kept in mind the possibility that an investigation into the causality of telepathy might aid in legitimating claims of reported thought-transference. It is important to note, Hewitt stresses, that in terms of investigating the causality of telepathy Freud was not advocating supernatural explanatory

---

53. Kripal, *Authors of the Impossible*, 74, Kindle.
54. Scherer, "The 'Scientific' Presentation," 673.
55. Scherer, "The 'Scientific' Presentation," 673.
56. Hewitt, *Freud on Religion*, 86.
57. Hewitt, *Freud on Religion*, 86.

forces.[58] Unlike the notion in parapsychology of *as of yet unexplained*, where a residual category of supernormal explanatory forces is permitted, Freud felt the inability to elucidate the causality of telepathy was "a temporary state of affairs,"[59] one that might eventually be overcome by way of natural explanations. Freud's interpretation of telepathy as an affective mode of transfer—unconscious communication between two minds with the help of a *conscious* "bridge," embedded in emotional human relationships[60]—allowed him to distance his interpretation of telepathy from other notions of the occult which seemed more fraudulent.[61]

This concludes the survey of substantive belief claims in some world religions and philosophical and psychical traditions. Also surveyed were examples of legitimation strategies, used by some religious, philosophical, and psychical groups to attempt to "justify" their claims relative to the epistemology and method of modern science. It is to that topic—the epistemology and method of modern science—that I now turn.

EPISTEMIC JUSTIFICATION OF SCIENTIFIC BELIEFS

Olav Hammer and James R. Lewis, in their introduction to the very provocative *Handbook of Religion and the Authority of Science*,[62] point out how the rhetorical strength of science—the institutional backing of science; the ability of science to employ intersubjective scrutiny in experiments—means a harmony between science *and* religion seems desired by religious institutions and religious people.[63] To that end, when assessing any epistemic relationships between scientific and religious modes of thought, it is worth noting that the word *and* in the phrase "science *and* religion" is not merely

---

58. Hewitt, *Freud on Religion*, 86.
59. Hewitt, *Freud on Religion*, 87.
60. Hewitt, *Freud on Religion*, 87.
61. In addition to his work on telepathy, it is worth noting Freud's methodology in the study of religion, which interestingly helps clarify the particular aims of methodological atheism in general. About this, Hewitt observes, "He [Freud] was an atheist in the double sense that he did not believe in God and he had no direct, subjective experience that might be called mystical . . . *Yet it does not automatically follow that he was invested in promoting atheism*" (Hewitt, *Freud on Religion*, 6; emphasis added). Like other etic scholars of religion, Freud's projects are *non-confessional*, but are also different from projects espousing a so-called "fundamentalist atheism."
62. Much of the content used in the survey of belief claims and legitimation strategies in chapter 2 included references from essays contained in *Handbook of Religion and the Authority of Science*.
63. Hammer and Lewis, "Introduction," 4–5.

a conjunction connecting the term *science* with the term *religion*. Like the terms *science* and *religion*, the intended meaning of the word *and* in the context of "science *and* religion" is important to consider.[64] For example, the potential conjoining of the word *Islam* with the word *science*—rendering the phrase "Islam *and* science"—may suggest for some an attempted conjoining of Islamic epistemic values with the cognitive values of science, or a substantive conjoining of scientific and Islamic claims. The notion of an "Islamic science," then, would include an epistemic connotation as well as faith-imbued substantive claims; the same would apply for "Christian science," "Jewish science," or "Hindu science," etc. *Prima facie* attempted epistemic and substantive conjoining of the empirical thought of science with the mythopoeic thought of religion(s) seems problematic.

Winner of the Nobel Prize in Physics (1979) *and* self-proclaimed Muslim believer, Mohammed Abdus Salam, writing the Foreword to Pervez Hoodbhoy's *Islam and Science* (mentioned previously), makes the point well when he states, "There is only one universal science, its problems and modalities are international and there is no such thing as Islamic science just as there is no Hindu science, no Jewish science, no Confucian science, nor Christian science."[65] As Salam points out, so long as it is understood that the apologetic aims of religious beliefs have no role to play in testing scientific beliefs, problems of "Islamic science" or "Christian science" are nonexistent (even if people do choose to combine these concepts, epistemically and/or substantively, for personal use). Recognizing an epistemic distinction between knowledge claims and belief claims would suggest that, when "science *and* religion" are studied, the academic analysis takes on the character of a *comparing and contrasting* rather than an attempted substantive conjoining of science and religion (i.e., implications of different meanings of the word *and* in "science *and* religion"). The only question is, how acceptable is an epistemic distinction between knowledge claims (science) and belief claims (religion) for practicing scientists, engineers, and religious devotees? With this in mind, in the remainder of this chapter, and as a lead-in to chapter 3, I take up the topic of the epistemic justification of scientific beliefs. In doing so, I focus on the more abstract elements of the philosophy of scientific theories rather than possible conceptions of science that find a consensus in everyday practice.[66] (At a later stage I discuss the question

---

64. Lopez, *Buddhism and Science*, 2.

65. Salam, foreword to *Islam and Science*, ix.

66. In this book, I function, in part, as a writer in the philosophy of science: my analysis of scientific products and method may be different from the analysis which a practicing scientist or engineer would provide about the same topics. Likewise, my analysis of religious products and discourse may be different from the analysis which

of consensus in science, a topic central to the post-Kuhnian compatibility system.)

In the epistemic justification of scientific beliefs, the concept of a *scientific theory*[67] indicates a methodological form for human beliefs, used to identify and express propositional claims about states of affairs in the physical world. In *Personal Knowledge: Towards a Post-Critical Philosophy*, Michael Polanyi explains a *theory* as follows: "A theory is something other than myself. It may be set out on paper as a system of rules, and it is the more truly a theory the more completely it can be put down in such terms."[68] Polanyi also notes, "Indeed, all theory may be regarded as a kind of map extended over space and time."[69] Similarly, philosopher of science, Karl R. Popper, presents the notion that "theories are nets cast to catch what we call 'the world.'"[70] Furthermore, Popper urges, "We endeavour to make the mesh [of the nets] even finer and finer."[71] In terms of the ontological status of the external, physical world, which is thought to be revealed by tested, scientific theories, various philosophies of science have been put forward:

- For *realists*, a scientific theory provides a substantive description of physical reality *as* reality is. This view is perhaps the view closest to

---

a practicing religious devotee would provide about the same topics. It is also possible, however, that in some cases the analyses of philosophers of science and scientific practitioners may overlap. Also that in some cases the analyses of philosophers of religion and religious devotees may overlap.

67. In the context of this book, the concept of a *theory*, of course, pertains to the analysis of *scientific theory* in the field of the philosophy of science. It is also worth noting how the concept of a *theory* is applied differently in other areas of academia: For example, in the Frankfurt School, Max Horkheimer seems to agree with the notion of theory as a methodological form of knowledge, at least in its traditional sense. In his "*Traditional and Critical Theory*," Horkheimer notes, "Theory is stored-up knowledge, put in a *form* that makes it useful for the closest possible *description* of facts" (188; emphasis added). However, in addition to theory in its traditional sense, Horkheimer (197) asks, what does *theory* mean for human life? While traditional theory provides an epistemic platform for expressing the methodological form of scientific knowledge, traditional theory, from Horkheimer's perspective, also possesses the disadvantage that it includes no direct connection to the activities of society, at least in so far as how society might influence a theory. To appreciate more fully the concept of *theory*, then, Horkheimer argues a social mechanism—"critical theory"—must be included. In summary, critical theory, in the context of the Frankfurt School, connects abstract "theory" to a social framework which includes a concern for human life, rendering critical theory a project with an emancipatory character: critical theory includes concerns for elements of human work and circumstances of production in society.

68. Polanyi, *Personal Knowledge*, 4.
69. Polanyi, *Personal Knowledge*, 4.
70. Popper, *The Logic of Scientific Discovery*, 37.
71. Popper, *The Logic of Scientific Discovery*, 38.

maintaining that scientific theories are substantive truths (the view which I exclude from the assumptions of this book). Popper, who defends realism,[72] describes the realists as those who believe "the laws of nature reveal to us an inner, a structural, simplicity of our world beneath its outer appearance of lavish variety."[73] However, from the nuances of his methodology to be sketched further on, Popper stops short of equating scientific theories with absolute truth claims.[74] It is likely the case that many practicing scientists and engineers function as realists (whether or not they would use that label to describe themselves is a different matter).

- For *critical realists*, there is a physical object to be studied, and a scientific theory can provide an abstract description of that object; however, the theory may not provide a complete, foolproof description of physical reality *as* reality is. For some theologians and philosophers of religion, critical realism is seen as lending itself well toward conceptualizing science as an activity which provides, at best, tentative descriptions of physical reality.[75] Similarly, Ian Barbour, who defends critical realism, explains that, for critical realists, religion provides, at best, analogical models for metaphysical reality.[76] In both cases, neither science nor religion are seen to provide foolproof, literal descriptions of physical or metaphysical objects. However, it seems critical realists accept that science and religion possess at least realist intents: i.e., so far as is possible, science and religion seek to know and interpret reality *as* reality is.

- For *instrumentalists*, a scientific theory serves as a model for predicting states of affairs in the physical world. Here, a theory has shifted from providing a description of physical reality to serving as a model for predicting some aspect of reality or demonstrating the usefulness of some aspect of reality. For this reason, instrumentalists may claim physical "reality" is unknowable or that "reality"—independent of the theory-ladenness of perception—is meaningless. For instrumentalists, the scientific enterprise provides useful opportunities to model

---

72. Popper, *Conjectures and Refutations*, 157.

73. Popper, *The Logic of Scientific Discovery*, 58.

74. See also Geoffrey Stokes in his *Popper: Philosophy, Politics and Scientific Method*. Regarding Popper's methodology, Stokes remarks, "If a theory is judged to have more empirical content [i.e., a higher degree of falsifiability], it may be designated as *closer to the truth even though it may be a false theory*" (140; emphasis added).

75. Barbour, *Religion and Science*, 117.

76. Barbour, *Religion and Science*, 119.

the physical world, but scientific theories cannot provide descriptions, substantive or abstract, of physical reality *as* reality is. In a curious twist, Nancy Cartwright, an instrumentalist, suggests the difference between realists and instrumentalists has a kind of theological character:[77] According to Cartwright, realists are prepared to interpret physical reality in an abstract, yet elegant and unified, form. In contrast, instrumentalists will accept physical details and components of scientific theories as useful, but will not impose very much (if any) abstract organization over particular details. Hence, in theological terms, the question of whether God places highly organized laws of nature over physical reality (realist) *or* whether God functions in a more sporadic, untidy manner (instrumentalist), becomes interesting. I shall return briefly to a discussion of the interface of religion and instrumentalism in chapter 3.

- Finally, for *conventionalists*, scientific theories are mere intellectual inventions—so-called "laws of nature" created by humans. For conventionalists, Popper remarks how "theoretical natural science is not a picture of nature but merely a logical construction."[78] Furthermore, "laws of nature" invented by conventionalists determine what an observation or measurement is—the "world" which conventionalist science speaks to is an intellectual world invented by humans. (This is an important difference between conventionalists and instrumentalists: Although, for instrumentalists, scientific theories and laws are intellectual tools, the world which science speaks to remains, for instrumentalists, a world with a physical existence independent from observers. For conventionalists, however, the world which science speaks to is an "artificial world"—a world invented by observers, stipulated, as it were, by laws of nature invented by observers.[79])

Outlining his philosophy of science as a "theory of theories,"[80] or a "theory of experience,"[81] in *The Logic of Scientific Discovery* and other essays, Popper suggests that, even though a scientific theory may be falsified, the theory was still a great intellectual achievement.[82] Put simply, a theory which is falsified provides researchers with an opportunity to modify the

77. Cartwright, *How the Laws of Physics Lie*, 19.
78. Popper, *The Logic of Scientific Discovery*, 58.
79. Popper, *The Logic of Scientific Discovery*, 58.
80. Popper, *The Logic of Scientific Discovery*, 37.
81. Popper, *The Logic of Scientific Discovery*, 35.
82. Popper, "Back to the Presocratics," 190.

"old" theory and develop a new, more accurate, theory. It is the case that a lot of existing ("old") scientific theories possess high degrees of certitude, so they are unlikely to be discarded, but even scientific theories with high degrees of certitude are continuously subject to ruthless, critical tests. In a Popperian fashion, this continuous subjecting of scientific theories to critical, empirical tests is thought to accomplish the following aims: (i) Testing a scientific theory ensures that a theory does in fact describe or predict real-life states of affairs in the physical world. (ii) Testing a scientific theory ensures that, if a theory is false and does not describe or predict real-life states of affairs in the physical world, this falsity will in fact be uncovered.

According to Popper, for a scientific theory to be tested, a theory should have the potential to be falsified. A brief digression is in order: How can a scientific theory have the potential to be falsified? A theory predicts real-life states of affairs in the physical world. A real-life experiment, based on the theory in question, is performed. In this real-life experiment, should the theory *not* predict as expected, the theory may be false.[83] Of course, Popper is careful to point out that a theory is not falsified if a single time the theory does not predict as expected—random experimental anomalies can occur.[84] However, if a theory *repeatedly* fails to predict as expected, we may consider seriously the possibility that the theory is false.

Concerning scientific testing, empirical information requires we observe evidence of a causal connection in the physical world. The purpose of such an exercise is to demonstrate, with as high a degree of certitude as possible, that the causal connection is in fact an accurate description of some aspect of physical reality or a useful model for predicting states of affairs in the physical world. To collect empirical information we sometimes read the mass of an object on a scale, we assess the acidity of a solution using a chemical test, or we read the temperature off a thermometer. In addition, empirical information collected from laboratory devices and techniques such as scales, chemical tests, or thermometers, must be collected multiple times. Experimental designs and the execution of experimental set-ups must be capable of being repeated as many times as is necessary to collect multiple sets of experimental values—multiple sets of experimental values comprise the empirical information (data) for a project. After empirical information is collected, a rigorous process of data interpretation ensues. For example, the mathematical modelling of experimental values using equations and spreadsheets, the completion of statistical analyses to determine

---

83. Popper, *The Logic of Scientific Discovery*, 95–96.

84. For example, random experimental anomalies may occur because of a compromised experimental apparatus or because of unintentional negligence on the part of the researcher.

confidence intervals for values, comparisons of experimental values with values previously reported in literature, and the formulation of conclusions which either corroborate or (sometimes) falsify initial hypotheses. In this fashion, scientific testing and data interpretation presume an epistemic realism—the view that consistent empirical support for a scientific theory means we are justified in concluding the theory provides a description of physical reality which is (at the very least) close to accurate.[85] In summary, scientific researchers must have all experimental design and data interpretation options mentioned in this paragraph available to them so they can adequately and convincingly test beliefs.

However, no commitment *per se* to belief entails knowledge, including commitments to previously tested beliefs. A hallmark of the scientific method includes a continuous level of skepticism toward all beliefs.[86] As Imre Lakatos[87] explains, "Thus a statement may be pseudoscientific even if it is eminently 'plausible' and everybody believes in it [i.e., is committed to it], and it may be scientifically valuable [testable] even if it is unbelievable and nobody believes in it."[88] To that end, although commitments generated by the experiences of religiosity, dreams, or myths, could all (potentially) stimulate the conjectural nature of scientific thought, testing beliefs—elucidating causal connections to explain claims—is an empirical process only. The possible influence of religiosity, dreams, or myths on scientific thought, although potentially important for human creativity, *ends* after one moves out of the realm of discovery and into the realm of justification.[89] Consider August Kekulé's reported dream of a snake biting its tail—the supposed inspiration for the *discovery* of the molecular structure of benzene—but hardly a *justification* for benzene's structure. Scientific epistemology, even in simple, everyday practice, cannot allow different "rationalities" to influence the process of epistemic justification.

Finally, this leads me to point out that philosopher of science, Thomas S. Kuhn, in his seminal book *The Structure of Scientific Revolutions* (1962;

---

85. Laudan, *Science and Values*, 105–6.

86. Lakatos, *The Methodology of Scientific Research Programmes*, 1:1.

87. Imre Lakatos is known for his notion of *research programs*. Research programs are attempts to understand the scientific practice in a more highly organized conceptual scheme than Popper's falsifiability criterion only: Lakatosian "hard core" theories are protected from falsification by a "protective belt" of auxiliary hypotheses (Lakatos 1978, 4).

88. Lakatos, *The Methodology of Scientific Research Programmes*, 1:1.

89. This characterization is Reichenbachian: i.e., the scientific realms of *discovery* versus *justification*.

4th ed., 2012), describes *normal science*[90] as *new* scientific research based on *past*, successful scientific achievements. Successful achievements are those acknowledged by a *scientific community*[91] as being a strong foundation for future research. Kuhn popularized the term *paradigm*, using the concept of paradigms to explain his interpretation of scientific thinking. In simple terms, a *paradigm*[92] is a pattern, such as a pattern in grammar which allows one to conjugate a verb using a series of pre-established verb endings.[93] In Kuhn's philosophy of science, a paradigm possesses two qualities: (i) the *initial* achievement of the paradigm was unprecedented,[94] and (ii) the initial achievement of the paradigm includes space for *new* research.[95] Examples of paradigms include atomic theory and molecular orbital diagrams (chemistry), quantum mechanics and general relativity (physics), and Darwinian theories of natural selection and common descent (biology). In modern universities, the study of paradigms prepares natural sciences and engineering students to join professional scientific and engineering communities. Furthermore, Kuhn points out, paradigms help researchers resolve disagreements over the foundations of their work (e.g., disagreements over the scientific laws[96] they follow); to share rules that resolve methodological ambiguities.[97] All in all, paradigms allow researchers to find a *common* experimental ground in their practice.

90. Kuhn, *The Structure of Scientific Revolutions*, 10.

91. The notion of a *scientific community*, composed of scientific practitioners with shared research goals, is Kuhnian: e.g., see Kuhn's *The Essential Tension*, 296, or his Postscript to *The Structure of Scientific Revolutions*, 175–77.

92. The etymology of *paradigm* is the Greek *parádeigma*, meaning *pattern*.

93. Kuhn, *The Structure of Scientific Revolutions*, 23.

94. Kuhn, *The Structure of Scientific Revolutions*, 10.

95. Kuhn, *The Structure of Scientific Revolutions*, 11.

96. Paul Feyerabend maintains that a clear distinction between the terms *theory* and *law* has eluded contemporary philosophy of science. For example, the phrases Newton's "Theory" of Gravitation and Kepler's "Laws" are both used. The only apparent distinction between the terms *theory* and *laws* as applied in the preceding phrases is that Newton's Theory of Gravitation applies to all physical phenomena whereas Kepler's Laws apply to the planets only. However, that distinction—*theory* applied to all phenomena; *law* reserved for some phenomena only—fails when one considers, for example, that the Second *Law* of Thermodynamics applies to all physical phenomena. In conclusion, Feyerabend (*The Tyranny of Science*, 131) suggests the task of formulating a foolproof distinction between the terms *theory* and *law* should not be taken very seriously.

97. Kuhn, *The Structure of Scientific Revolutions*, 11.

3

Attitudes of Mind toward Testing Beliefs

A MODEST NATURALISM AND CONTEMPORARY RELIGION

As MENTIONED, EMPIRICAL INFORMATION requires we observe evidence of a causal connection in the physical world. In this chapter, I attempt to show that evidence for a causal connection is a distinguishing feature of knowledge claims (science), separating knowledge claims, epistemically, from belief claims (religion). This analysis of knowledge claims continues to open up for us a wider discussion about the philosophy of belief in general. Our study of the philosophy of belief goes on to include: tested beliefs further compared with non-tested beliefs (this comparison was started in chapter 1), the psychological state of believing as opposed to the content of beliefs, and basic beliefs contrasted with derived beliefs. During this time I shall begin to assess the cogency of an epistemology of belief claims relative to knowledge claims. This assessment considers the relationship of belief claims to knowledge claims within an epistemic stance like what Susan Haack calls a "modestly naturalistic"[1] epistemology. Finally, these topics and assessments set the overall stage for the continuation of the book.

Recall my previous comment near the end of the preceding chapter that "no commitment *per se* to belief entails knowledge, including

---

1. Haack, *Evidence and Inquiry*, 169.

commitments to previously tested beliefs." This point is important: the histories of philosophy and theology are saturated with "retreats to commitments," as the title of philosopher William Warren Bartley's book, *The Retreat to Commitment*,[2] alludes. Thus, as I attempt to show that evidence for a causal connection is a distinguishing feature of knowledge claims (and their tested beliefs), I shall also be attempting to show that intellectual assent to evidence is not the same as unwavering commitment to evidence. In order to distance myself, as far as is possible, from the inherent tendency to unwaveringly commit oneself to the tenets of any one philosophy (or theology), I strive to maintain a sufficient level of skepticism even toward the observed, tested evidence which supports knowledge claims. Throughout the continuation of this book, the epistemological projects of Karl R. Popper,[3] William Warren Bartley,[4] and Susan Haack,[5] will help me to accomplish my goal. Twentieth-century and early twenty-first-century philosophies of science to be utilized, then, in order of historical development, are as follows: (i) Popper's *critical rationalism*, (ii) Bartley's *pancritical rationalism*, and most recently (iii) Haack's *foundherentism* and *innocent realism*. Popper's, Bartley's, and Haack's philosophies of science share common themes: (a) they embrace and/or utilize a hypothetico-deductive method, (b) they avoid scientistic tendencies, and (c) for my use (which I shall be arguing), they provide methodological approaches well suited to discussing the epistemic possibility of a religious epistemology *contextualized* in a modern research university. Moreover, the possibility of a compatibility system specifically between a scientific study of religion and a religious epistemology.

Attempting to distinguish *knowledge* from *belief*, Wiebe notes, "That distinction cannot be based simply on the attendance of 'complete conviction,' for that reveals merely a psychological (subjective) certainty. One must

2. Bartley, *The Retreat to Commitment*, 4.

3. Sir Karl R. Popper is arguably one of the greatest philosophers of science of the twentieth century. Popper's seminal book *The Logic of Scientific Discovery* presents his epistemology termed *critical rationalism* and his famous demarcation criterion of falsifiability.

4. William Warren Bartley III was one of Karl Popper's students at the London School of Economics. Bartley expands Popperian epistemology in his *The Retreat to Commitment*, decoupling justification and criticism to propose a non-justificatory philosophy of criticism termed *pancritical rationalism*. Bartley's work includes analyses of theology and philosophy of science.

5. Susan Haack is Cooper Senior Scholar in Arts and Sciences, Distinguished Professor in the Humanities, Professor of Philosophy, and Professor of Law at the University of Miami. Following what she calls a modestly naturalistic epistemology, Haack's projects termed *foundherentism* and *innocent realism* are presented in her *Evidence and Inquiry* and *Defending Science—Within Reason*, respectively.

always, that is, distinguish between knowledge and the *claim to knowledge*."[6] For a *scientific explanation* to accomplish the epistemic task of distinguishing knowledge claims from belief claims, a scientific explanation, as I see it, must accomplish three goals:[7]

1. An explanation reveals the *cause* for how a state of affairs in the physical world occurred.
2. An explanation articulates the *cause* in a meaningful or useful fashion.
3. An explanation presents a *cause* which can be repeated and reproduced during an experiment. This ensures that the cause is a justified cause.

Popper's epistemology, which is skeptical about induction,[8] characterizes the rationality of scientific explanations (science) as a rationality marked by—indeed, a rationality possible because of—our ability to subject all beliefs to ruthless, critical tests—hence the label *critical rationalism*. Popper's criterion of *falsifiability*, considered in chapter 2 and defended by Popper as a form of deduction,[9] is a method that separates tested beliefs from non-tested beliefs, as well as knowledge claims from belief claims (per the typology adopted in this book). Like Wiebe's caution in the preceding quotation in this paragraph, Popper's distinction between claims to knowledge and any other claims is a distinction not centred on one's conviction (or unwavering commitment) toward the beliefs one makes claims about. Furthermore, the critical tests Popper proposes never cease—indeed never cease even after a belief has reached a high degree of certitude. About this, Popper states, "A system such as classical mechanics may be 'scientific' to any degree you like; but those who uphold it dogmatically—believing, perhaps, that it is their business to defend such a successful system against criticism as long as it is not *conclusively disproved*—are adopting the very reverse of that critical attitude which in my view is the proper one for the scientist."[10] As such, Popper's philosophy of science seeks always to increase the degree of

---

6. Wiebe, "Is Religious Belief Problematic," 24; emphasis added.
7. Woodward, *Adventure*, 67.
8. David Stove (*Scientific Irrationalism*, 111–12), who traces Popper's skepticism about induction to Hume's own skepticism about induction, describes an inductive argument as follows: "In an inductive argument, the premises are simply reports of something which has been (or could have been) observed; the conclusion is a contingent proposition about what has not been (and perhaps could not be) observed. In addition, of course, what the conclusion of an inductive argument says about the unobserved is *like* what the premises say about the observed."
9. Popper, *The Logic of Scientific Discovery*, 19, 55–56.
10. Popper, *The Logic of Scientific Discovery*, 28.

testability of a scientific theory—to increase the number of states of affairs ruled out by a theory.

For example, Popper suggests, (i) one might introduce to a theoretical system *ad hoc* hypotheses which increase the degree of falsifiability:[11] the formulation of a new theory permitting *fewer* events in the physical world than the previous theory permitted. Or, (ii) one might introduce changes to the ostensive definitions[12] of higher-level concepts especially if a change is thought to be useful or helpful in testing:[13] e.g., the term *energy* and its corresponding definition and conceptual scheme are established by linguistic usage; however, if another term and conceptual scheme are thought to be more useful in representing the higher-level physical concept known as *energy*, a change toward the new term (symbol) and scheme would be permitted. In another option (iii), which regards the possible lack of competence on the parts of the researcher or the theoretician, one might implement a rigorous system of intersubjective testing to determine whether counter-experiments and counter-theories are to be accepted or discarded.[14] This third option seems to represent the focal point of the Popperian worldview, although it is supported by the preceding two options regarding *ad hoc* hypotheses and ostensive definitions.

Are knowledge claims an epistemic benchmark for belief claims? Is the acceptability of belief claims assessed by their ability to conform to the epistemic structure of knowledge claims—by their ability to stand up to the unforgiving, ruthless, critical tests faced by knowledge claims? Centrally my project concerns the design of a religious epistemology contextualized in a modern research university—the possibility of a compatibility system specifically between a scientific study of religion and a religious epistemology. Given the number of theologically oriented readers I may have perusing this book, and given my awareness of the importance of faith-imbued experiences in many people's lives (as testimonies of religious devotees inform me), I do not wish to provide at this stage an explicit answer to the question *are knowledge claims an epistemic benchmark for belief claims?* My intention (and hope) is that further development in this book will speak for itself, suggesting possibilities for answering this question as well as limitations. What I can say quite assuredly at this point, however, is that the epistemic

---

11. Popper, *The Logic of Scientific Discovery*, 62.

12. In this context, ostensive definitions are empirical meanings assigned to concepts by linking concepts to physical objects/realities. Ostensive definitions function, then, as symbols (Popper, *The Logic of Scientific Discovery*, 54).

13. Popper, *The Logic of Scientific Discovery*, 63.

14. Popper, *The Logic of Scientific Discovery*, 63.

structure of an *explanation* in scientific causation is radically different from the structure of agentic "explanations" applied to formulate religious claims.

Clarifying another possibility to contextualize the concept of an *explanation*, religion classified instrumentally (vis-à-vis the philosophy called instrumentalism) seems to elude the explanatory challenge created by CPS-agentic modes of thought. Religious models of physical reality interpreted as psychological constructions need not be explained by CPS-agents but can be explained through performative, instrumentalist functions: e.g., religion helps to make sense of reality; to bring to conscious awareness ethical attitudes that seem desirable in a civilized life. Bartley, though, sees instrumentalism applied to religion to be an escape hatch, but not because instrumentalist religion eschews the need for CPS-agents. For now, in simple terms, Bartley's *pancritical rationalism*, whose tenets I shall sketch fully and apply in chapter 6, refers to a thesis that rationality is unlimited in terms of criticism. Bartley decouples the philosophical concepts of *justification* and *criticism*, arguing that in the history of Western philosophy these concepts have become confused; that we should not attempt to justify our beliefs (which invariably requires some commitment), but should strive primarily to *criticize* our beliefs, even to the point of criticizing the concept of criticism itself—hence the label *pancritical rationalism*.[15]

Bartley's concern with instrumentalism is that instrumentalism applied in scientific practice directly counteracts the very pancritical attitude toward beliefs he proposes. With instrumentalism, Bartley suggests, "Scientific activity is a sort of 'glorified plumbing,' but never glorified enough to 'plumb the depths.' Moreover, if such notions [scientific theories] are just tools, their internal troubles hardly matter; we can use them when they are useful and discard them for other tools when they break down."[16] Thus, that instrumentalism does not provide tested descriptions, substantive or abstract, of physical reality *as* reality is, that instrumentalism does not impose very much (if any) organization over particular details, instrumentalism for Bartley furthers an irrationalist cause.[17] As instrumentalist religion or instrumentalist science appear to psychologically choose different beliefs when they are useful rather than being too concerned with the substan-

---

15. Bartley's *pancritical rationalism* is by some accounts epistemically radical; perhaps even dangerous. By my account, as a writer in the philosophy of science and religion, his work is unusually fantastic, yet the nuances of his work need to be unpacked to fully appreciate his thesis. When I first read Bartley I felt led to label him my "new epistemic hero." I devote portions of chapter 6 to pancritical rationalism and to Bartley's arguments.

16. Bartley, *The Retreat to Commitment*, 91.

17. Bartley, *The Retreat to Commitment*, 93.

tive content of beliefs, Bartley's concern with instrumentalism unexpectedly opens up a new discussion about the psychological state of believing contrasted with the content of beliefs. Moving toward an initial orientation with Haack's projects in the following paragraph, these different aspects of the general concept of *belief* become apparent.

At the core of scientific and religious epistemologies is the question of realism and, in the case of a religious epistemology, whether or not an ontological reality for perceived religious revelation is permitted? If revelation is permitted, *a priori* there must be a realist understanding of revelation. To respond adequately to this question, then, *realism* is first in need of some disambiguation. In its simplest version, the term *realism* implies that "something" exists independent from what you or I think about the "something," whether or not you or I think the "something" exists. However, I note that from this fairly simple concept many brands of realism exist within the philosophies of science and religion. In *Religion, Science and Naturalism*, philosopher of science and religion, Willem B. Drees, comments that differing brands of realism perhaps do all agree that "something" exists independent from us, but they disagree about how accurately our current knowledge claims or our current belief claims describe the constitution of the "something," the *quality* of our knowledge claims and belief claims, so to speak.[18] As examples, for a religious person, the "something" in question might be an ontology for religious revelation; for a scientific person, the "something" might be an ontology for a molecular orbital system in quantum mechanics. For a scientific-religious person, the "something" might be an ontology for (a) contents of religious revelation coalesced with (b) quantitative information from quantum mechanics (whatever that would look like).

In *Defending Science—Within Reason*, Susan Haack outlines her particular brand of realism, called *innocent realism*. In a tone strikingly similar to Berger's and Luckmann's thesis of the social construction of reality, Haack presents innocent realism:

> There is one, real world; and the sciences aim to discover something of how this world is. Of course, human beings intervene in the world, and we, and our physical and mental activities, are part of the world. The world we humans inhabit is not brute nature, but nature modified by our physical activities and overlaid by our semiotic webs, including the imaginative constructions of writers and artists, and the explanations, descriptions, and theories of detectives, historians, theologians, etc.—and of scientists. The imaginative constructions of novelists and artists,

---

18. Drees, *Religion, Science and Naturalism*, 7–8.

their fictional characters and events, are both imaginative and imaginary. *But, when they are successful, the imaginative constructions of inquirers, their theoretical entities and categories, are not imaginary but real, and their explanations true.*[19]

Following Haack's lead to distinguish the brute nature of the one, real world from our physical activities and from the semiotic webs of our mental activities, it seems that in innocent realism one might *characterize* a belief about a real "something" in the physical world in a three-fold manner: (i) *realize* the "something," (ii) *identify* a belief about the "something," and (iii) *explain* the "something." Inspired by Haack, I suggest we implement this three-fold characterization as follows:

1. *Realize* the "something" physiologically and/or psychologically.

2. *Identify* a belief about the "something" by locating the "something" in sociocultural institutions: e.g., locating the "something" in religious or scientific communities. For Haack, the task of *identifying* requires a capacity for intentional language, an intentionality—i.e., the use of intentional words (vocabulary) in the believer's language and the relating of those words to objects in the physical world.[20]

3. *Explain* the "something" using tested, scientific theories about states of affairs in the physical world.[21]

From the preceding three-fold characterization, Haack's innocent realism allows for a "metaphysics," but a "metaphysics" she argues is about *the one, real world*,[22] centred on *natural human experience* in the physical world. In terms of explanations for states of affairs in the physical world, Haack eschews the reported actions of CPS-agents as explanatory forces, for as she rightly points out the reported actions of CPS-agents do not mechanically explain.[23] What Haack does allow, however, is for sociocultural institutions, which include religious institutions, to identify and locate objects of human belief *as* objects of natural human experience. These objects, which include the theoretical entities of artists, theologians, historians, novelists, and scientists, take on existences of their own which could be *physical* but are also *social*. Examples of these theoretical entities might include paint-

19. Haack, *Defending Science—Within Reason*, 123–24; emphasis added.
20. Haack, *Defending Science—Within Reason*, 157–58.
21. In this characterization, the third suggestion to classify belief about a real "something," where explanation is connected to tested, scientific theories, is my own suggestion.
22. Haack, *Defending Science—Within Reason*, 123.
23. Haack, "Fallibilism and Faith," 205.

ings (artists), myths (theologians), timelines (historians), literary characters (novelists), or atomic models (scientists). Finally, as mentioned, experiences of these objects of human belief are realized (felt/observed) in the physiological and/or psychological states of human life. In summary, as I understand it, Haack's innocent realism permits the *a priori* assumption that "something" exists independent from you or me, but this version of realism appears "innocent" in the sense that the "something" which exists is about the phenomenal world as perceived and constructed by *us*: how *we*—as fallible and imperfect, yet rational and sophisticated creatures—know, interpret, and construct the phenomenal world to be. (Haack's innocent realism, like all elements of her pragmatic philosophy of science, presumes her epistemology, foundherentism, linking basic and derived beliefs. Chapter 6 includes this topic along with Bartley's pancritical rationalism.)

Although, by definition, innocent realism does not make claims about any supposed realities outside of natural human experiences, innocent realism is also, according to Haack, non-reductionistic. Innocent realism does not reduce human experiences—or public testimonies about those experiences—to mere causal interactions among physical particles only. It appears this aspect of innocent realism is ambiguous. Yes, innocent realism might explain human experiences (or testimonies) in terms of causal interactions among physical particles; however, in Haack's defense, I would like to aver that what innocent realism does not do is erase all *meaning* or *social significance* from human experiences. That sociocultural institutions, including religions, exist in the first place points to the fact that human experiences carry greater weight for individuals when experiences are contextualized in the meaning-structures of these communities[24]—greater weight than experiences would carry if they were interpreted as outcomes of neurobiology only.[25] A completely reductionist account of human experiences would

---

24. My suggestion that human experiences carry greater *weight* for individuals when experiences are contextualized in the meaning-structures of sociocultural institutions refers to degrees of importance, quality, and value that humans attach to their experiences. In choosing the term *weight*, I am thinking of experiences that are memorable, emotionally charged, and built into the individual's personal value system: e.g., experiences that are passed down through generations, for example, participation in religious rituals introduced to offspring by their parents; experiences of secular holidays that also include religious elements, such as Christmas. Or, purely secular events, such as the experiences of secular school graduations or other formalized rites of passage.

25. This point will become more apparent when we consider, for example, the role of the hypersensitive agency detection device (HADD), an evolutionary-based, cognitive device, in attempting to explain religious activity. Even still, when proposed neurophysiological, cognitive devices from our evolutionary past are employed to attempt to "explain" religion, human experiences generated by religious activity can still take on *social* existences of their own. Finding a balance, then, between (a) attempting

have to deny that objects of human belief (the "somethings") have significance independent from you or me. However, innocent realism—a kind of modest naturalism—permits objects of human belief, including objects which are socially constructed, to inhabit a "level" of reality of their own.

The "level" of reality inhabited by objects of belief in innocent realism is best alluded to by Haack's statement about the imaginative constructions of inquirers, whether they be artistic, theological, historical, literary, or scientific inquirers: Haack remarks, "When they are successful, the imaginative constructions of inquirers, their theoretical entities and categories [e.g., paintings (artists), myths (theologians), timelines (historians), literary characters (novelists), or atomic models (scientists)], are not imaginary but real, and their explanations true."[26] This leads me to say that, when applied to the interface of science and religion and the potential design of a religious epistemology, Haack's innocent realism presents some very interesting and useful possibilities. In part 3, where the philosophical design of a religious epistemology is the specific goal, I shall consider in detail what contribution innocent realism has to my project about compatibility between a scientific study of religion and a religious epistemology. Haack's innocent realism, for our purposes, helps to cut open, if you will, a new, alternative philosophy of science and religion—one that gets us outside of the usual polarized options of either traditional, *a priori* theism or radical, *scientistic* naturalism. About these polarized options, Schellenberg remarks, "Even when opposed, traditional theism's idea of God has been influential: the naturalistic picture of metaphysics has been developed more or less by contrast with it. To one degree or another, we have *all* been influenced by the narrative of an ongoing struggle between theism and naturalism."[27] Getting beyond this "ongoing struggle between theism and naturalism,"[28] which has become so blasé, is a goal of part 3. Prior to that stage, however, I would like the material in chapters 4 and 5 (part 2) to speak for itself, as there are a number of concepts, including the concept of *myth*, which still need to be unpacked before the attractiveness of innocent realism toward the design of a religious epistemology—and consequently a new philosophy of science and religion—can be fully digested. My purpose, however, in introducing innocent realism at this stage in the book was so that an awareness of the central tenets of innocent realism can permeate the following chapters. As we shall

---

to "explain" religious activity and (b) receiving meaning and orientation in life from religious experience, will play into the analysis in part 3.

26. Haack, *Defending Science—Within Reason*, 124.
27. Schellenberg, "Philosophy of Religion," 98.
28. Schellenberg, "Philosophy of Religion," 98.

soon see in part 2, Haack's innocent realism dialogues quite naturally with additional theses to be considered from such interlocutors as Peter Berger, Ninian Smart, and John Searle.

SCIENCE AND SCIENTISM

Before part 2, a consideration of the relationship between science and scientism is necessary. At the core of Drees's thesis in *Religion, Science and Naturalism* (mentioned in the preceding section) is that religious phenomena are part and parcel of nature. Religion, then, amounts to *constitutive reductionism*,[29] but not a complete reductionism for Drees's work also includes *conceptual and explanatory non-reductionism*,[30] such that concepts and explanations for religion are permitted in levels of reality outside of physical reality. Although intriguing, it is difficult to figure out what precisely Drees is getting at: Drees does not advocate superhuman agency (his ontology is naturalistic), but he also keeps open the possibility that concepts and explanations for religion exist outside the domain of natural science. This distinction, between a completely reductionist account of religious phenomena and allowing religious phenomena to inhabit their own "level" of reality (with their own concepts and "explanations") while also being constituted by nature only, is perhaps best articulated by Drees's suggestion that "humans [including humans' religious and scientific enterprises] . . . 'are the earth in one of its manifestations.'"[31] (Drees is reflecting on a quotation from John Dewey's *Art as Experience* (1934) that natural phenomena, such as mountain peaks, "do not flow unsupported; they do not even just rest upon the earth. They *are* the earth in one of its manifest operations."[32]) So, in Drees's view, religious phenomena are more *significant* than mere causal interactions in the physical world, but religious phenomena nevertheless remain constituted by nature only.

Along a similar but not identical vein to Haack, it seems that Drees presents a kind of "innocent realism" himself but he proposes a different possibility from Haack to *identify* an object of belief: In terms of our threefold characterization to *realize*, *identify*, and *explain* beliefs about the physical world, both Drees and Haack would have to agree that experiences of objects of belief are realized physiologically and/or psychologically for the simple reason that both Drees and Haack are ontological naturalists. While

---

29. Drees, *Religion, Science and Naturalism*, 14.
30. Drees, *Religion, Science and Naturalism*, 16.
31. Drees, *Religion, Science and Naturalism*, 1.
32. Dewey, *Art as Experience*, 2.

Haack identifies a belief by locating its object in sociocultural institutions, Drees instead distinguishes between *existence* and *access*, noting that, although human cognitive capacities limit *access* to possible trans-empirical worlds, this limitation need not exclude the possibility that metaphysical objects *exist* outside of sense perceptions.[33] So, Drees keeps open the possibility of identifying a belief by locating its object in a trans-empirical world, albeit a world we do not have substantive access to and so we cannot affirm anything, positive or negative, about its existence. Conveniently, we are now provided with two possibilities to identify an object of belief from two philosophers who agree at least that *realizations* (*experiences*) of objects of belief occur in the natural world only. In addition, after realization has occurred, Haack suggests objects be *identified* in sociocultural institutions, while Drees keeps open the possibility of *identifying* objects in trans-empirical worlds (stopping short, however, of affirming the existence of such worlds).[34]

---

33. Drees, *Religion, Science and Naturalism*, 140.

34. Although it seems difficult to figure out what precisely Drees is proposing in his balancing act between *constitutive reductionism* and *conceptual and explanatory non-reductionism*, the point here, about Drees keeping open the possibility to identify objects of belief in trans-empirical worlds although experiences of those objects are realized naturally, may shed some light on his position articulated in *Religion, Science and Naturalism*. It may not be so much that Drees is proposing to explicitly allow into one's conceptual scheme those concepts and explanatory forces thought to originate from trans-empirical worlds, but that, in acknowledging our fallible physiology (the limitations of our cognitive capacities), although we cannot access such concepts/explanatory forces we also cannot rule them out. What this amounts to on a practical level may not be any different from Haack's recommendation to identify objects of belief in sociocultural institutions: if we cannot access hypothesized trans-empirical worlds, but can acknowledge only that affirming their existence is beyond our cognitive ability, it seems our next option is to follow Haack's lead and to identify objects of belief in sociocultural institutions. In my *Adventure in Human Knowledges and Beliefs*, I did, however, express a view similar to the view which I think Drees is articulating, as least how this view might actualize itself when lived out practically. Commenting on my faith position at the time of writing *Adventure*, I stated, "Even if I end up having to say that 'God' does not exist (because to believe in something I have never seen is really so hard for me to do), the action of faith that I possess in my life opens me up to the real 'GOD' who is beyond my grasp of knowledge; the real 'GOD' who I cannot really ever know or understand. I can never stop growing in a relationship with this 'GOD'—the 'GOD' who escapes the boundaries of my human mind and the boundaries of human knowledge" (Woodward 2014, 57–58). Thus, the point I make in the preceding quotation and the point that Drees's view seems to imply if lived out practically is that, yes, the observed world is the world that humans know about, the world humans experience, and intersubjectively within this world one would have to conclude that no evidence suggests the existence of a CPS-agent (e.g., "God"). At the same time, and in an apophatic fashion, wondering about the limitations of human knowledge, an activity made possible through faith, perhaps opens one up in some partial way to a more

According to Mikael Stenmark's notion of an epistemic scientism,[35] both Haack's and Drees's projects outlined in this chapter would have to be classified as *scientistic*—a claim I refute in the remainder of this section by arguing that what Stenmark calls epistemic scientism should not be classified as a type of scientism. My argument draws on Popper's critical rationalism: I attempt to show the tenets of Stenmark's epistemic scientism to be in fact the tenets of the modern scientific method, which, if understood and applied with epistemic modesty, is not a scientistic endeavour at all. Epistemic scientism is described by Stenmark as "the view that the only reality that we can *know* anything about is the one science has access to."[36] My summary of epistemic scientism (also included in chapter 1) is that within this worldview it is not irrational to hold religious beliefs in one's personal life; however, we cannot test religious beliefs as we can test scientific beliefs. Therefore, we cannot *know* if our non-tested, religious beliefs are accurate descriptions of physical reality.

Stenmark maintains that his problem with this view is that it makes the overall assumption "all *knowledge* is *scientific*," but that assumption, he points out, is a philosophical statement and not a scientific one. Therefore, Stenmark avers, the assumption "all *knowledge* is *scientific*" is not in fact *knowledge*.[37] In a backhanded manner, then, Stenmark goes on to claim that the philosophical assumption "all *knowledge* is *scientific*" weakens the case for epistemic scientism.[38] As I see it, Stenmark's argument against epistemic scientism, then, includes two points: (i) If taken seriously, "all *knowledge* is *scientific*" implies that philosophical questions were handed over to the relevant science to resolve, as if to say philosophy proper was repudiated, that philosophy is now part and parcel of science. (ii) Stenmark goes on, the implication that philosophy is now part of science weakens the case for epistemic scientism, because if philosophy (which was not *knowledge* per the assumption "all *knowledge* is *scientific*") suddenly becomes "knowledge,"

abstract, ineffable theological realism ("GOD") that otherwise would be left unknowable. Drees (1998, 18) summarizes this aspect by explaining that questions which exist at the ontological boundaries of natural science (e.g., boundaries of particle physics, cosmology) may require concepts or explanatory accounts which do in fact transcend the natural world. It is not my intention to try to coalesce Drees's and my views but it does seem plausible to me that when Drees talks about concepts or explanatory accounts transcending the natural world, and when I talk about the "GOD" who escapes the boundaries of my human mind, Drees and I may in fact be trying to express the same idea but in different words.

35. Stenmark, *Scientism*, 4.
36. Stenmark, *Scientism*, 4; emphasis added.
37. Stenmark, *Scientism*, 5.
38. Stenmark, *Scientism*, 5.

absorbed by science, the assumption "all *knowledge* is *scientific*" no longer stands as a lone arbiter, independent from science itself.

Stenmark's rebuttal of epistemic scientism is tiresome. On the one hand he formulates the view he calls epistemic scientism, but then goes on to criticize the view in effect by pointing out that epistemic scientism is a "weak" type of scientism. He contends the definition of *science* provided by epistemic scientism is too broad, causing epistemic scientism to fall apart once we acknowledge that epistemic scientism requires philosophy to be science, too, to permit the philosophical assumption "all *knowledge* is *scientific*" into the tenets of epistemic scientism.[39] However, in this complicated rebuttal of epistemic scientism, Stenmark trades on a doubleness in his use of the concept of *knowledge*. In doing so, he fails to see the import of Popper's critical rationalism in the assumption "all *knowledge* is *scientific*"— which does not require philosophy be handed over to science to preserve the integrity of philosophy as another *type* of *knowledge*.

Stenmark's double use of the concept of *knowledge* involves (a) use of the concept of *knowledge* as it pertains to various fields of inquiry, local knowledges, counter-knowledges, etc., and (b) use of the concept of *knowledge* as it pertains to the "*claim to* knowledge," a trait peculiar to science. In trading on this double use, Stenmark contends, "The expansion of the boundaries of science . . . consists of the move from accepting that 'Science gives us knowledge of reality,' to maintaining that 'Nothing but science gives us knowledge of reality.'"[40] This quotation is confusing: For one, the methodological boundaries of science, which concern belief testing, expand nothing; moreover, they cannot be expanded.[41] Secondly, to assert that "Science gives us knowledge of reality,"[42] fails to point out what *type* of knowledge this refers to: e.g., does it refer to local knowledge; to counter-knowledge? Finally, anyone who has learned their Popper understands that science does not give us knowledge of physical reality, but science, as one particular (and peculiar) *type* of *knowledge*, gives us "*tested beliefs* about physical reality."

39. To build his argument against the view he calls epistemic scientism, Stenmark (*Scientism*, 5) contends, "If science were defined by the advocates of Scientism in such a way that philosophy is considered a part of science proper, this criticism [that "all *knowledge* is *scientific*" is a philosophical statement and not a scientific one] would lose its point and, of course, Scientism would also lose its point; it would not be a very controversial view."

40. Stenmark, *Scientism*, 25.

41. I am assuming the "boundaries" mentioned here are *methodological boundaries*: in this instance, there is no mention of ontological scientism; the concern is about science providing knowledge of physical reality—a *methodological* question which is centred on the testing of beliefs.

42. Stenmark, *Scientism*, 25.

(The *tested* element in the preceding phrase is the Popperian feature.[43]) As science gives us tested beliefs about physical reality, and given that intersubjectively testing beliefs is possible by way of observed experiences only, the extension toward maintaining that *nothing but* science gives us tested beliefs about physical reality is natural. Indeed, it is not really an extension at all because the fact that intersubjectively testing beliefs is possible by way of observed experiences only implies no other human enterprise can provide tested beliefs about states of affairs in the physical world.

Given Stenmark's other concern, that philosophical assumptions cannot dictate what knowledge is or isn't (because then they would have to be scientific assumptions),[44] for one, my pointing out of Stenmark's double use of the concept of knowledge already alleviates this concern: science does not speak to the general concept of knowledge; science speaks to the *claim to* knowledge. Therefore, with the precise nature of the epistemology of science resolved, philosophy, religion, folklore, magic, alchemy, fortune-telling, sexism, racism, homophobia, and transphobia all constitute types of knowledge. Indeed, in the preceding sentence, I could replace the term *knowledge* with the term *belief*, but there is no need to—I already resolved how science, another type of knowledge, is epistemically different from the other types mentioned (and, of course, other types mentioned are also substantively different from one another). In closing, Popper's critical rationalism as *philosophy* is a *type* of *knowledge*, which I suppose, for some, is no better than folklore. Given, however, that intrinsic to critical rationalism is the notion that all beliefs are subject to ruthless, critical tests, and, following Bartley's lead, that even the concept of *criticism* is subject to criticism,[45] it seems difficult to then come back and say that Popper's philosophy does not set appropriate standards for establishing the rationality of science. One would have to attack Bartley directly since he formally extends the Popperian project to criticize the philosophy of criticism, too. Thus I conclude this case study by noting that what Stenmark calls epistemic scientism—the view that we cannot test religious beliefs as we can test scientific beliefs; therefore, we cannot know if our non-tested, religious beliefs are accurate descriptions of physical reality—is not an example of scientism, but is an epistemic *effect* of the modern scientific method.

Finally, it is worth noting that, in addition to epistemic scientism, Stenmark proposes five other types of scientism—all much less "belief-friendly" than epistemic scientism. Although his classification system

---

43. Popper, *The Logic of Scientific Discovery*, 79–80.
44. Stenmark, *Scientism*, 5.
45. Bartley, *The Retreat to Commitment*, 122.

is admirable—he categorizes what he sees to be six different types of scientism—in doing so he also gives the impression that religious devotees ought to feel threatened by science. It's almost as though the six types of scientism are like a secret code to religious believers: if faced with any scientific claim, religious believers can choose any one of the six types of scientism and effortlessly shun any scientific claim as *scientistic*; in effect "saving" religion from any and all of science. All the while, we have no indication from Stenmark about how religion might in fact abuse the cognitive values of science (but, in fairness to him, that question does not seem to be one of his interests). Note also that *scientism* is defined in a more straightforward manner by other scholars: According to Hammer, a different, but straightforward, definition of *scientism* is that scientism is the use of legitimation strategies—the positioning of one's claims relative to science to "legitimate" one's claims.[46] (Examples of legitimation strategies were presented in chapter 2.) As Hammer points out, the positioning of non-scientific claims relative to science requires a reinterpreting, a manipulating, of the scientific method and/or scientific results:[47] whatever the legitimation strategy amounts to is no longer "science" as science is understood and accepted by academic and professional scientific communities. For Hammer, this irresponsible act of manipulating science is scientism. Or consider Haack's pragmatic definition of *scientism* (different from Hammer's but also very simple) that scientism points out "an exaggerated kind of deference towards science, an excessive readiness to accept as authoritative any claim made by the sciences, and to dismiss every kind of criticism of science or its practitioners as anti-scientific prejudice."[48] To me, these definitions get to the hearts of the situations Hammer and Haack are reflecting on, without picking apart belief claims (Hammer's situation only) and also without picking apart every aspect of the scientific method—what Stenmark has done in categorizing six different types of scientism.

For completeness, though, a concluding word to Stenmark's other five (more severe) types of scientism. In rationalistic scientism, it is irrational to hold religious beliefs or any beliefs which are not empirically tested:[49] in rationalistic scientism, the criterion for accepting a belief claim as being a reasonable belief claim to "*believe*" is the same criterion for accepting a knowledge claim as being a reasonable knowledge claim to "*know*"—the criterion being tested evidence. Next, in ontological scientism, some phi-

---

46. Hammer, *Claiming Knowledge*, 206.
47. Hammer, *Claiming Knowledge*, 207.
48. Haack, *Defending Science—Within Reason*, 17–18.
49. Stenmark, *Scientism*, 6.

losophers go a step further to argue the *only* ontological reality which exists is the reality revealed to us by scientific theories:[50] this is a more severe position; it is different from stating that the existence of a physical world or ontological naturalism are *assumptions* with high initial plausibilities through which academic work proceeds. Ontological scientism rather makes an *absolute* statement that no reality exists except physical reality. Not surprisingly, ontological scientism and its related conclusions are not very popular in the philosophy of religion. For example, Schellenberg makes clear his suspicions about a view like ontological scientism when he writes, "We in the modern world tend to be completely preoccupied with things that can be provided with natural causes. In our finite way, this has become 'everything.' Perhaps it really *is* everything; but, equally, perhaps we are simply in a phase where we are draining dry the scientific approach, seeing nature only from the peculiar slant our preoccupation affords."[51] Moving on further still, another more severe version of scientism, I suggest, is Stenmark's comprehensive scientism, arguing that in time science will solve all human problems: questions about human meaning and purpose, which, for some, are more suited to religious life, will eventually be solved by science.[52] Stenmark also classifies what he calls existential scientism, the view that eventually science will explain and replace religion:[53] to simplify matters, what he calls existential scientism could be equated with comprehensive scientism—the view that science has annexed fields of inquiry not traditionally thought to be amenable to science. Finally, Stenmark also proposes axiological scientism which, put simply, is the view that science is the most valuable human activity:[54] again, this type of scientism could be grouped with comprehensive scientism and existential scientism, because if science is thought to be the most valuable human activity then any field of inquiry would be assessed through science. Like all labels, these categories are useful when taken as guides—they should not prevent us from thinking beyond their definitions or from appreciating how the content of any category presents itself in degrees along a spectrum.

∼

50. Stenmark, *Scientism*, 7.
51. Schellenberg, *The Wisdom to Doubt*, 143, Kindle.
52. Stenmark, *Scientism*, 15.
53. Stenmark, *Scientism*, 14.
54. Stenmark, *Scientism*, 11.

This concludes part 1. With this material covered, and with some grasp on its complexity, we are now ready to tackle some of the more nuanced concepts and (I hope) provocative analyses which await us in part 2.

PART 2

Science and Religion Compatibility Systems

A rationally persuasive compatibility system . . . is simply not possible no matter how much modern Western societies desire it, though this is not to say that the quest for that elusive structure will come to a halt. Society, if it is not to disintegrate, it appears, requires it—and it will, therefore, "find" it.

—DONALD WIEBE, *BEYOND LEGITIMATION*

4

What Is a Compatibility System? Who Is It For?

OUTLINE AND DESCRIPTION OF A COMPATIBILITY SYSTEM

IN THIS CHAPTER I begin to extend my project to wider intellectual groups of academics, professionals, and scientific and/or religious people. As such, this chapter will address overall questions including: (i) Does science and religion compatibility matter? (ii) Who is interested in possible science and religion compatibility? These questions help to contextualize this project at practical as well as theoretical levels. Comparisons and contrasts of the modern scientific enterprise with Christian modes of thought have permeated much of the academic and popular debate referred to colloquially as "science and religion." Over the past 150 years or so, notable aspects of the science and religion debate have included the following:

- Nineteenth-century, popular debates: e.g., Anglican bishop of Oxford, Samuel Wilberforce, participated in a public debate with biologist, Thomas Henry Huxley (1860). This debate was a struggle for Christianity in the face of modern science, or, as some might wish to phrase it, a struggle for modern science in the face of Christianity. Wilberforce argued for a biblical account of the origin of life whereas Huxley argued for the biological mechanisms of natural selection and common descent. At the end of the debate, it was not clear which side had won, but rather it seems both sides went away feeling like winners.[1]

- Nineteenth-century books which argue a "conflict"[2] thesis between science and religion: e.g., John William Draper's *History of the Conflict Between Religion and Science* (1874),[3] or Andrew Dickson White's *A History of the Warfare of Science With Theology in Christendom* (1896).[4]

- A twentieth-century legal trial: the Scopes "Monkey Trial" in Tennessee (1925), centred on the allegation that a high school teacher, John T. Scopes, had taught the scientific theory of evolution in a state-funded ("Christian"-state-funded) school. Scopes was convicted and fined $100, but in the end did not have to pay the fine.[5]

- Present-day, popular debates: e.g., polarized debates in the media between self-proclaimed atheist and theist debaters, including Richard Dawkins, Victor J. Stenger, Alister McGrath, and William Lane Craig.[6]

- Twenty-first-century books, written from seemingly faith-imbued perspectives, which argue a "non-conflict"[7] thesis between science

---

1. Luscombe, *Groundwork of Science and Religion*, 2.

2. The notion of a "conflict" thesis between science and religion (science and Christianity) has been portrayed by some writers as misguided. For example, Michael J. Murray (2009, 234) maintains that both the Galileo Affair and the Scopes Trial have been historically misrepresented to the point that common portrayals of these events are actually scams. Be that as it may, what is the case is that knowledge claims from science and belief claims from religion provide different descriptions of shared states of affairs in one, physical world. Whether it is fair to label that a "conflict" may be debatable; however, there are substantive and epistemic *differences* between claims from science and claims from religion.

3. Draper, *History of the Conflict Between Religion and Science*, 1.

4. White, *A History of the Warfare of Science With Theology*, 1.

5. Stenger, *God and the Folly of Faith*, 112.

6. A quick internet search about "science and religion debates" returns links to videos of present-day, popular debates between these speakers and others. Most common are debates contrasting modern science with Christianity.

7. Here I use the term *non-conflict* rather than *compatibility* to describe the apparent aims of such faith-imbued projects, because I would like to reserve the term *compatibility* for two reasons: (i) Compatibility systems, to be discussed beginning in this chapter, are attempts to provide intellectual justification for the accepting of two apparently conflicting modes of thought. The task of designing a compatibility system may draw on resources from such fields as epistemology, sociology, academic theology, and analytic philosophy. (ii) In the scientific study of religion, compatibility systems are not designed merely by the invoking of a faith position—the invoking of one's faith to argue for the harmony of science *and* religion is what I instead call a "non-conflict"

and religion: e.g., John C. Polkinghorne's *One World: The Interaction of Science and Theology*,[8] or Alvin Plantinga's *Where the Conflict Really Lies: Science, Religion, and Naturalism*.[9]

Put simply, it seems most comparisons and contrasts of "science *and* religion" are really comparisons and contrasts of "science *and* Christianity." Also, the brand of Christianity which is compared and contrasted with modern science is often a Christianity which makes belief claims about metaphysical objects, rather than a demythologized Christianity regarding the Christian worldview more as an ethical system or a way of life, arising from ancient Hebrew and Greek modes of thought. Beginning with an outline of the compatibility system concept, I shall be presenting a comparison and contrast of "science *and* religiosity *simpliciter*"—a comparison and contrast of modern science with what is (by many accounts) the universal activity of the simple deference of the human mind to the actions of CPS-agents. My comparison and contrast of "science *and* religiosity," then, might also be described as a comparison and contrast of *disenchanted* (scientific) thinking with *agentic* (religious) thinking. I shall continue to use the term *religion* when mentioning the academic debate I am partaking in; that is, the science and religion debate. The term *religion*, though, is not meant to signify a faith tradition, but points to the agentic thinking characteristic of the human behaviour scholars call "religion."

Ninian Smart's concept of *compatibility systems*, which I utilize in this chapter, involves articulating the precise nature of the relationship between science and religion. Whether that relationship is one of agreement, where science and religion are in fact compatible systems of belief, or whether that relationship is one of disagreement, where science and religion are incompatible, remains to be seen. Indeed, much of what it means to be "compatible," or "incompatible," will need to be unpacked before a decision can be made as to whether science and religion are compatible, incompatible, or paradoxically both compatible and incompatible.[10] In addition, we must

---

thesis. (Note: This distinction is not meant to belittle the invoking of a faith position to "create" harmony between science and religion; however, the invoking of a faith position is still a different matter from designing, on academic grounds, a compatibility system between science and religion.)

8. Polkinghorne, *One World*, 1.

9. Plantinga, *Where the Conflict Really Lies*, 1.

10. The task of attempting to design a compatibility system between science and religion may find science and religion to be in fact compatible, but also incompatible, or paradoxically both compatible and incompatible. These are *possible* options for describing the relationship between science and religion. At this stage, I am not arguing which of these options, if any, is academically sound in terms of the epistemologies of science

consider how science and religion might be *commensurable* or *incommensurable*: only after that matter is resolved can any useful discussion really be had about compatibility or incompatibility between science and religion.

In *The Science of Religion and the Sociology of Knowledge: Some Methodological Questions*, Smart identifies the overall goal of designing a compatibility system as one of establishing, on an intellectual basis, a compatibility between religion and modern science.[11] That task, he maintains, amounts to a modern strategy for contextualizing and placing the sacred in modern life.[12] Indeed, much of the motivation in attempting to design a compatibility system arises from the realization that the scientific enterprise has ushered in a "new," disenchanted cosmos,[13] incommensurable with the pre-scientific cosmologies of antiquity.[14] As Smart candidly observes, "The shifting perspective on the cosmos provided by modern science and social science poses questions not dreamed of in Paul's letters or in the Vedic hymns."[15] Similar to the role of science in legitimating religion (examples of which were mentioned previously), compatibility systems also function as types of legitimation strategies.[16] Compatibility systems seek to legitimate styles of human behaviour—they contribute toward human activities of world-construction and meaning-making. Also, it is worth noting that a compatibility system need not be concerned about whether one *should* believe the claims of science or the claims of religion. Rather the primary concern of a compatibility system is whether one can in fact *consistently* maintain beliefs about science *and* beliefs about religion in one's personal life and/or academic work.

Interestingly, from the outset, Smart is aware the proposed task to design a compatibility system will be difficult. He remarks, "It does not matter particularly for my argument here whether compatibility systems fully work, in the sense of correctly handling the relationship between religion and religion.

11. Smart, *The Science of Religion*, 82–83.

12. Smart, *The Science of Religion*, 82.

13. That the disenchanted cosmos of modern science be described as "new" is not such a stretch: modern science has existed in a few human societies for about 400 years only.

14. In this context, *incommensurability* suggests the modern scientific cosmos cannot be compared with pre-scientific cosmologies. To that end, Lucien Lévy-Bruhl's dichotomy thesis of pre-logical minds contrasted with logical minds is defensible only with the assumption that, at the substantive level, mythopoeic thought is incommensurable with scientific thought (Wiebe, *The Irony of Theology*, 5).

15. Smart, *The Science of Religion*, 91.

16. Smart, *The Science of Religion*, 88.

and science. What is important is that they provide an account which intelligent and honest people can accept."[17] Furthermore, as Wiebe reminds us, if a *prima facie* conflict between science and religion did not exist, there would be no impetus to design a compatibility system.[18] With these observations in mind, we are wise to consider whether our proposed task to design a compatibility system is faced with complications even before we begin? This appears to be the case for (i) the impetus to construct a compatibility system assumes *prima facie* a conflict between science and religion and (ii) Smart himself, the originator of the compatibility system concept, alludes to the fact that compatibility systems may not "fully work."[19] Despite these initial complications, however, when religious life is intellectually cut off from the scientific enterprise, religious life is, in effect, practically cut off from modern, Western life itself.[20] Hence, I suggest it would be a mistake to dismiss *a priori* the possibility that a useful compatibility system could be developed, just as it would be a mistake to dismiss the possibility that religious life and modern life might coexist in a meaningful or useful way. Smart also points out the self-reflexive nature of the scientific study of religion as lending itself well toward the designing of compatibility systems.[21] All in all, the task of designing a compatibility system is what the academic study of science and religion amounts to, although the task is fraught with some difficulty.

According to Smart, the splitting of a myth into its component parts of *fact* and *symbol*, and the attempted rejoining of *fact* and *symbol* in the modern scientific cosmos, is what a compatibility system amounts to.[22] Thus, in a compatibility system, the following two steps occur: (i) the splitting of *fact* and *symbol* from their origins in a pre-scientific myth; followed by (ii) the realization and attempted rejoining of *fact* and *symbol* in a compatibility system in the modern scientific cosmos. My treatment of the concept of a *myth* is grounded in Harry Slochower's,[23] and Don Wiebe's, assessments of the activity of mythopoesis.[24] As Slochower and Wiebe understand it, myths

17. Smart, *The Science of Religion*, 83.
18. Wiebe, "Science and Religion," 58.
19. Smart, *The Science of Religion*, 83.
20. Smart, *The Science of Religion*, 105.
21. Smart, *The Science of Religion*, 90.
22. Smart, *The Science of Religion*, 90–91.
23. Slochower, *Mythopoesis*, 12.
24. The etymology of *mythopoesis* includes the Greek *poiesis*, which means *making*. The activity of mythopoesis is thought to indicate the making (formulating) of a symbolic reality through the telling of the myth itself. Thus the act of telling the myth is a participation in the social reality of the myth, which itself creates a social model for human thought and action.

(stories) function as pictorial hypotheses about human emotions, especially as emotions (e.g., hopes, fears, and loves) are related to a concrete human existence.[25] What is most important, however, is the role myths play—that is, mythopoesis—in formulating a *symbolic* reality for the religious observer. As Smart points out, the myth-maker picks out contingent features of the universe and then arranges those features in a particular symbolic fashion.[26] In *Origins of the Modern Mind* (1991), psychologist Merlin Donald speaks of *myth* as the prototype of an integrative mind tool.[27] Myth-making, a kind of modelling of the physical world,[28] integrates various events in nature, forming conceptual models of the universe. Mythical models developed might include creation stories, thoughts about physical death, and ideas about cosmology.[29] Concerning the splitting of *myth* into component parts of *fact* and *symbol*, a viable relationship between *fact* and *symbol* (for the purpose of this book) must be ascertained.

To start, I note that Ian Hacking points out that facts are not objects *in* the world, but facts nevertheless may be in the world in some other way.[30] In a similar fashion, Norwood Russell Hanson remarks, "Facts are not picturable, observable entities."[31] To further complicate matters (although only slightly), philosopher John R. Searle in *The Construction of Social Reality* (1995) speaks of *brute facts, social facts,* and *institutional facts*:[32] institutional facts are created out of social facts, while social facts depend first upon the existence of brute (physical) facts. Take, for instance, the example of money, an institutional fact: regarding the pieces of paper we call "money," Searle contends, "If everybody stops believing it is money, it ceases to function as money, and eventually ceases to be money."[33] Brute facts, in contrast, at least presume an external realism: unlike social and institutional facts, brute

---

25. Wiebe, *The Irony of Theology*, 39.
26. Smart, *The Science of Religion*, 79.
27. Donald, *Origins of the Modern Mind*, 215.
28. Myth-making as modelling begins to occur in stage (ii), *mimetic to mythic culture*, of Merlin Donald's three stages of the evolution of the modern human mind, outlined in his *Origins of the Modern Mind*. Donald's three stages are as follows: (i) episodic to mimetic culture, (ii) mimetic to mythic culture, and (iii) development of external symbolic storage (e.g., use of graphic symbols) and a theoretic culture (Donald, *Origins of the Modern Mind*, 162–360).
29. Donald, *Origins of the Modern Mind*, 213.
30. Hacking, *The Social Construction of What*, 22–23.
31. Hanson, *Patterns of Discovery*, 31.
32. Searle, *The Construction of Social Reality*, 113–14.
33. Searle, *The Construction of Social Reality*, 32.

facts exist independent from any human thought or action.[34] Social facts, on the other hand, imply some collective intentionality.[35] Finally, collective recognition of a phenomenon *and* collective imposition of a function onto a phenomenon (even if the imposition is unconscious[36]) result in the creation of an institutional fact. Searle considers that phenomena onto which functions are imposed may be either non-mental brute facts or mental facts (states).[37] Furthermore, Searle goes on, institutional facts can be discerned by their subject matter (e.g., whether they are legal or religious facts), by their continued social maintenance (an institution's temporal status), or by any logical operations internal to the institutional fact itself.[38]

I suggest that, in accordance with Searle's thesis of the creation and maintenance of institutional facts, one might conceptualize *objects of religious knowledge*, e.g., CPS-agents, as *types of institutional facts*. My reasons for proposing this characterization are as follows:

1. The existence of CPS-agents is reported in a collective fashion—from the testimonies of religious devotees, we find a *collective* recognition of the existence of CPS-agents.

2. CPS-agents are reported to possess beliefs and desires—they possess supposed *functions* related to reported supernatural events thought to occur in the natural world.

3. Religious experiences, which involve purported CPS-agents, are realized physiologically and/or psychologically: hence it could be argued the apparent "functions" of CPS-agents are, in actuality, socially constructed functions imposed upon *non-mental brute facts* (physiological experiences) and/or *mental brute facts* (psychological states)[39]—rendering CPS-agents as types of institutional facts. In addition, human

---

34. Marc Lange, in his chapter "*Laws of Nature*," 235, furthermore classifies *brute facts* into three categories: (i) logical necessities, (ii) nomological necessities derived from laws of nature, and (iii) accidents/properties which do not depend on laws of nature.

35. Searle, *The Construction of Social Reality*, 122.

36. Searle, *The Construction of Social Reality*, 125.

37. Searle, *The Construction of Social Reality*, 122.

38. Searle, *The Construction of Social Reality*, 124–25.

39. For example, Hewitt characterizes functions of religious beliefs in the contexts of psychodynamics and contemporary attachment theory: Hewitt (*Freud on Religion*, 27) explains, "The need to restore a sense of felt security can be achieved through personal relationships with figures conjured by the mind, such as gods." Or, for example, consider the Feuerbachian conception of God whereby "God" is a psychological projection of humanity's ultimate concern, the function of which is to objectify humanity's most ideal qualities.

beliefs about CPS-agents are maintained and strengthened within the institutional frameworks of modern religions: the cultural sharing of history between members of any religious community produces a body of knowledge passed between generations, ensuring the survival (albeit unwittingly) of CPS-agents *as* institutional facts.

At this point I hope the relationship between *fact* and *symbol* I am proposing will become clear. The splitting of a myth (which originated in a pre-scientific cosmos) into its component parts of *fact* and *symbol* no doubt occurs because at some point in the history of a human society it becomes no longer possible for the "fact" element of a myth to be believed—or at least believed in the *way* it was believed when the myth was contextualized in a pre-scientific cosmos only. An example of a "fact" in a pre-scientific myth would be the reported "fact" that the god, El, of the ancient Near Eastern religions is an ontological reality. The "fact" of a myth is closely related to (if not equated with) the purported substantive reality of the myth. When *fact* is split from *symbol* (or when *fact* is discarded completely), the *symbol* element of a myth takes on an existence of its own—an existence which is *social* rather than substantive. Then, in a compatibility system in the modern scientific cosmos, where attempted rejoining of *fact* and *symbol* occurs, *symbol* takes precedence, recovering any values contained within the pre-scientific myth and, most importantly, recontextualizing those values in the compatibility system. According to Wiebe, "In this sense mythopoesis refers to the recovering of the value of the ancient stories (myths) for a culture that can no longer believe that what the stories narrate actually took place."[40] To that end, Wiebe goes on, "The values the stories contain are transposed into symbolic meaning."[41] In real-life scenarios, social institutions are experienced by the symbolic meanings of institutions.[42] Symbols express the "ultimate"[43] by implying their own lack of ultimacy: the most important aspect of symbols,

---

40. Wiebe, *The Irony of Theology*, 39.
41. Wiebe, *The Irony of Theology*, 39.
42. Berger and Luckmann, *The Social Construction of Reality*, 75.
43. Here, I deliberately place the term *ultimate* in scare quotes to point out the ambiguous nature of *ultimate*—to be considered again in part 3 vis-à-vis the design of a religious epistemology. As I bracket ontological realities for religious concepts, any substantive reality for the "ultimate," to which symbols point, also remains bracketed. Note, however, that in this section I argue how, in a compatibility system, the symbol element of a myth is *social* rather than substantive: in a compatibility system, the concept of an "ultimate," then, is also taken to be a *social* reality—one that is constructed, realized, and identified in the physical world—which includes the sociocultural world of natural human experience.

then, is the ultimate reality to which they point.[44] In addition, symbols allow societies to move beyond typical space-time perspectives,[45] serving as cultural mediums through which the testimonies of religious devotees can be relayed to those not privy to experiences reported by religious devotees.

We conclude the analysis in the preceding paragraph by recognizing that, in a pre-scientific myth, *fact* indicates a purported substantive reality (e.g., El is an ontological reality), while *symbol* takes on a more subordinate role, serving as a consequence of *fact* (or *fact* and *symbol* are simply equated). Following the splitting of *fact* and *symbol*, and their attempted rejoining in a modern compatibility system, *symbol* takes precedence, recovering and representing whatever "ultimacy" was intended by the original myth. Finally, in the compatibility system, *fact* is rendered an institutional fact—which may have always been the case; however, in the modern scientific cosmos, the realization of mythological facts as institutional facts becomes possible. Returning briefly to Peter Berger's work, we are reminded by Berger how the "other worlds"[46] of religious life, although not available as empirical realities, are nevertheless realized by humans as "meaning-enclaves within *this* world, the world of human experience in nature and history."[47] In this sense, both Berger and Smart contribute toward an understanding of the concept of *myth* although Smart's critique of Berger's work sets the two professors apart. However, as I see it, where Berger and Smart differ is also where the precise, yet ambiguous, nature of myths conceptualized in the modern world is best articulated. I take up this analysis in the following section.

MYTHS AND IGMYTHICISTS

The goal, then, is to understand myths as articulations of human values when values are located in a modestly naturalistic epistemology. Unlike Berger, Smart understands "*this* world"[48]—i.e., the physical world of human experience—as a cosmos which is socially constructed.[49] Distinguishing *facts* from *human products*, Smart seems less reluctant than Berger to separate completely (a) the independent, physical world and (b) human projections placed onto the physical world through the activities of world-

---

44. Bartley, *The Retreat to Commitment*, 54.
45. Kurtz, *The New Skepticism*, 101.
46. Berger, *The Sacred Canopy*, 88.
47. Berger, *The Sacred Canopy*, 88–89.
48. Berger, *The Sacred Canopy*, 89.
49. Smart, *The Science of Religion*, 75.

construction and meaning-making.⁵⁰ Rather, for Smart, to conceptualize the physical world (universe) in a completely neutral, objective fashion is somewhat naive. Smart's primary concern with Berger's neutral universe amounts to the observation that many physical objects, such as the sun or mountains, are included in religious belief systems, fulfilling functions *not* as human products, but as *what appear to be religious brute facts*.⁵¹ Thus Smart sees a degree of subjectivizing as concerns the physical world itself. In his view, not only are human projections placed onto a "neutral" world (the term *neutral* is now seen to be tendentious), but also the physical world undergoes some form of social construction *prior* to additional human projections being placed onto the physical world. It would be more precise, Smart argues, to consider the possibility that brute facts may lead to human products followed by those products *acting back* upon their producers as *new* brute facts. This process, resulting in what Smart calls "outbreaks of the experience of the numinous,"⁵² continually produces new facts from human projections onto a physical world of "old" facts. In turn, the new facts become the "neutral" physical world (universe) onto which additional human projections are then produced and actualized. (A biblical example of this process is perhaps the theophanies experienced by Isaiah in the Temple.⁵³)

For my purposes, Smart's distancing of himself from Berger's neutral universe is interesting for two reasons:

1. Although Smart disapproves of a conception of the physical world where the physical world is seen to be completely independent and objective, Smart's separation of religious "brute" facts from human products helps to point out what is, for some, the faith-imbued status of myths—stories already dependent upon an enchanted, physical world. Or, even more importantly, Smart's separation of religious "brute" facts from human products points out the *influence* that myths

50. Recall that, for Berger, meaning-structures of a social world are projected onto the physical world such that events existing in brute nature *only* are generally meaningless, although events in brute nature may be similar to events in the projected, social world: Berger (*The Sacred Canopy*, 82) presents a clear, albeit extreme, example whereby in brute nature a person can be killed by a falling rock—an accident; whereas in a social world a person can be killed by the state—an execution (assuming the state permits such a barbaric practice). However, *constructed* meaning attached to an execution is different from meaning attached to a natural accident (indeed if there is any meaning at all attached to a natural accident). In the social world, constructed meaning, being reified as objective, means the person killed in an execution is thought to die "correctly," an interpretation which cannot be made if the person is killed in a natural accident.

51. Smart, *The Science of Religion*, 90.
52. Smart, *The Science of Religion*, 79.
53. See the biblical narrative in Isaiah 6.

(religious stories) continue to have on perceptions and mental states of humans who live in the *modern*, natural world (as testimonies of religious devotees inform us). If the physical world is not subjectivized, myths must be *entirely* human creations (projected onto a neutral world) whose origins must be either mere psychological delusions, or, alternatively, reflections of what is an ontological reality for the gods (the latter option assuming, of course, that such a reality exists and could serve as the origin of reflections).

2. Rather than being mere delusions or reflections of an ontological reality for the gods, Smart's distancing of himself from Berger unwittingly opens up a third option to contextualize the nature of myths and an approach I argue is really fitting to both Smart's and Berger's projects. I call this approach the *igmythicist* approach.[54] In the following paragraphs I defend the igmythicist approach—a.k.a. *igmythicism*—which, on a psychological scale, seems to fall halfway between acceptance of myths as mere delusions and belief about myths as reflections of an ontological reality for the gods.

Berger's notion of "meaning-enclaves"[55] within the *sociocultural world of natural human experience* is particularly helpful here. Indeed, although Smart parts company with Berger, regarding the extent to which tested beliefs about states of affairs in the physical world (brute facts) can echo the physical world itself, Smart's critique of Berger's neutral universe is untenable: Unlike Berger, Smart allows human products to serve as "new" (albeit faith-imbued) brute facts, but then, like Berger, Smart also allows human projections onto those "new" facts. Thus it could be demonstrated that even Smart's initial acceptance of human products created out of brute facts is itself a type of projection—the faith-imbued projection/realization of brute facts as being constituted by something other than brute physical reality only. (For example, the physical object of a burning bush,[56] which, by way of a faith-oriented human projection, is "imbued" with sacred qualities.) In this way, then, Smart is no different from Berger; both Smart and Berger approach the notion of meaning-enclaves as social realities initiated, at least in part, by human projection. Although I do appreciate Smart's more nuanced distinction between *facts* and *human products*, he and Berger deal fundamentally with the same topic—i.e., human projection onto the physical world. The only major difference between Smart and Berger, so far as

---

54. To be outlined in this section, my coining of the term *igmythicist* is inspired by Paul Kurtz's term *igtheist*.

55. Berger, *The Sacred Canopy*, 88–89.

56. See the biblical narrative in Exodus 3.

I can tell, is that Berger seems less inclined than Smart to recognize the possible *faith-imbued* element at play in the social construction of human products from brute facts.[57] (However, in a more ambiguous way and not concerning any mechanisms for social construction, Berger is prepared to speak generally about possible theological reflection of some unseen, superhuman reality.)[58]

I suggest that, falling halfway between acceptance of myths as delusions and belief about myths as reflections of an ontological reality for the gods, we conceptualize myths in a *practical* sense—as the *application* of meaning-enclaves enclosed in the world of natural human experience. For one, this particular conception of myths is in keeping with my previous statement that in this book I function as a methodological atheist, bracketing ontological realities for religious concepts. (The bracketing imperative separates me from the academic camp that would identify myths as reflections of an ontological reality for the gods.) At the same time, however, and especially in a real-life and *practical* sense, my approach concerning myths as realizations of meaning-enclaves in the sociocultural world of natural human experience places me in an academic camp which is perhaps more appropriately termed *methodological igtheism*.[59]

---

57. As a methodological atheist, Berger, of course, brackets ontological realities for religious concepts from his academic analysis. Thus, the possibility of a faith-imbued element at play in the mechanisms of social construction (as in Smart's thought) is also excluded from Berger's analysis. In contrast, Smart prefers what he calls a *methodological agnosticism*. In *Worldviews: Crosscultural Explorations of Human Beliefs*, Smart explains his contrasting position: "It is one thing *not to assume that God does exist*; it is another thing *to assume that he does not*. If we assume, more generally, that there is no Ultimate, no Beyond, then we assume that religion is false. Religion, then, is a finger that points, but at nothing. There is no moon for it to point to. It does not seem especially scientific to begin with the assumption that religion is false, nor need we begin with the assumption that it is true" (135; emphasis added). The latter aspect of Smart's position, in the last sentence in the preceding quotation, aligns with my view in this book whereby I do not affirm either way the truth or falsity of ontological realities for religious concepts. The first aspect of Smart's position, in the first sentence in the preceding quotation, where Smart places the emphasis on one *not assuming God exists* rather than one *assuming God does not exist* points to a methodological quandary: regardless of where the emphasis of the assumption is placed, in *not assuming God exists* one still intends to bracket ontological realities for CPS-agents as does the person who *assumes God does not exist*. In that way, the methodological atheist and methodological agnostic are the same. Smart's methodological agnosticism, however, seems to direct us to the possibility that in our personal lives we might affirm the existence of God, but in our academic work we bracket God's existence. The methodological atheist, though, might in fact do the same. In that case, then, it is really a matter of personal choice of terms: e.g., *methodological atheist* or *methodological agnostic*.

58. Berger, *A Rumor of Angels*, 46–47.

59. So far as I am aware, the particular phrase *methodological igtheism* is my own,

In the term *igtheism*, the prefix *ig* is derived from the word *ignorant*, although in this sense *ignorant* does not imply a negative attitude *per se* toward theism. Paul Kurtz, who coined the term *igtheism*,[60] describes the life of the igtheist, a follower of igtheism, in this way: "I [as an igtheist] cannot say whether or not such a being [God] exists since *I do not comprehend what is being asserted*."[61] About the igtheist's unique "ignorance," put simply, the igtheist is a person who argues that the statement "*God exists*" is a meaningless statement. Thus the igtheist is "ignorant" of whatever the statement *God exists* could possibly mean since, for the igtheist, that statement is academically nonsensical. Kurtz outlined the tenets of what he called *igtheism* in 1992 in his book *The New Skepticism: Inquiry and Reliable Knowledge*. Almost sixty years earlier, a young A. J. Ayer, in *Language, Truth, and Logic*, spoke of a similar school of thought to Kurtz's, although Ayer's outline of the position (now called *igtheism*) seems to present a stronger version of logical positivism than does Kurtz's characterization.[62] I shall comment briefly on Ayer's epistemic approach toward propositional claims about superhuman agents for indeed Ayer's approach is very clear—and for that reason is helpful in clarifying what is now called *igtheism*. This is followed by a discussion of how the notion of a methodological igtheism is useful in characterizing my own *practical* approach toward myths—myths conceptualized as meaning-enclaves within a modestly naturalistic epistemology.

As mentioned, the igtheist is one who argues the statement *God exists* is a meaningless statement. In *Language, Truth, and Logic*, Ayer maintains

---

although the concept of *igtheism* (also called *ignosticism*) is discussed in some schools of philosophical theology and philosophy of belief.

60. As stated, in *igtheism*, the prefix *ig* is derived from the word *ignorant* although *ignorant* in this sense is not meant to imply a negative attitude *per se* toward theism. Rather the "ignorance" of *igtheism* refers to the group of igtheists' realization that "we are totally incapable of knowing what is meant by 'theism' when we use the term 'God' to denote a transcendent being or the 'ground' of being" (Kurtz, *The New Skepticism*, 196).

61. Kurtz, *The New Skepticism*, 197; emphasis added.

62. By Kurtz's own admission, religious devotees will likely criticize the igtheistic position as positivistic (*The New Skepticism*, 196). However, Kurtz also explains that he accepts that the term *God* may include some meaningful content so long as *God* is defined as the anthropomorphic God of the Abrahamic religions (questions of the truth or falsity of claims about "God" remain irrelevant). Kurtz considers that, since an anthropomorphic God includes seemingly physical descriptors, such as "God the Father," "God the Son," or the claim that human beings are created in the image of God, such an anthropomorphic God may include some quasi-empirical content. In that way, the statement *God exists* could be a meaningful statement since *God* defined as an anthropomorphic God may not completely violate standards of meaningful language and observed experience (*The New Skepticism*, 197–98).

the statement *God exists* is a metaphysical statement which cannot be either true or false.[63] As in logical positivism, central to Ayer's epistemology is the notion that meaningful propositions are only those hypotheses which can be tested empirically. It is no surprise, then, that Ayer would classify the statement *God exists* as a proposition which is nonsensical: the statement *God exists* is a hypothesis that cannot be tested empirically.[64] However, it is my sense that most observers, including the most pious of religious devotees, would have to agree with Ayer's conclusion. After all, "God-talk," the expression of the substantive reality of religious life, is meant primarily to indicate a reality *not* intended to be known through empirical observation but a reality intended to be known and accessed through the activity of faith.[65] At any rate, it would be premature to dismiss Ayer's epistemic approach toward propositional claims about CPS-agents. Ayer's approach, although seen to be inimical to the faith-based aspirations of religious life (he maintains "God-talk" is nonsensical), is at the same time an approach which opens up a wider range of epistemic issues concerning what precisely we are doing when we attempt to define the term (or the supposed reality of) *God*, especially vis-à-vis the academic study of science and religion.

In outlining the tenets of the view which later becomes known as *igtheism*,[66] Ayer meticulously notes:

> For it is characteristic of an agnostic to hold that the existence of a god is a possibility in which there is no good reason either to believe or disbelieve; and it is characteristic of an atheist to hold that it is at least probable that no god exists. And our view [the view which later becomes *igtheism*], that all utterances about

---

63. Ayer, *Language, Truth, and Logic*, 115, Kindle.

64. For Ayer, as for other logical positivists, propositions involving non-tested beliefs, such as "religious knowledge," are not only non-verifiable, but also constitute nonsensical language.

65. However, as discussed in chapter 1, while it is the case that some religious testimonies refer to objects of belief residing in a trans-empirical world—a "world" thought to exist beyond the limits of empirical observation—it is also the case that many religious testimonies involve claims made about an interplay between that so-called trans-empirical world and the observed, empirical world (e.g., religious miracles as violations of the laws of nature). At any rate, the distinction made here, between empirical observation and the activity of faith, serves to point out that in religious life the *emphasis* is toward the activity of faith as being one's source for knowledge about the physical world.

66. Ayer died in 1989, so he never knew the term *igtheism* that Kurtz coined a few years later in 1992. It should also be noted that Kurtz, in developing the concept of igtheism in *The New Skepticism*, does not mention Ayer. It seems, then, that Kurtz's formulation of the igtheistic position evolved independent of Ayer, although Ayer and Kurtz do more or less present and explain the same position.

the nature of God are nonsensical, so far from being identical with, or even lending support to, either of these familiar contentions, is actually incompatible with them. For if the assertion that there is a god is nonsensical, then the atheist's assertion that there is no god is equally nonsensical, *since it is only a significant proposition that can be significantly contradicted.* As for the agnostic, although he refrains from saying either that there is or that there is not a god, he does not deny that the question whether a transcendent god exists is a genuine question.[67]

From Ayer's remarks in the preceding quotation, we come to appreciate that a definition for any physical or metaphysical object must be established prior to any discussion about whether the object (a) does exist, (b) does not exist, (c) presents "good reasons" for us to believe or disbelieve it exists,[68] or finally (d) constitutes sensical or nonsensical language. Choosing from among these four options represents the core of the igtheist's position. The igtheist would be willing to engage in debate about the existence of God should a suitable definition for the term *God* be presented. However, until such a definition is presented, the statement *God exists* remains (to the igtheist) a meaningless statement. Of course, in the case of the metaphysical object called *God*, what constitutes a suitable definition for *God* will likely vary among faith traditions, religious sects, and academic contexts. For example, in the context of Christianity, where *God* is often defined as a "transcendent and immanent agent" (one that has feelings and desires), I would maintain that I am an igtheist—"CPS-agent-talk" is nonsensical to me. However, in the context of an academic classroom in a modern research university, where *God* is perhaps defined as an *institutional fact* (for the purpose of

---

67. Ayer, *Language, Truth, and Logic*, 115, Kindle; emphasis added.

68. The notion that "good reasons" be available to believe *or* disbelieve that a physical or metaphysical object exists amounts to the theory of rationality referred to as *evidentialism*. In his *How to Relate Science and Religion*, Stenmark (89) rejects unwavering support for evidentialism: he argues judgement-based evidentialism (which he sees as amounting to an attitude of mind whereby beliefs are "*intellectually guilty* until proven innocent") cannot be applied in *all* aspects of one's practical life. In contrast to judgement-based evidentialism, Stenmark (90) suggests a presumptionism model of rationality whereby belief-forming processes and beliefs are taken as justified ("*intellectually innocent* until proven guilty") until such a time as good reasons not to accept one's belief-forming processes and/or beliefs are presented. In addition, Stenmark makes a case that possessing "good reasons" to accept or reject belief-forming processes and/or beliefs involves more practical factors than possessing tested evidence only. Stenmark (91) cites additional factors such as one being consciously aware of one's evidence, one assessing the quality of one's evidence, and one comparing one's evidence to the evidence of alternative beliefs.

academic research), I might change my position from that of the igtheist to that of the theist.

As mentioned, I suggest the notion of a methodological igtheism is useful in characterizing a practical approach toward myths, conceptualizing myths as meaning-enclaves within a modestly naturalistic epistemology. However, to specify in what sense a methodological igtheism might apply to myths, I need to unpack what I see to be potential applications of the igtheistic position in contemporary religious life. (These potential applications transcend uses of igtheism discussed already.) For one, in a rhetorical fashion, igtheism speaks primarily to matters of definition, stressing the importance of providing a definition for an object. Also, igtheism emphasizes how the activity of *defining* must occur prior to any discussion about an object's purported reality (or lack thereof). Although igtheism speaks to the object of *God* directly, I suggest we apply the tenets of igtheism toward other religious concepts as well, such as adopting an igtheistic position vis-à-vis the concept of *myth*. Indeed, this is not such a stretch for religious myths involve a superhuman agent called *God* who intervenes in the physical world—i.e., the concepts of *myth* and *God* are intimately related. To identify as an igtheist about the concept of *God* implies that one would likely also identify in an igtheistic manner about the concept of *myth*. Sound intriguing? Read on.

Similar to the statement *God exists*, which the igtheist maintains is a meaningless statement (until perhaps a definition for *God* suitable to the igtheist is presented), we can propose a statement that "*myths are descriptions of physical reality.*" About the statement "*myths are descriptions of physical reality,*" the igtheist—in this case, the "igmythicist," if you will—would maintain that such a statement is nonsensical (initially, even if just for rhetorical purposes). However, like the igtheist, the *igmythicist* would be willing to engage in debate about the existence of myths should a *suitable definition* for *myth* be presented. What I call the igmythicist approach to myths relates more widely to the topic of compatibility systems: the igmythicist approach to myths involves my attempt to conceptualize religious life (and non-tested beliefs) within the realm of natural human experience. Recall from earlier in this chapter that Smart identifies the primary function of compatibility systems as one of recontextualizing, of replacing, the "sacred" in modern life.[69] About this, Smart observes:

> For in order to translate the beliefs of one age for the benefit of another age, members of the faith will always be presented with a certain dilemma, namely how far transitions can be made

---

69. Smart, *The Science of Religion*, 82.

without sacrificing the essential meaning of the original faith. Further, it happens that religions on the whole, in order to preserve the past upon which they partly depend, have conservative tendencies. Insecurity in a changing world may also introduce a conservative literalism.[70]

In the preceding quotation, Smart's emphasis on the notion of a "changing world"—a fluctuating, evolving human world immersed within the faith-imbued realities of religious life—is striking. Indeed, in setting the stage in this fashion, so to speak, Smart is outlining a rationale for the academic study of science and religion—an academic discipline, which, unlike other aspects of philosophy and theology, only has relevance (indeed only has meaning) since the modern scientific cosmos arose. Smart's rationale in a nutshell amounts to the realization that, with the development of the modern scientific cosmos, the need arises to "translate" religious myths from pre-scientific cosmologies into systems of values compatible with the epistemic standards of the modern scientific cosmos. To that end, the notion of "value maintenance"[71] is central to Smart's project. In summary, compatibility systems serve (i) to identify religious values from the pre-scientific past and (ii) to maintain the qualities of those values while also recognizing our life in the modern scientific cosmos.[72]

In addition, according to philosopher Owen Flanagan, the modern scientific outlook need not be deflating or even disenchanting:[73] naturalism continues to accept that humans are conscious creatures; human goals and interests are preserved. Although the physical constitutions and cognitive capacities of humans are explained by the natural sciences, potential remains for humans to construct and appreciate meaning; to have some control over their fluctuating circumstances.[74] Germane to my project, Fla-

70. Smart, *The Science of Religion*, 101.

71. Smart, *The Science of Religion*, 87.

72. Drees comments on the project to "translate" pre-scientific myths (beliefs) into systems of values compatible with the modern scientific cosmos. He points out that understanding one's motivations for attempting this kind of "translating" work is important: Drees (1998, 4) states, "That such beliefs arose in certain circumstances does not imply that they must be wrong, but their historical contingency in relation to human history and human nature raises the question of why we would consider particular beliefs of an earlier epoch as serious candidates for truth or as existentially relevant insights, worth reformulating in our time." It is my sense that, since religious people's testimonies inform us that religious people possess beliefs about superhuman agents and/or beliefs about trans-empirical worlds, that realization is sufficient enough to consider "translating" pre-scientific myths into values compatible with modern science.

73. Flanagan, *The Really Hard Problem*, loc. 1469, Kindle.

74. Flanagan, *The Really Hard Problem*, loc. 1469, Kindle.

nagan articulates well the aims of value maintenance in a naturalistic ontology. He writes, "We are biological beings living in a material world that we have constructed. *Our norms and values are designed to serve our purposes as social mammals living in different social worlds.* History, and possibly our psychology, has led us to mystify norms and values."[75] It is precisely this "mystification" of norms and values, alluded to by Flanagan, that modern compatibility systems seek to delimit and clarify. As mentioned, this process of value maintenance recovers the *symbolic*, leaving behind the metaphysical/religious "brute" facts we no longer can assent to.[76]

Returning to our statement "*myths are descriptions of physical reality*," which the igmythicist says is nonsensical, I acknowledge that, like the concept of *God*, when myths are conceptualized as metaphysical "brute" facts, myths lack existential import. However, that myths be conceptualized as metaphysical facts is one possibility only. We have seen already how the splitting of a myth into *fact* and *symbol* in the modern scientific cosmos presents another possibility to conceptualize myths: as mentioned, in this case, the *symbol* element of a myth takes precedence, recovering the "ultimacy" of values in the myth, but doing so in a representational fashion which does not require any explicit substantive claims. When myths are understood to function in a representational fashion, the statement "*myths are descriptions of physical reality*" is contextualized differently: *Descriptions* in the preceding statement are no longer descriptions of metaphysical "brute" facts, but are *symbolic* descriptions. Symbolic descriptions do not include claims about trans-empirical worlds, but rather are *human-sourced*

---

75. Flanagan, *The Really Hard Problem*, loc. 1469, Kindle; emphasis added.

76. That it becomes difficult to assent to metaphysical/religious "brute" facts occurs not merely because the modern scientific enterprise exists, but occurs because of what I see to be two main epistemic reasons, alluded to in various sections of this book: (i) Religious and scientific exercises make conflicting claims about *shared* states of affairs in one, physical world—this produces epistemic tension but that is still not enough to maintain that it is in fact difficult to assent to the metaphysical objects of religious claims. (ii) However, unlike religious exercises, scientific exercises are inherently *open to change*, permitting modification of beliefs and worldviews—a process which makes learning possible. As I note in *Adventure*, "In our everyday learning we need opportunities to work out inconsistencies and mistakes as we uncover them. This leads us, ultimately, to deeper and more mature understandings of the [physical] world. A denial of this type of attitude of mind is a denial of the purpose of learning, a denial of intellect, and a denial of ourselves" (Woodward 2014, 57). Thus, in light of point (i) and with the motivation toward learning expressed in point (ii), vis-à-vis modern science, it does become difficult to *continue* to assent to metaphysical/religious "brute" facts. This, however, does not preclude the possibility that myths play a role in a symbolic fashion, as *representations* of physical reality: I am not suggesting a dismissal of religious myths, but I am advocating for a reconfiguration of the precise nature of myths as myths are contextualized in a modestly naturalistic epistemology.

or *human-inspired* representations of physical reality. Also, while they are "representations" realized physiologically and/or psychologically and "representations" identified and located in the sociocultural institutions of modern religions, these symbolic descriptions (myths) remain representations only. Similar, though, to the notion of an anthropomorphic God, symbolically oriented myths may include some "observed" fact in the sense that their physiological and/or psychological realizations *and* their identification in sociocultural institutions are part and parcel of what have already been called brute facts *and* institutional facts (Searle), respectively.

~

Revisiting once again the ongoing struggle between theism and naturalism, Schellenberg notes, "It's not a coincidence that what Ayer was primarily concerned to declare meaningless in his 1936 positivistic manifesto *Language, Truth, and Logic*, when he came to matters religious, was talk about *God*. And when you have only two main alternatives or live options [theism and naturalism], it's always possible for the one that has fallen out of favour [i.e., theism], through quirks of history no one would have foreseen, to gain the upper hand once more."[77] Despite the fact that traditional theism seems to have regained some popularity in analytic philosophy, especially because of its stark contrast to naturalism, neither *a priori* theism nor a strict, *scientistic* naturalism will do for our project of designing a religious epistemology in a modern research university. In summary, Kurtz's igtheism has brought to the fore the realization that the non-tested beliefs of belief claims perhaps *will not ever* be tested—belief claims are empirically meaningless! *However*, belief claims, in our current, twenty-first century, retain some emotional and psychological value—thus, belief claims could be *emotionally* and *psychologically* meaningful! This is the direction in which we are heading. Without wishing to overdo the point too much, I will leave this argument to rest here, revisiting these themes in part 3 where the philosophical design of a religious epistemology is the specific goal.

INITIAL RESPONSES TO SCIENCE AND RELIGION INTERFACES

The upcoming chapter 5 will address examples of compatibility systems existing in science and religion literature, developed from analytic philosophy, philosophical theology, and sociology. To begin with here, I note that, in a

77. Schellenberg, "Philosophy of Religion," 99.

general sense, theories of rationality serve as attempts to design compatibility systems. In addition, Smart suggests that examples of projects within the discipline of systematic theology are attempts at designing compatibility systems.[78] For example, in natural theology, Smart goes on, attempts are made to relate the tenets of religious faith toward developments in modern scientific knowledge, to the evolving nature of human perceptions of physical reality, and to overall changes in the *Zeitgeist*. Despite the main imperative of compatibility systems to "translate" pre-scientific myths into values compatible with the modern scientific cosmos, there is *some* leeway. For example, Smart notes how a faith-imbued compatibility system would be open to continue to treat the cosmos as sacred—that is, derived from the actions of CPS-agents. However, the metaphysics of such compatibility systems would be similar to pre-scientific cosmologies,[79] and, I would add, sensible to individuals functioning under the presuppositions of faith-imbued communities only. Conversely, notions of the sacred or other metaphysics are often removed from compatibility system design. In this way, the focus of the compatibility system is not toward an attempted reconciliation of the substantive beliefs of either science or religion, but rather toward an etically oriented philosophical or sociological comparison of science and religion. Most compatibility systems assessed in chapter 5 are attempts to fit this last category, though they remain attempts.

Smart models five initial responses one might experience toward the relationship of science and religion as one *begins* the task of compatibility system design.[80] For each model, in the following pages, I summarize the nature of the response, including a brief practical example, illustrating how the response might be actualized in religious and/or scientific life. (My examples are current, twenty-first-century examples; not necessarily examples relevant to Smart's era a few decades ago.) There is, of course, much variation among the commitments, experiences, and beliefs of different religious devotees and scientific practitioners. For that reason, the examples I include in the following pages may seem polarized or stereotypical; however, they serve well the purpose of illustrating what the epistemic implications of each response would be.

1. *Reject the modern scientific enterprise*: Accept an incompatibility between science and religion, although in a state of what Smart calls a "paradoxical tension."[81] For some religious devotees, this model re-

78. Smart, *The Science of Religion*, 100.
79. Smart, *The Science of Religion*, 83.
80. Smart, *The Science of Religion*, 104–5.
81. Smart, *The Science of Religion*, 104.

sults in a rejection of tested beliefs about states of affairs in the physical world—a rejection of the modern scientific enterprise.[82] An example which fits this model would be the claim made by young-earth creationists that the creation narratives in Genesis are accurate descriptions of the origin of physical reality[83]—that the earth was created in six, 24-hour days, sometime around 4004 BCE, per James Usher's "calculation" made in 1650.[84] To honestly make the claim made by young-earth creationists requires one to reject tested geological dating and hence reject modern science.[85]

2. *Attempt to make religion "fit" science*: Contextualize the non-tested beliefs of religious life relative to the tested beliefs of scientific practice.[86] This model accepts the method of the modern scientific enterprise, replacing any pre-scientific cosmologies with the contemporary scientific cosmos. Nevertheless this option also recognizes that religious beliefs continue to permeate modern societies, as testimonies of religious devotees inform us.[87] An example which fits this model would be the day-age theory of old-earth creationists. Day-age theory maintains that each of the six "days" in Genesis is actually a very long period of time, accommodating ages of modern geological dating:[88] here, the modern scientific enterprise sets a benchmark in terms of method (geological dating is permitted), while the six "days" in Genesis are contextualized in a figurative (non-literal) sense for the purpose of religious life. Yet, still being *influenced* by traditional religious proclivities, this model still maintains that CPS-agents *are* ontological realities. This model

---

82. Dubbed the "Bible belt reaction," Smart (2015, 104) points out how a rejection of the modern scientific enterprise, enhanced by a strong emotional attachment to a conservative religious literalism, is and only can be a contemporary phenomenon: it is only in face of modern science that such a response exists; such an emotional response is not applicable to, for example, what Smart calls "medieval belief."

83. Haack, "Point of Honor: On Science and Religion," 273.

84. White, *A History of the Warfare of Science with Theology*, 1:253.

85. Unless, of course, one chooses to accept the method of modern science as an epistemic benchmark for testing beliefs in some matters but not in others: e.g., one rejects modern geological dating, but more generally accepts quantum physics. Such an option, however, would amount to an inconsistent application of the scientific method.

86. Smart, *The Science of Religion*, 104.

87. That religious beliefs continue to permeate modern societies is a theme in works such as Peter Berger's *A Rumor of Angels: Modern Society and the Rediscovery of the Supernatural*. More recently see, for example, Jürgen Habermas's essays in *Between Naturalism and Religion*, in particular his "Religion in the Public Sphere: Cognitive Presuppositions for the 'Public Use of Reason' by Religious and Secular Citizens."

88. Haack, "Point of Honor: On Science and Religion," 273.

maintains that the actions of CPS-agents *can* provide explanations for states of affairs in the physical world.

3. *Attempt to make science "fit" religion*: Contextualize the tested beliefs of scientific practice relative to the non-tested beliefs of religious life.[89] This model accepts the method of modern science but only in a limited, quasi-intellectual sense, amounting to what Smart calls "deviant scientific ideas,"[90] and, in my view, suppressed learning and growth in modern society. In this model, it seems tested information from scientific theories is acknowledged, but, due to religious motivations, constraints are placed on how such information may be utilized. An example which fits this model would be the claim of some religious groups that, although scientific theories describe same-sex attraction as inborn, in accordance with religious proscriptions non-heterosexual individuals should nevertheless resist their natural sexual interests: here the modern scientific enterprise sets a benchmark at least in terms of method (i.e., information from scientific theories is acknowledged), but religious motivations limit modern science, suppressing the extent to which scientific findings are allowed to promote intellectual growth and betterment in society.[91]

4. *Place science and religion in separate "compartments"*: Place science and religion in separate "compartments" such that each enterprise neither communicates with the other nor even knows the other exists. Although this model may elude the epistemic tension which motivates the formulating of preceding models, Smart is concerned this model tends toward an over-compartmentalized worldview.[92] An over-compartmentalized worldview may lead to an over-compartmentalized practical life. An example which fits this model would be Stephen Jay Gould's non-overlapping magisteria (NOMA) principle outlined in his *Rocks of Ages: Science and Religion in the Fullness of Life* (1999):[93] here, science and religion exist in separate domains (magisteria), fulfilling separate, incommensurable roles in society. Stenmark com-

---

89. Smart, *The Science of Religion*, 104.
90. Smart, *The Science of Religion*, 104.
91. It is worth mentioning that, like all examples presented in these paragraphs, the example regarding religious proscriptions against non-heterosexual individuals applies to some religious groups only. Other religious groups have adjusted their positions on sexual orientation vis-à-vis new information obtained from modern science: For example, see Rayside, *Queer Inclusions, Continental Divisions*, 153.
92. Smart, *The Science of Religion*, 104–5.
93. Gould, *Rocks of Ages*, 1.

ments on Gould's NOMA, remarking that, while Gould accepts that evidentialism is mandatory in science,[94] evidentialism is a *possibility* only in religion.[95] Thus, in terms of Gould's notion of incommensurable domains for science and religion, it is not an epistemic problem in this model that science accepts evidentialism as mandatory whereas religion does not.

5. *Reject the non-tested beliefs of religious life*: Undergo a complete rejection of the non-tested beliefs of religious life[96]—the epistemic tension experienced by the *attempted* design of a compatibility system between science and religion was too great and the tested beliefs of modern scientific life are chosen exclusively. An example which fits this model would be the proposed abandonment of the academic project to attempt to design a compatibility system, as proposed by Don Wiebe in his essay "*Is Science Really an Implicit Religion?*" in his *Beyond Legitimation: Essays on the Problem of Religious Knowledge*:[97] here, it is concluded that compatibility systems fulfill a social function, however, the attainment of a compatibility system which is logically justified is deemed not possible.[98] Since the ideals of the Popperian attitude of mind toward learning are built into the epistemic structure of modern science—beliefs can be proposed, tested, and then accepted or discarded[99]—the tested beliefs of modern science are chosen exclusively and the non-tested beliefs of religious life rejected.

Before progressing to examples of potential compatibility systems in chapter 5, our final task in this chapter is to consider that discussions about *compatibility* or *incompatibility* between science and religion presuppose that science and religion are *commensurable* human enterprises—i.e.,

---

94. The notion of evidentialism is, of course, only one aspect of a theory of rationality. To treat the scientific method as a method governed by evidentialism only (or primarily) is to limit one's understanding of the scope and purpose of the scientific method. In its wider scope, the scientific method includes inherent capacities to allow intellectual growth, permit new learning, and (if required) modification of existing beliefs. These goals are possible because of evidentialism (which makes testing beliefs possible), but the motivation to apply the scientific method in one's life need not be evidentialism only (or at all), but rather an attitude of mind of being open to the possibility of *new* learning . . . to the possibility of a more mature understanding of the physical world.

95. Stenmark, *How to Relate Science and Religion*, 54.

96. Smart, *The Science of Religion*, 105.

97. Wiebe, "Is Science Really an Implicit Religion," 99.

98. Wiebe, "Is Science Really an Implicit Religion," 99.

99. Wiebe, *The Irony of Theology*, 38.

that science and religion can be compared in the first place. However, as I mentioned near the start of this chapter, only after we resolve whether science and religion are in fact commensurable *or* incommensurable can any useful discussion about compatibility or incompatibility really be had. This is an interesting point: it seems most academic and popular debates about science and religion jump right to the question of compatibility or incompatibility without first asking whether the project of comparing science and religion is even tenable. For example, should scientific and religious modes of thought be in fact incommensurable, comparing and contrasting them would be a senseless endeavour. About incommensurability, Wiebe notes, "Neither requires justification outside itself—they simply are what they are, neither better nor worse than the other."[100] Also, science and religion deemed incommensurable might be an intellectual escape hatch—an avoidance or denial of the science and religion question. Alternatively, for some, science and religion deemed incommensurable means the individual roles of science and religion can be most clearly articulated (e.g., Gould's NOMA principle). The question for us, however, is not whether we possess a preference either way toward the commensurability or incommensurability of science and religion. Rather, the question at hand is whether the internal structures of science and religion—their *substantive beliefs*; their *cognitive intentionalities*, etc.—can help us to determine if science and religion are commensurable or incommensurable human enterprises.

As is now pointed out, generally in philosophical theology, for two different beliefs to be rendered compatible or incompatible, those two beliefs must first be commensurable beliefs. In response to the question of science's and religion's alleged commensurability or incommensurability, *à la* Wiebe, a consideration of human modes of communication is helpful. In *The Domestication of the Savage Mind*, a twentieth-century anthropological text, Jack Goody contends that culture amounts to "a series of communicative acts."[101] Similarly, for Steven Mithen, cultures are "not just lists of facts about the world, but specific ways of thinking and understanding."[102] Differences in modes of communication and ways of thinking are crucial to analyze differences among societies where critical attitudes are normative and those where *any* beliefs freely dominate. For example, exclusively oral societies (what Goody terms *traditional societies*) would find it difficult to practice skepticism:[103] a critical attitude toward beliefs can hardly exist (if at

---

100. Wiebe, "Is Science Really an Implicit Religion," 98.
101. Goody, *The Domestication of the Savage Mind*, 37.
102. Mithen, *The Prehistory of the Mind*, 34.
103. The concept of *skepticism* includes various schools of thought, including

all) when one's substantive beliefs are not physically recorded.[104] As Goody's argument goes, the invention of written language ushers in a *new* mode of communication whereby the contents of beliefs are written down, allowing critical reflection about beliefs in both communal and private settings.[105] Written language, however, is not the only component at play. In addition to written language, Wiebe points out that an explicit, *conscious* intent to know the physical world ushers in a radical, alternative mode of thought in contrast to the *unconscious* intentions of mythopoeic thought.[106] The well-known Popperian thesis of a new mode of thought (alternative to myth) appearing among the Presocratics supports this view. According to Popper, the Presocratics ventured to make simple, yet bold, theories about the physical world.[107] Initiating a tradition of critical discussion,[108] the view that free and open criticism of beliefs be tolerated, the Presocratics transitioned from the medium of myth toward a new method of *consciously* critiquing their theories. Wiebe summarizes this venture as follows:

> The easiest way to summarize this discussion is to say that the emergence of [Presocratic] philosophy signals the emergence of a more purely cognitive intentionality in human thought. "Beliefs" come to function in an *essentially* cognitive capacity rather than in what has been called a "catechismic" one. Primitive thought certainly produces and operates with beliefs, but their beliefs function primarily socially rather than epistemically;

---

nihilism, mitigated skepticism, and Paul Kurtz's "new skepticism" (Kurtz, *The New Skepticism*, 23–30). In the sense employed in the current discussion about modes of communication which include language, *skepticism* refers to *inquiry* where the focus of the "skeptic" is on pragmatic, methodological concerns and the testing of beliefs. In addition, Asbjørn Dyrendal ("Oh No, It Isn't," 897) points out that modern skeptical rhetoric serves as a "counter-rhetoric," acting to naturalize controversial claims about supernatural phenomena. This counter-rhetorical strategy ("counter" because it aims to delegitimate the rhetorical strategy employed by belief communities whereby they "appeal" to science to attempt to legitimate their own claims) often amounts to the skeptic's counter-argument that a natural explanation for the controversial claim in question has simply not yet been uncovered.

104. Goody, *The Domestication of the Savage Mind*, 43.

105. The continued existence of *theology*, too, requires the invention of written language much more than does the continued existence of religiosity. Theology is systematic, polemical, and analytic; these features seem to be supported by (may even require) written language. Religiosity, in contrast, is cognitively natural *with or without* recording and/or systematizing its claims. See also McCauley's analysis of what he terms "popular religion" compared with theology (McCauley 2011, 153–54).

106. Wiebe, "Is Science Really an Implicit Religion," 97.

107. Popper, "Back to the Presocratics," 183–85.

108. Popper, "Back to the Presocratics," 200.

they function as a social bond amongst the members of the group rather than merely supplying them with knowledge.[109]

For Wiebe, "religious knowledge" (e.g., catechismic belief) functions as a local knowledge, because with "religious knowledge" no distinction between the concepts of *knowledge* and *meaning* is maintained.[110] However, although "religious knowledge" cannot be tested,[111] it nevertheless remains, for religious devotees, "knowledge" about the physical world. Conveniently, it is this distinction—between *impersonal, tested knowledge* and *socially bonded meaning ("religious knowledge")*—which helps elucidate the question of science's and religion's alleged commensurability or incommensurability.

Put simply, mythopoeic (religious) thought is not concerned with testing beliefs.[112] Or, if there is any intentionality toward testing beliefs (any at all), the intentionality is *unconscious*. In mythopoeic thought, there seems to be no explicit desire to know and interpret the physical world—for if there was, beliefs would be freely and openly critiqued.[113] Granted, the argument here is not trying to say that persons employing mythopoeic thought are inherently inferior to persons employing modern science (the argument is not a "racist" one), but the goal of the argument is to point out that individuals employing mythopoeic thought are capitalizing on cognitive capacities different from those cognitive capacities utilized by persons employing modern science. In this sense, some individuals could experience cognitive capacities responsible for both mythopoeic thought *and* scientific thought.

---

109. Wiebe, "Is Science Really an Implicit Religion," 96.

110. Wiebe, "Religion, Science, and the Transformation of 'Knowledge,'" 107.

111. I note that, for some, a noncognitivist interpretation of religious objects of knowledge may appear to capitulate too easily toward positivism. (Ironically, such concerns reveal what Wiebe calls a "lack of nerve" in the scientific study of religion.) In this section, the highlighting of *socially bonded meaning*, a goal and outcome of religious life, may help to ease the concerns of those who feel my distinction between knowledge claims and belief claims tends toward positivism. I'm not a closet positivist—I openly admit that, in terms of epistemology, my work includes a positivistic flavour. In terms of the social realities of religious life, however, my work allows the possibility of "religious knowledge" as *socially bonded meaning* located in a religious/belief community. These ideas and their implications for the possibility of a religious epistemology are considered extensively in part 3.

112. Wiebe, "Is Science Really an Implicit Religion," 92.

113. To add to the point here, as *H. sapiens sapiens*, we are not infallible creatures, but we are fallible and imperfect—so by extension we need to freely and openly critique our beliefs to ensure that our beliefs are tested and open to modification, if need be. Otherwise, as this argument goes, tested human knowledge would not even be epistemically possible. Since, in mythopoeic thought, beliefs are not freely and openly critiqued, in mythopoeic thought there seems to be no *explicit* desire (no conscious intentionality) to know and interpret the physical world.

What Is a Compatibility System? Who Is It For? 103

Depending on personal preference, or, perhaps more importantly, an inculcated *awareness* of these different cognitive capacities, one may or may not display a *conscious* desire to know and interpret the physical world. It might also be argued that persons seeking to incorporate both science *and* religion in their lives are attempting to mentally utilize different cognitive capacities at the same time—cognitive capacities responsible for mythopoeic thought *and* those required for scientific thought.

Continuing with the theme in the preceding paragraph, we observe that in scientific thought there is an explicit desire to test beliefs—an explicit, indeed self-proclaimed, interest to know and interpret the physical world. Also, this explicit interest to know the physical world motivates critical belief testing. The intentionality, then, toward testing beliefs in science is *conscious*. In terms of *intentionality*, scientific thought and mythopoeic thought are incommensurable:[114] As science and religion are grounded in different cognitive capacities, resulting in different desires and motivations to know and interpret the physical world (explicit, conscious desire *versus* unconscious desire), scientific thought and mythopoeic thought cannot be compared. Neither one is more "correct" than the other. To say one is more "correct" than the other would be to say that some cognitive capacities are more superior or more "right" than others—a claim I am not willing to make. In addition, one's methodology (one's systematic procedure for analyzing and/or testing beliefs) presupposes an intentionality, whether an intentionality which is conscious or unconscious. Thus, it would seem that science and religion are incommensurable in terms of *methodology*, too. However, in light of these realizations—that, in terms of intentionality and methodology, science and religion are incommensurable—has our project foundered? Shall I close the curtain and stop the show?

Perhaps a short intermission, but not a complete ending just yet. For surely, and following Wiebe's lead, in terms of *mentation*, scientific thought and mythopoeic thought are commensurable:[115] Both science and religion, although arising from different cognitive capacities, include *shared* mental functions—a *shared* mentation. Through our awareness of science's substantive beliefs (about the physical world) and by way of our exposure to religion's substantive beliefs (about the physical world), we can see that science and religion include shared mental functions. For example, by way of their substantive beliefs, we observe that both science and religion possess shared mental functions in their shared attempts to *know* and *interpret* the one, physical world. In fact, we already considered this in chapter 1 when

---

114. Wiebe, "Is Science Really an Implicit Religion," 98.
115. Wiebe, "Is Science Really an Implicit Religion," 98.

I made the case that both science and religion make claims about *shared* states of affairs in one, physical world. In doing so, science and religion epistemically conflict, but they display a shared mentation: yes, science and religion claim to know and interpret the physical world in radically different ways (we find that they epistemically conflict), but nevertheless science and religion display a shared mentation—noticed by way of their substantive beliefs, made known to us through the verbal statements of knowledge claims (science) and belief claims (religion). As science and religion scholars, we are justified, then, in comparing and contrasting science and religion at the *level of mentation*—my departure point in chapter 5. Potential compatibility systems will assess compatibility or incompatibility by way of mentation—i.e., an analysis of the mental functions shared by science and religion.[116]

Finally, I noted earlier in this chapter that notions of the sacred or other metaphysics are often removed from compatibility system design; that preferably the focus of a compatibility system be not toward an attempted reconciliation of the substantive beliefs of science and the substantive beliefs of religion. I hope it is more clear now why in my work I choose to distance myself from what I call the *faith-imbued* projects[117] of other science and

---

116. In 2016, Wiebe and I discussed his essay "Is Science Really an Implicit Religion?"—found in his book *Beyond Legitimation*. In this essay, about mythopoeic thought compared with scientific thought, Wiebe notes that "the two modes of thought, mythopoeic and scientific, are incommensurable with respect to intention but commensurable with respect to function" (98). I have clarified with Wiebe that, in the preceding quotation, when he writes "commensurable with respect to function" he is referring to possible commensurability with respect to mental functions—i.e., with respect to mentation. In addition, in the preceding quotation, when Wiebe writes "incommensurable with respect to intention" he is referring to incommensurability with respect to both intentionality *and* methodology, too—since one's methodology presupposes an intentionality, whether one that is conscious or unconscious. Generally in philosophical theology, for two different beliefs to be rendered compatible or incompatible, those two beliefs must first be commensurable beliefs. In Wiebe's essay, he concludes that science and religion are both *incommensurable* and *incompatible* human enterprises (98). To reach this unusual conclusion, Wiebe first required himself to argue that science and religion are incommensurable (with respect to intentionality and methodology), but also that science and religion are commensurable (with respect to mentation). After arguing that science and religion are commensurable (with respect to mentation), he was then able to argue that science and religion are incompatible—as well as incommensurable.

117. Examples of various *faith-imbued* science and religion projects include projects of young-earth and old-earth creationists; projects which attempt to equate religious miracles with violations of the physical laws of nature; Fritjof Capra's attempt to find parallels between physics and Eastern mysticism in Capra, *The Tao of Physics*; theosophist Helena Blavatsky's esoteric theory of evolution, drawing on the theory of evolution and Hindu cosmology; and the Christian-centred projects of Polkinghorne, *One World*, or Plantinga, *Where the Conflict Really Lies*.

religion scholars—those projects which propose either (a) a reconciliation between the substantive beliefs of science and the substantive beliefs of religion or (b) an attempted reconciliation of the respective methodologies of science and religion. In short, those projects are misguided: those projects fail to realize that, in terms of intentionality (explicit, conscious desire *versus* unconscious desire to know the physical world), science and religion are incommensurable. However, as science and religion *are* commensurable in terms of mentation, compatibility or incompatibility can be assessed by way of the mental functions shared by science and religion.[118] It must be noted, however, that this possible assessment—by way of mentation—is still different from an attempted reconciliation of science and religion at the level of science's and religion's substantive beliefs, respectively, or at the level of science's and religion's methodologies, respectively. Furthermore, although we can conclude that science and religion are commensurable in terms of mentation, the question of science's and religion's alleged compatibility or incompatibility still remains to be seen. For that elusive analysis, we now turn to chapter 5!

---

118. Note also from Smart's five initial responses toward an attempted reconciliation between science and religion, and from the examples I provided to highlight the epistemic implications of each response, the following: Response (i)—*rejection of the modern scientific enterprise*, and response (v)—*rejection of the non-tested beliefs of religious life*, presume (albeit unknowingly) that science and religion are commensurable in terms of mentation, making their assessments (in part) by way of mental functions. In contrast, response (ii)—*attempt to make religion "fit" science*, and response (iii)—*attempt to make science "fit" religion*, presume (albeit unknowingly) that science and religion can be compared on substantive grounds or methodological grounds (by manipulating the substantive beliefs of either science or religion, or manipulating the methodologies of either science or religion), even though science and religion are in fact incommensurable in terms of intentionality and methodology. Finally, response (iv)—*place science and religion in separate "compartments"* evades the academic assessment of compatibility or incompatibility by assuming that science and religion are incommensurable. Note, however, that this assumption in response (iv) is not necessarily based on the realization that science and religion cannot be compared because they employ different intentionalities and cognitive capacities, but just that it has been determined *a priori* that science and religion are incommensurable. As science and religion are in fact commensurable in terms of mentation, the *a priori* assumption of incommensurability made in response (iv) is questionable.

5

Presentation of Potential Compatibility Systems

KNOWLEDGE COMMUNITIES AND BELIEF COMMUNITIES: "YOU TOO!"

SOCIOLOGIST JÜRGEN HABERMAS'S PRESENTATION of postmetaphysical thinking in his *Between Naturalism and Religion* (2008) is strikingly similar to Smart's concept of compatibility systems. In fact, the tenets of postmetaphysical thinking align quite well with the aims of compatibility system design. Habermas, a methodological atheist, alerts us in a general sense toward not passing judgement too quickly on religious motivations, but rather encourages us to orient ourselves toward the observation that religious communities, in one form or another, continue to permeate secular society.[1] While he does insist on an epistemic separation between scientific beliefs and religious beliefs, Habermas's motivation to orient his readers to the continued existence of religious communities is centred on a realization of what religions, in a personal, non-scientific fashion, might offer a *postsecular* society. About this, Habermas notes:

> It would be unreasonable to reject out of hand the idea that the major world religions—as the only surviving element of the now alien cultures of the Ancient Empires—can claim a place within the differentiated architecture of modernity, because their

---

1. Habermas, "Religion in the Public Sphere," 139–40.

cognitive substance has not yet been exhausted. At any rate, we cannot exclude that they involve semantic potentials capable of exercising an inspirational force on society *as a whole* as soon as they divulge their profane truth contents.[2]

Consider carefully Habermas's suggestions, in the preceding quotation, (i) of making known the "profane truth contents"[3] of religious statements, including (ii) the exercising of religion's "inspirational force on society."[4] A brief digression is in order: In the context of postmetaphysical thinking, precisely what it means to make known the truth contents of religious statements must be unpacked. Similar to compatibility system design, postmetaphysical modes of thought, for one, avoid substantive assumptions about ontological realities—the substantive truth contents of statements (if any) are irrelevant. (For example, as Habermas puts it, "Postmetaphysical thinking refrains from making ontological pronouncements on the constitution of being.")[5] But secondly, and this aspect of postmetaphysical thinking is also similar to Haack's innocent realism, postmetaphysical thinking avoids a devaluation of those statements—moral, religious, artistic, or emotional, etc.—which seem to resist reduction to natural, causal interactions only.[6] It appears that, like potential compatibility systems, postmetaphysical thinking vis-à-vis religion embraces the possibility that religious values can be recontextualized (replaced) in the modern scientific cosmos—e.g., Habermas's proposed divulging of the "profane truth contents"[7] of religions. I would like, then, to think of this chapter as an extension of the postmetaphysical project; that potential compatibility systems are attempts to actualize some of the aims of a postsecular society.

Following the argument in chapter 4, ideal compatibility systems assess compatibility or incompatibility by way of *mentation*—a consideration of mental functions shared between science and religion. In the upcoming compatibility system assessments, along with the concept *mentation*, the concepts *intentionality* and *methodology* will also appear at times. For each potential compatibility system presented, I shall endeavour to show how the proposed compatibility system assesses compatibility, or incompatibility, by way of mentation, or, if it does not, why it does not. I must also mention that the examples to be presented, although taken from literature, are

2. Habermas, "Religion in the Public Sphere," 142.
3. Habermas, "Religion in the Public Sphere," 142.
4. Habermas, "Religion in the Public Sphere," 142.
5. Habermas, "Religion in the Public Sphere," 140.
6. Habermas, "Religion in the Public Sphere," 141.
7. Habermas, "Religion in the Public Sphere," 142.

not termed *compatibility systems* in the respective literature. Rather, I apply Smart's phrase *compatibility system* to systems of thought deemed by myself and/or the scholars mentioned to be examples of projects which attempt a reconciliation between science and religion. My purpose for doing this is so that a more organized and helpful structure might be applied to the various projects I have come across which seek to, in some way, unite science and religion, or distance them. Merits and downfalls of potential compatibility systems are also addressed.

The Post-Kuhnian Compatibility System

We begin with a compatibility system which I call the *post-Kuhnian compatibility system*—made possible by Thomas Kuhn's philosophy of science formulated in *The Structure of Scientific Revolutions*, and then alluded to in various contributions to science and religion literature.[8] Post-Kuhnian compatibility systems, which in most general terms argue a subjectivist interpretation of the scientific enterprise, are similar to traditional, religious apologetics.[9] Whereas prior to Kuhn, religious beliefs were argued to share cognitive values with science, post-Kuhn, compatibility system enthusiasts began to argue that science is no more rational than religion. As the argument goes, if religion is irrational, science is irrational too.[10] Another version of this approach to compatibility system design replaces Kuhnian paradigms with Lakatosian research programs, but in effect the gist of the argument vis-à-vis Lakatos remains the same: i.e., the mantra *if religion is irrational, science is irrational too*. Classifying scientific practitioners as members of a *knowledge community* and religious devotees as members of a *belief community*,[11] the post-Kuhnian compatibility system allows members in each community to make use of the rather fashionable *tu quoque* argument: "you too!" Various scholars, including Ian Barbour,[12] Hans Küng,[13]

---

8. Various scholars, including Ian Barbour, Hans Küng, and Don Wiebe, have proposed post-Kuhnian compatibility systems. (Wiebe has since abandoned compatibility system design altogether.)

9. Wiebe, "Is Science Really an Implicit Religion," 93.

10. Wiebe, "Science and Religion," 71–72.

11. This classification of scientific practitioners into a *knowledge community* and religious devotees into a *belief community* is in keeping with my Thomistic-flavoured *knowledge claim* and *belief claim* typology.

12. Barbour, *Religion and Science*, 93–94.

13. Küng, *Theology for the Third Millennium*, 123–26.

Nancey Murphy,[14] and Don Wiebe,[15] have proposed compatibility systems based on knowledge communities and belief communities.[16] (Wiebe has since abandoned the project of compatibility system design altogether.)

The relevance of the *tu quoque* argument to our purposes here is that the *tu quoque* speaks to the mental functions (mentation) shared by science and religion—science's and religion's shared attempts to (i) *know* and (ii) *interpret* the one, physical world. The focus of this potential compatibility system—the *tu quoque*—suggests that, by way of Kuhn's philosophy, modern science does not attempt to know and interpret the one, physical world in a mental fashion which could be deemed any more rational than religion when religion attempts to know and interpret the one, physical world. Again, as stated, in the post-Kuhnian compatibility system, if religion is irrational, science is deemed irrational, too (and vice versa). Applying Kuhnian paradigms, in the following paragraphs, I outline my own take on the argument which supports a compatibility system centred on knowledge communities and belief communities.

Kuhn describes three modes of research through which scientific work is accomplished in a scientific paradigm.[17] Using my own examples,[18] I summarize these modes as follows:

1. Apply facts, known through previous research, to solve scientific problems. Facts may be numerical constants—e.g., Planck's constant, a fundamental physical constant, which is $6.63 \times 10^{-34}\,m^2 \cdot kg \cdot s^{-1}$. Or, facts may be formulas—e.g., Newton's second law that force is mass multiplied by acceleration, expressed by the formula $F=ma$. Alternatively, facts may be other laws—e.g., the second law of thermodynamics which states that the disorder of an isolated system will always become more disordered or remain the same.

2. Apply the scientific theories of a paradigm to solve a real-life problem. For example, applying the theories of electrochemistry to solve a chemical engineering problem.

3. Work toward resolving ambiguities in a scientific theory which helps to make the theory stronger and more reliable. Kuhn believes

---

14. Murphy, *Theology in the Age of Scientific Reasoning*, 88–129.
15. Wiebe, *Beyond Legitimation*, 13, 72.
16. In proposing compatibility systems based on knowledge communities and belief communities, Barbour, Küng, and Wiebe draw primarily on Kuhnian paradigms, while Murphy draws primarily on Lakatosian research programs.
17. Kuhn, *The Structure of Scientific Revolutions*, 25–27.
18. Woodward, *Adventure*, 53.

this method to be the most common method in modern scientific research.[19]

Reflecting on the preceding research modes, and especially the third mode, Kuhn sees the paradigmatic work of normal science as the work, not of formulating new scientific theories, but of re-expressing previous theories.[20] A "revolution" in science, Kuhn goes on, is a rare chance for a new paradigm to be formulated, referred to by Kuhn as *extraordinary science*.[21] Curiously, and it is this aspect of Kuhn's philosophy most amenable to compatibility system design, Kuhn avers, "The transition between competing paradigms cannot be made a step at a time, forced by logic and neutral experience. Like the gestalt switch, it must occur all at once (though not necessarily in an instant) or not at all."[22] In addition, Lakatos, commenting on Kuhn's extraordinary science, confirms that "scientific change [for Kuhn] is *a kind of religious change*."[23] The question, then, of *consensus* (or lack thereof) in science is central to the post-Kuhnian compatibility system: Religious life notoriously lacks consensus, except possibly for whatever *stated* consensus is published by belief/religious communities in community documents or on community websites; however, that information concerns nothing about personal religious experiences or the individual beliefs of religious devotees, which, invariably, lack consensus. Post Kuhn, a hermeneutic of suspicion is applied to scientific life. As the argument goes, not counting whatever stated consensus is published by knowledge/scientific communities in community documents or on community websites, perceptions of experimental practice among scientific practitioners lack consensus—except for those internal to a single paradigm. The implications for compatibility system design are epistemically attractive: if accused by knowledge communities of being internally inconsistent, belief communities can respond by saying, "you too!"—and, vis-à-vis Kuhn, they would be right. For enthusiasts of the post-Kuhnian compatibility system, this compatibility system provides a simple and elegant comparison of science and religion by way of mentation (mental functions)—in this comparison, via the *tu quoque*, science and religion could be rendered *compatible*.[24]

---

19. Kuhn, *The Structure of Scientific Revolutions*, 27.

20. Kuhn, *The Structure of Scientific Revolutions*, 24.

21. Kuhn, *The Structure of Scientific Revolutions*, 83.

22. Kuhn, *The Structure of Scientific Revolutions*, 149.

23. Lakatos, *The Methodology of Scientific Research Programmes*, 1:9; emphasis added.

24. Here, my choice of words *could be rendered* is meant to point out that, in this analysis, my motivation is not to convince you—my readers—that, by way of the

Despite the attractiveness of the post-Kuhnian compatibility system, it is worth mentioning that *extraordinary science*—the concept which helps to ground this compatibility system—has faced critique. In *Science and Values*, which includes a critique of extraordinary science, Larry Laudan disparagingly asks: "Did he [Kuhn] really believe that accepting a new theory was a 'conversion experience,' subject only to the Gestalt-like exigencies of the religious life?"[25] Also, since revolutions are not determined by external logical factors,[26] revolutions are not rational events. It is here, Laudan emphasizes, that Kuhn breaks away from typical modes of rationality.[27] Kuhn relativizes rationality by insisting there is no supra-paradigmatic framework to adjudicate the various ontologies, methodologies, and cognitive values characteristic of different paradigms. As Laudan puts it, Kuhn's failure to acknowledge *any* universal standards to adjudicate different paradigms produces "a kind of self-reinforcing solipsism in science."[28] In addition, although Kuhn himself notes that he and Popper agree that adherence to tradition is fairly essential in the scientific enterprise,[29] about normal science and extraordinary science, Popper parts company with Kuhn: while Popper sees criticism as the hallmark of science during any phase of scientific practice, Kuhn sees criticism as occurring during periods of extraordinary science (revolutions) only, then leveling out during periods of normal science (so, for Kuhn, normal science is not really a critical enterprise).

Moreover, philosophical notions of revolutions in science are gradually being replaced with notions of stability in science. Hacking explains, "From now on (it is already being said) future large-scale instability seems quite unlikely. We will witness radical developments at present unforeseen. But what we have may persist, modified and built upon."[30] Hacking speaks of a "robust fit"[31] occurring among a plethora of factors including one's

post-Kuhnian compatibility system, science and religion are compatible. Nor is that necessarily my own definite conclusion either. Rather, my motivation in this analysis is to assess compatibility systems presented in science and religion literature and determine how justified proponents of each compatibility system are in their conclusion that science and religion are compatible. So, here, that *science and religion could be rendered compatible* means that, for post-Kuhnian compatibility system enthusiasts, there do seem to be some reasons available to those enthusiasts to justify their compatibility system—to justify *their* conclusion that science and religion are compatible.

25. Laudan, *Science and Values*, 67.
26. Hacking, *The Social Construction of What*, 97.
27. Laudan, *Science and Values*, 69.
28. Laudan, *Science and Values*, 72.
29. Kuhn, *The Essential Tension*, 267–68.
30. Hacking, *The Social Construction of What*, 85.
31. Hacking, *The Social Construction of What*, 73.

experimental apparatus, background beliefs about the apparatus, the scientific theory being tested, and interpretation and analysis of experimental results.[32] Granted, Hacking contends that a robust fit is not determined by however the inherent-structurism[33] of the physical world really is.[34] Rather, different research programs—accommodating and/or resisting different adjustments to one's apparatus, theory, or method of data interpretation—produce various robust fits. Temporary halts to processes of accommodating and/or resisting various adjustments to auxiliary hypotheses (which pertain to apparatus, theory, etc.) result in these robust fits. However, at any rate, minor changes to auxiliary hypotheses—whether they apply to apparatus *or* theory—are different from radical revolutions ushering in new paradigms with new scientific theories and new perceptions of the physical world.[35]

It seems that, within the everyday life of the scientific community, shifts toward a supra-paradigmatic rationality, overall stability, and minor adjustments to auxiliary hypotheses are the orders of the day. These trends, however, are no reason for belief communities to refrain from maintaining a hermeneutic of suspicion toward science (should they choose to), from applying the coveted *tu quoque*: Paul Feyerabend, known for his "anarchic" epistemology, claims that events and developments in the history of science occurred because scientific practitioners deliberately chose not to follow some methodological rules or unwittingly broke rules.[36] As examples, Feyerabend cites the invention of atomism, the Copernican Revolution, and the formulation of nineteenth-century and twentieth-century scientific theories such as the kinetic theories of gases and quantum mechanics. Another example of a radically counterintuitive scientific revolution is the delayed acceptance of the germ theory of disease.[37] As philosopher of science, Robert N. McCauley, notes, it took over 200 years since microorganisms were first discovered for Louis Pasteur to then propose germ theory. The radi-

32. Hacking, *The Social Construction of What*, 72–73.
33. Hacking, *The Social Construction of What*, 83.
34. Hacking, *The Social Construction of What*, 74.
35. Regarding scientific revolutions, Kuhn remarks that, after a paradigm change, one perhaps responds to a different world, suggesting also that, for Kuhn, the ontological status of *scientific truth* depends on the paradigm one is working under. Kuhn explains, "Paradigm changes do cause scientists to see the world of their research-engagement differently. In so far as their only recourse to that world is through what they see and do, we may want to say that *after a revolution scientists are responding to a different world*" (*The Structure of Scientific Revolutions*, 111; emphasis added). Minor changes to auxiliary hypotheses, however, do not constitute a response to a different physical world.
36. Feyerabend, *Against Method*, 7.
37. McCauley, *Why Religion Is Natural and Science Is Not*, 108.

cal causality of germ theory—microorganisms—seemed disproportionate to effects of diseases.[38] Even toward the end of the nineteenth century, Canadian physician, Sir William Osler, although aware of germ theory, continued to recommend bleeding to treat pneumonia.[39] If anything, what these examples do point out is that different paradigms have existed during the history of science. These examples, in and of themselves, do not make a case that twenty-first-century science will produce radical paradigm changes; however, it would also be naive to believe that science has not experienced considerable changes. Indeed, the very notion that science is open to change, intrinsic to its epistemology, suggests that science and the evolution of learning go hand in hand.[40]

FURTHER EXAMPLES OF COMPATIBILITY (OR INCOMPATIBILITY) SYSTEMS

The Neo-Tylorean Compatibility System

Applying what he terms *African traditionalism* and *Western modernity* as departure points, anthropologist Robin Horton presents a thesis of the continuity of human thought and discourse among "traditional," religious modes of thought (which utilize CPS-agents) and modern science.[41] Horton's work in this regard, described by Wiebe as a kind of neo-Tyloreanism[42]— it suggests a resurgence of the nineteenth-century assumption of Edward Burnett Tylor of the uniformity of the human mind across all space and time—amounts to the attempted design of a compatibility system. I call it the *neo-Tylorean compatibility system*. In his essay *"Tradition and Modernity Revisited,"* in the volume *Rationality and Relativism*, Horton philosophizes two types of *theory*:

---

38. McCauley, *Why Religion Is Natural and Science Is Not*, 108.
39. McCauley, *Why Religion Is Natural and Science Is Not*, 108.
40. My point here is not that, given that modern science is open to change, we may be surprised and one day find out that scientific data in fact suggest the existence of a CPS-agent (the hypothesis that CPS-agents are ontological realities is not falsifiable anyway). However, I also do not wish to deny to belief communities the option to employ the *tu quoque*: so long as one is aware of the possible drawbacks of Kuhn's philosophy of science, there remain some grounds for religious devotees to argue that consensus in science is perhaps not as cut-and-dried as some scientists or engineers would like those external to the scientific enterprise to think.
41. Horton, "Tradition and Modernity Revisited," 228.
42. Wiebe, *The Irony of Theology*, 68.

1. A *primary theory* as one's commonsense, everyday encounter with the physical world—a kind of encounter which is constant across all cultures and historical periods.[43] Elements encountered in primary theory include a foreground of physical objects, related by "push-pull"[44] causal interactions in space and time. Essentially, the physical objects and causal interactions of primary theory are *brute facts*.

2. A *secondary theory* as abstract and conceptual, providing what Horton calls a "vastly enlarged causal vision,"[45] which transcends the limited, "push-pull" causality of primary theory. Elements in secondary theory include the personal entities of religion and the impersonal entities of science—but they remain hidden; unobserved.

The crux of the neo-Tylorean compatibility system is that this interest—to postulate hidden, unobserved entities to explain everyday experiences[46]—is shared by religious thought *and* modern science. Attempts to explain and predict everyday experience involve attempts to place simplicity, order, and regularity over one's encounters with the physical world; the unobserved entities of secondary theory help to accomplish these goals. In religious thought, personal entities postulated include gods, spirits, or ancestors, etc. In modern science, impersonal entities postulated include atoms, molecules, electrical currents, and light waves, etc. As Horton goes on, the entities of secondary theory, whether personal or impersonal, depend on analogies from primary theory: for example, models of gods and spirits are analogous to real-life human interactions with other humans; likewise models of atoms, electrical currents, and light waves are analogous to observed phenomena such as traveling objects, water currents, and water waves.[47]

As outlined, the neo-Tylorean compatibility system contends that, since both religious thought and modern science postulate hidden, unobserved entities to explain everyday experience, science and religion are compatible. This conclusion presumes that human encounters with the physical world are constant across cultures, that the human mind is uniform across space and time. Personally, at first glance, I resonate well with the neo-Tylorean compatibility system—the conceptual equating of gods, atoms, spirits, and waves, is emotionally appealing. I think you would get a

---

43. Horton, "Tradition and Modernity Revisited," 228.
44. Horton, "Tradition and Modernity Revisited," 228.
45. Horton, "Tradition and Modernity Revisited," 229.
46. Horton, "Tradition and Modernity Revisited," 230.
47. Horton, "Tradition and Modernity Revisited," 230.

lot of religiously minded scientists, or scientifically minded religious people, jumping on to this compatibility system. *There is, however, a slight academic problem*: according to our previous work in chapter 4, *science and religion are incommensurable at the level of intentionality*—in terms of intentionality, science and religion cannot be compared. What is at issue here is that to go about postulating hidden, unobserved entities—the *focus* of this potential compatibility system—*presupposes an intentionality* which undergirds one's postulations about the physical world and one's reasoning strategies for making those postulations. In other words, as mentioned previously, *one's methodology presupposes an intentionality*. What Horton's work does not consider, then, is how the mythopoeic thought of religion amounts to an unconscious desire (unconscious intentionality) to know the physical world and how that mode of thought cannot be compared, for better or for worse, with the explicit, conscious desire (conscious intentionality) to know the physical world employed in modern science.

We have, then, an example of a "compatibility system" which is perhaps not really a compatibility system after all—at least not in academic terms. I do wish, however, to retain the terminology *neo-Tylorean "compatibility system"* because, as mentioned, what this chapter is providing are *assessments* of potential compatibility systems in science and religion literature. As these are assessments, each compatibility system presented is evaluated for potential commensurability or incommensurability; then, *if deemed commensurable*, potential compatibility or incompatibility in terms of mentation (in terms of mental activity/functions). As such, it will not always be clear from the start how a potential compatibility system will fare vis-à-vis the preceding options. So, in summary, for personal use, the neo-Tylorean compatibility system provides an emotionally attractive comparison of science and religion: a proposed similarity between science's and religion's unobserved entities (Horton's secondary theory) may permit science and religion to be rendered compatible for personal use. On the other hand, on academic grounds (the context of this book), we find the neo-Tylorean compatibility system to be in fact a system where the tenets applied actually show science and religion to be incommensurable. For this reason, we conclude that, in this system, science and religion cannot be rendered compatible *or* incompatible.

The "Will to Power" Incompatibility System

For all the difficulty involved in such an elusive analysis as this, so far life is not too bad: By way of the post-Kuhnian compatibility system we have assessed that science and religion could be rendered compatible. Through our analysis of the neo-Tylorean compatibility system we have also assessed that science and religion cannot be rendered compatible or incompatible. As paradoxical as this may sound, I wish to make the point that individuals pursuing different *potential* compatibility systems will reach different conclusions about compatibility or incompatibility. This ambiguity is not such a bad thing—as least not for the practical outcomes of compatibility system design pursued (potentially) by all of theists, atheists, agnostics, and igtheists. That being said, far greater epistemic ructions still prevail: In *Islam and Science: Religious Orthodoxy and the Battle for Rationality* (1991), Pervez Hoodbhoy brings to our attention how it may seem odd—even bizarre—that, although Islam was a considerably advanced civilization between the ninth and thirteenth centuries, a scientific revolution in modern Islam has not occurred.[48] Hoodbhoy's thesis considers Islamic attitudes toward testing beliefs, concepts of education and research in Islamic universities, and the theological character of Islam when the worldly and other-worldly are combined.

To respond to the question of modern Islam's failure to produce a scientific revolution, Hoodbhoy appeals to Friedrich Nietzsche's contention that rationality is a psychological phenomenon:[49] according to Nietzsche, humans possess a psychological will to ascertain causes for states of affairs in the physical world—a "will to power."[50] In addition to Nietzsche's "will to power," various theories of mind in modern psychology and psychoanalysis agree that humans will go to great lengths to make sense of the unpredictable behaviour of the physical world, aiming to provide some psychological control over chaos, to allow some conscious change to occur. Psychological explanations for religious activity specifically are based on generalizations (though useful ones), such that religion is well suited to the lives of humans: human minds readily desire explanations, human societies prefer order, and human beings seek comfort. As odd as it may sound, in psychoanalysis, religious ritual practices are described by Freud as neurotic compulsions.[51] As Freud's argument goes, human civilization suppresses sexual impulses, so religious practices (neuroses), with their promise of a blissful afterlife, provide an escape hatch from an unbearable, suppressed reality (which ironically helps civilization accomplish further its goal of suppression). At any rate, the point to be made is that whether it is a theory of rationality, a

---

48. Hoodbhoy, *Islam and Science*, 118.
49. Hoodbhoy, *Islam and Science*, 119–20.
50. Hoodbhoy, *Islam and Science*, 120.
51. Hewitt, *Freud on Religion*, 19.

religion, a psychological "will to power," or a "theory of mind," all of these human endeavours serve to attempt to make sense of an unpredictable and often frightening reality; to attempt to reduce the felt tension which exists between brute nature and the constraints of civilization.

Returning to Hoodbhoy's assessment of Islamic attitudes toward testing beliefs vis-à-vis modern science and Nietzsche's "will to power," an extensive comparison of modern science and Islam is presented by Hoodbhoy, leading to his proposal of a science and religion *incompatibility system*. I call it the *"will to power" incompatibility system*. As a "will to power," rationality is a search for causal connections—a causal theory of knowledge. We might wonder, though, what maintains our curiosity for attempting to explain states of affairs in the physical world? Even though we might possess a psychological predisposition toward explaining the physical world, what prevents us from turning simply to agentic explanations? (Some, in fact, do turn to agentic explanations and in effect reject natural explanations.) The search for causal connections requires essentially unlimited mental "space" for continued and unsuppressed belief testing as well as opportunities for new causes to be ascertained in the future (perhaps some former causes also ruled out). Not surprisingly, as Hoodbhoy's argument goes, the inclusion of a medieval-type interventionist deity in one's worldview fills up one's mental "space," discouraging the elucidation of causal connections. As Hoodbhoy candidly puts it, "If divine intervention is complete, then curiosity, imagination, and ambition become superfluous."[52] According to Hoodbhoy, at times when Islamic society was producing intellectual work, e.g., medieval science in the thirteenth century,[53] fatalism did not dominate Islamic society.[54] Also, conflicting tension between schools of thought promoting free will and those teaching predestination tended to favour free will—as seems to be the case in liberal Christian communities today. Eventually, however, fatalism was promoted; beliefs about connections between causes and effects

---

52. Hoodbhoy, *Islam and Science*, 120.

53. In *Old Arts and New Theology: The Beginnings of Theology as an Academic Discipline*, Gillian Rosemary Evans (1980, 104) explains how in twelfth-century Europe the subject of academic theology opened up new discussion about differences between (i) the activity of faith proper—a desire to know God, and (ii) the activity of studying in a neutral fashion the substantive contents of faith—objects of belief to be known about God. Interestingly, medieval Islamic science may play into this also: Evans (1980, 56) points out that various scholars, in particular Étienne Gilson, have suggested that medieval Islamic science helped generally to clarify differences between domains of knowledge that were natural and domains of knowledge pertaining to religious philosophy.

54. Hoodbhoy, *Islam and Science*, 120.

repudiated[55]—severe detriments to the conscious employment of the attitude of mind termed one's "will to power."

Moreover, Hoodbhoy suggests that during the pinnacle of Islamic intellectual life, when the Caliphs sent their emissaries "far and wide to seek manuscripts on matters of learning and [medieval] science, the basic motive was altruistic rather than materialistic."[56] Any materialistic outcomes of testing beliefs, to support utilitarian, technological advances only, were not connected with the altruistic search for knowledge *for the sake of knowledge alone*. From Hoodbhoy we learn how a crucial difference between traditional education and modern education is that, in modern education, knowledge claims serve the purpose of problem solving—questions are freely asked and assessed. The contrast is that, in so-called traditional education, knowledge claims are thought to be received through divine revelation—the questioning of claims is not welcomed, for indeed there is no reason to search for knowledge if knowledge is already provided. Regarding modern Islam, Hoodbhoy draws on a rather revealing quotation from M. A. Kazi, a science advisor to Pakistan during the Zia regime. At a seminar on the "Islamization of knowledge," at International Islamic University (Islamabad, 1982), Kazi remarked, "In Islam there is no science for the sake of science and *there is no knowledge for the sake of knowledge.*"[57]

Firstly, we might conclude that the "will to power" incompatibility system provides a comparison of science and religion by way of mentation, capitalizing on the fact that science (in modern education) and religiosity (in traditional education) both include the making of types of knowledge claims—that is, both include a shared mental goal to attempt to know the physical world.[58] The mental activity of making knowledge claims, then, is a focal point of this potential incompatibility system, acting as a departure point for our analysis. Secondly, we also notice that, when we analyze how beliefs are tested within the problem solving modes of modern education

55. Hoodbhoy, *Islam and Science*, 120.
56. Hoodbhoy, *Islam and Science*, 121.
57. Hoodbhoy, *Islam and Science*, 122; emphasis added.
58. In so-called traditional education, although there may not be knowledge *for the sake of knowledge* (or science *for the sake of science*), there still is a mental goal to attempt to know the physical world: In traditional education, knowledge is thought to be already provided by way of divine revelation; however, it seems the mental goal to attempt to know the physical world would still be present in the mindset of the individual who participates in traditional education. Of course, the *source* of knowledge about the physical world in traditional education is different from the source of knowledge about the physical world in modern education, but the mental goal—to attempt to know the physical world—is mentally present in both traditional education and modern education.

and how, in contrast, the fatalism of an interventionist deity in traditional education may suppress one's will to test beliefs, our problem becomes redirected toward the level of intentionality—where science and religion are incommensurable. However, as it does seem possible to analyze the "will to power" incompatibility system by way of mentation, we can conclude that science and religion—as they are employed in Hoodbhoy's thesis—are commensurable. In this comparison, then, following Hoodbhoy's case illustration of Islam in relation to a psychological "will to power," science and some versions of religiosity could be rendered *incompatible*.[59]

The Demythologized Compatibility System

In *Buddhism and Science: A Guide for the Perplexed*, Donald Lopez explains how the term *Buddhism* has enjoyed a long kinship with the term *science*. Lopez's work is to uncover what the source(s) of this apparent kinship may be.[60] Late nineteenth-century attempts to legitimate Buddhism included the contextual placing of a demythologized Buddhism vis-à-vis Christianity, albeit a Christianity that remained mythologized.[61] The point being that such a legitimation strategy is possible only when one belief system is demythologized while the other remains mythologized: I call this approach the *demythologized compatibility system*. However, mythologized elements of Buddhism also remain, for some, important aspects of Buddhist tradition.[62] About the general tension surrounding the post-Enlightenment (and Presocratic!) project of demythologization, Lopez astutely notes, "Yet once the process of demythologizing begins, once the process of deciding between the essential and the inessential is under way, it is often difficult to know where to stop."[63] (This point, as it concerns any religion, is revisited in part 3.)

At the same time, those advocating a compatibility thesis between science and Buddhism have presented their project in various (and rather

---

59. Again, as mentioned, my choice of words *could be rendered* is meant to point out that my motivation is not to convince you that, by way of the "will to power" incompatibility system, science and religion are incompatible. Nor is that necessarily my own definite conclusion either. Rather, my motivation in this analysis is to assess compatibility systems presented in science and religion literature and determine how justified proponents of each compatibility system are in their conclusion that science and religion are compatible or, in this case, incompatible.

60. Lopez, *Buddhism and Science*, 3.

61. McMahan, "Buddhism as the 'Religion of Science,'" 121–22.

62. McMahan, "Buddhism as the 'Religion of Science,'" 125.

63. Lopez, *Buddhism and Science*, 72.

startling) forms, such that the contents of Buddhist faith are not contradicted by scientific theories or that the supposed historical Buddha anticipated current discoveries in modern science.[64] In designing such a compatibility system, it would seem the motivation of compatibility system enthusiasts is that scientific and religious beliefs coalesce, if not at the intentional level, then in terms of mental functions thought to be shared by science and by Buddhism—in their shared attempts to know and interpret the one, physical world. However, in a straightforward manner, the demythologized compatibility system does not seem to achieve either of those. In applying the preceding strategy—to keep one religion mythologized (Christianity) and the other demythologized (Buddhism)—in effect the argument being made is that Buddhism (now demythologized) is a "science" while Christianity remains mythopoeic and mythologized. We have, of course, already seen that, in terms of intentionality, science and religion are incommensurable—classifying the demythologized compatibility system as a comparison of science and religion in terms of intentionality is not possible.

However, in a general sense, it is possible to envision a sociocultural model to describe the evolutionary development of modern sociocultural institutions: communities of believers (call them *believers* for lack of a different word) transition gradually from mental states of superstition (e.g., animism, pantheism, or panentheism) toward more organized albeit primitive religions (e.g., totemism), then increasingly (over time) to mental states which employ the epistemology of modern science. During these stages, new mental goals include achieving logical coherence and high degrees of certitude for one's beliefs. Lopez touches on this idea when he points out that perhaps nineteenth-century Buddhist leaders were smart to market Buddhism as being compatible with science—this helped to alleviate the view presented by European missionaries that Buddhism was superstitious and primitive.[65] On the one hand, the transition from superstitious mental states to (eventually) mental states which employ modern science would involve changes in intentionality, likely from an unconscious intentionality to a conscious one. At the same time, however, whether we are dealing with superstitious mental states or mental states which employ modern science, we are still dealing nevertheless with mental functions shared between science and religion—shared attempts to know and interpret the physical world.

Having now moved to our final example of a potential compatibility system, the preceding point might now become a moot one—i.e., disregard or ignore differences in intentionality between science and religion (which

---

64. Lopez, *Buddhism and Science*, 2.
65. Lopez, *Buddhism and Science*, 24.

would render them incommensurable) and then focus instead on a shared mentation between science and religion to "make" science and religion commensurable; thereby "making" science and religion possibly compatible or incompatible. If my approach in this regard (for the third and fourth examples in particular) seems too salutary, then I accept that accusation. However, what I have been trying to do in this chapter, and what I am attempting to do with this final example, is make every last-ditch effort to consider how *any* proposed compatibility system or incompatibility system between science and religion (for the examples illustrated) might really be (if at all) persuasive. What is clear, I hope, is that with compatibility system design we are dealing with an elusive project—its results are not going to be always clear, nor will there (likely) be very much intersubjective agreement about whether science and religion really are compatible, or incompatible, or whether the project of comparing and contrasting science and religion was really viable from the start. Ironically, these important realizations might be the most useful take-home ideas from this chapter!

So, in summary, the demythologized compatibility system could provide a comparison of science and religion by way of mentation, but *prima facie* it rules in favour of Buddhism anyway. (From the start, this compatibility system was designed to accomplish that goal.) Likewise, we could reverse the situation—demythologize Christianity and keep Buddhism mythologized; the same type of compatibility system *prima facie* would then rule in favour of Christianity. At any rate, following Lopez's case illustration of Buddhism in relation to Christianity, science and some versions of religiosity could be rendered *compatible*. Yes, an elusive analysis indeed.

∼

Progressing forward in this book to better and brighter things, the demythologized compatibility system also brings to mind some interesting and often controversial questions about compatibility system design overall: Reflecting on *provisional* as opposed to *essential* parameters, as they relate to religious mythologies and the building of a demythologized compatibility system, when we demythologize a religion—removing metaphysical claims—do we still possess the "religion"? Moreover, do we still need to design a compatibility system? So, if one demythologizes Buddhist cosmology, or, say, the New Testament gospels, does one still require a compatibility system? This leaves us with yet again another pointed question: *how did the need for compatibility system design arise in the first place*? At this stage, these are open-ended, unanswered questions—they will be useful between now and the end of the book.

6

Philosophical Models in Scientific Life

AT THE CORE OF modern scientific theorizing is a willingness to adopt a *disengaged* perspective. As Charles Taylor succinctly puts it, "We are not trying to understand things merely as they impinge on us, or are relevant to the purposes we are pursuing, but rather grasp them as they are, outside the immediate perspective of our goals and desires and activities."[1] In this chapter, we assess those epistemic factors involved in developing a disengaged theory of rationality, in particular the implications of *consistently* testing the propositional beliefs of knowledge claims, and, if it were possible, testing the propositional beliefs of belief claims.[2] The concept *disengaged*—or *neutral, dispassionate, unbiased*, etc.—plays a complicated role in constructing a religious epistemology vis-à-vis modern science. The realist intents of both scientific and religious practitioners—whether they are traditional realists or critical realists—highlight what are thought to be the "disengaged," "neutral" aims[3] of science and religion in grasping physical reality *as* reality is.

1. Taylor, "Rationality," 89.

2. As outlined in chapter 1, this book includes the argument that, if a philosopher or theologian is successful in designing a compatibility system between science and religion, the compatibility system will be based on a theory of rationality which consistently tests the propositional beliefs of knowledge claims, and, if possible, the propositional beliefs of belief claims. Hence the requirement here to discuss the implications of consistently testing the propositional beliefs of knowledge claims, and, if it were possible, testing the propositional beliefs of belief claims, within a *disengaged* theory of rationality.

3. In this sentence, the terms *disengaged* and *neutral* in the phrase "'disengaged,' 'neutral' aims of science and religion" are placed in scare quotes to point out that, in this usage, the concepts *disengaged* and *neutral* may be seen to be tendentious: My point

In addition, I suggest the utilitarian goals of instrumentalism (i.e., *instrumentalism* applied to our *conceptions of objects of belief*[4]) require a "disengaged" perspective. Although instrumentalist science and religion may seem epistemically lackadaisical (e.g., in terms of Bartley's critique of instrumentalism,[5] instrumentalists seem to casually discard beliefs after beliefs no longer "fit" some *a priori* interests), instrumentalism does require that objects of belief are *in some sense* grasped as they are: instrumentally, objects of belief are not grasped substantively, but can be grasped statistically, or phenomenologically,[6] providing *models* for states of

---

here is that, for many humans, both scientific and religious exercises possess realist intents—both science and religion are thought to provide information about physical reality (the physical world) independent from personal human preference about how physical reality ought to be. In the case of modern science, realist intents of science suggest the purpose of many scientific exercises is to elucidate tested information indicating the nature, structure, constitution, etc., of physical reality—information obtained through experiments, equations, and/or statistical models. In the case of religious life, realist intents of religion suggest the purpose of many religious exercises is to receive supernatural information indicating a physical-world-transcending reality—information obtained through faith, revelation, and/or personal experience. In both cases, realist intents point out that whatever information is thought to be obtained from either science or religion, that information is thought to describe states of affairs existing independent from personal human preference, not influenced by personal human attitudes or behaviours. While realist intents of science and religion describe *ideal* situations for either the scientific or religious practitioner—where methodological aims are in fact *disengaged* and *neutral*—one cannot help but bring to science one's own background beliefs about the perceptual event itself: as Haack (2007, 126) puts it, "background beliefs that determine what experiential evidence they [scientists] take to be relevant to the claim in question." Similarly, one cannot help but bring to religious life one's own faith-imbued perceptions of physical reality: so, arguments held by faith convince no one unless one already believes arguments based on faith. With these points in mind, realist intents of science and religion are not disengaged or neutral *per se*: epistemic factors such as background beliefs in scientific practice or faith-imbued perceptions in religious life cause scientific and religious practitioners to possess beliefs, goals, and desires, which are established *prior* to one's participation in a particular scientific or religious exercise. So, while maintaining complete epistemic neutrality may be difficult, science and religion at least attempt to operate as realist modes of thought: making claims and testing beliefs about states of affairs in the physical world require that, so far as is possible, one functions in a *disengaged, neutral* fashion; at the very least, as a realist, one acknowledges this kind of methodological neutrality to be one's *ideal* method.

4. It is important to note that, as a type of pragmatism, instrumentalism applied to our conceptions of objects of belief is very different from other versions of pragmatism, such as Haack's pragmatism: in Haack's pragmatism, realist intents are maintained (Haack's philosophy of science is not instrumentalist); rather, Haack's pragmatism is situated within the tradition of Charles Sanders Peirce's pragmatism.

5. Bartley, *The Retreat to Commitment*, 91.

6. In the instrumentalist text *How the Laws of Physics Lie*, Cartwright (2002, 1) identifies the philosophical distinction between *phenomenological* and *substantive/*

affairs in the physical world. So, while instrumentalism does not employ substantive-based, realist intents, instrumentalist science and religion at least acknowledge there is an independent, physical world to study—that the goal of instrumentalism is to model (just not substantively describe) this physical world.[7] At any rate, a religious epistemology contextualized in a modern research university depends on the framework *and nuances* of a modestly naturalistic epistemology,[8] such as the epistemic framework which undergirds Susan Haack's innocent realism. Firstly, though, some background on William Bartley's project, pancritical rationalism, to provide some orientation to Bartley's work and the epistemic generalities underly-

---

theoretical statements as the distinction between the *observable* and the *unobservable*, respectively. About scientific theories conceived as instrumentalist models of physical reality, Cartwright goes on, "The fundamental laws of the theory are true of the objects in the model [constructed model to fit observed phenomenon into a theory], and they are used to derive a specific account of how these objects behave. But the objects of the model have only *'the form or appearance of things' and, in a very strong sense, not their 'substance or proper qualities'*" (Cartwright 2002, 17; emphasis added). Like *simulacra*, objects of belief modeled instrumentally, perhaps allow us to grasp the observable forms of objects, but not their unobservable substances—phenomenological descriptions of objects as objects exist (or might exist) in physical reality, but not substantive/theoretical descriptions of objects (Cartwright 2002, 4).

7. Note, however, that neither Popper nor Bartley would agree with a defence of statistical models for objects of belief in terms of the instrumentalism presented here: Bartley (1984, 91) reminds us that, for Popper, all scientific theories (or laws) have *zero* probability of providing accurate descriptions of states of affairs in the physical world. This principle relates to Popper's falsifiability criterion whereby scientific theories cannot be demonstrated to be true (although they can reach high degrees of certitude); theories can be demonstrated to be false only. So, vis-à-vis Popper, physical *objects* in scientific theories—types of *objects* of belief—cannot be modeled as statistical representations of physical reality, because all scientific theories have *zero* probability of providing accurate descriptions of the physical world. However, while I accept this to be an important Popperian principle, it does not (necessarily) prevent us from acknowledging potential benefits of instrumentalism applied in the practical aspects of scientific lives and faith-imbued religious lives. Within instrumentalist versions of science and religion, although (*à la* Popper) we cannot model objects of belief statistically, we can model objects of belief *phenomenologically*—an option which fits the epistemic framework I propose and utilize in this book.

8. Scientific exercises and the cognitive values of a scientific epistemology provide an intellectual benchmark for testing many beliefs in modern research universities. A religious epistemology contextualized in a modern research university, then, depends on the framework *and nuances* of a modestly naturalistic epistemology. A modestly naturalistic epistemology—as a model for a religious epistemology—presumes the two substantive assumptions which undergird this book: namely, (i) that phenomenal reality provides a standard of observed experiences used for testing beliefs about states of affairs in the physical world, and (ii) that religious people's testimonies inform us that religious people possess beliefs about superhuman agents and/or beliefs about transempirical worlds.

ing any theory of rationality. This analysis is followed by a discussion about Haack's foundherentism and Haack's assessments of epistemic frameworks linking basic and derived beliefs.

Epistemological assumptions are built into the reasoning processes of scientific practice. At the same time, tested beliefs from scientific theories influence epistemology's role in science. This two-way philosophical dialogue, between the enterprises of epistemology and science, helps to point out the role of *experience* in testing beliefs.[9] The ability of *natural human experience* to serve as a platform through which beliefs are tested is an epistemological question—as are questions about the quality and reliability of the scientific method. On the other hand, scientific information obtained from disciplines such as psychology or cognitive science helps to point out the *limitations* of the human intellect. In this fashion, then, information from science might influence epistemology's role in science; pointing out, for example, that human experience is not brute nature, but nature modified by our background beliefs, the apparatus and instruments we use to "collect" and test experience (empirical data), and one's particular educational background that persuades one to interpret experience in any one particular way. While the development of background beliefs, apparatus, and education, are remarkable human achievements—indeed, they are what make scientific practice possible—these achievements are designed, constructed, and utilized by humans, thus, they are fallible and imperfect. As epistemology is also a human invention, any theory of rationality (an aspect of epistemology) is also fallible and imperfect. However, like the other human achievements mentioned in this paragraph, if an appropriate theory of rationality could be developed—in this book, a theory of rationality which seeks to incorporate the aims of both knowledge claims and belief claims—the theory of rationality[10] would be a very remarkable achievement indeed.

In *The Retreat to Commitment* (introduced previously), William Bartley would like to develop a theory of rationality allowing us to move beyond

---

9. Haack, *Evidence and Inquiry*, 144.

10. Indeed, about the fallible and imperfect nature of epistemology (and other academic inventions), note that a *"theory* of rationality" is not a *"tested, scientific theory* of rationality," but a *"philosophical theory* of rationality"—an aspect of "epistemology"—which functions in a two-way dialogue between the enterprises of *science-influenced epistemology* and *epistemology-influenced science*. As mentioned, epistemological assumptions are built into the reasoning processes of scientific practice while tested beliefs from scientific theories also *influence* epistemology's role in science. Contextualizing epistemology in this fashion places me within the framework of Haack's *modestly naturalistic epistemology*—an epistemic position which lies between traditionalist apriorism and those more radical versions of naturalism which repudiate epistemology altogether (Haack 2009, 169).

the theoretical limitations of criticism. Bartley argues that even traditional criticism is limited—e.g., criticism expressed in the common maxim *you must be critical* (heard throughout the entire history of Western philosophy) is limited. Traditional modes of rationality, which equate epistemic *justification* and *criticism*, are epistemically limited. In a theory of rationality, a retreat to an ultimate commitment is required in the attempt to avoid an infinite regress. For religious devotees and/or scientific practitioners, the *tu quoque* ("you too!") is invoked to protect one's choice of commitment from competing choices. Bartley's project, then, is an attempt to develop a theory of rationality epistemically immune from the *tu quoque*. Bartley would like to develop a method whereby it becomes irrational to invoke the *tu quoque*, making one's "retreat to commitment" a non-arbitrary decision. Bartley's motivation for attempting such a project is that Bartley is frustrated by what he calls the religious devotee's "rational" excuse for irrational commitment:[11] i.e., in terms of the post-Kuhnian compatibility system, religious devotees apply the *tu quoque*; however, can we defeat the *tu quoque*, Bartley asks, allowing ourselves to be *actually* rational—to experience a non-arbitrariness in our choice of commitment? Granted, proponents of the post-Kuhnian compatibility system might argue that, in applying the *tu quoque*, scientific practitioners also employ a "rational" excuse for irrational commitment. Although Bartley initiates his project by pointing out his frustration with what is thought to be the religious devotee's "rational" excuse for irrational commitment, a similar frustration might be experienced regarding what is thought to be the scientific practitioner's "rational" excuse for irrational commitment. In summary, then, for either religious devotees *or* scientific practitioners, Bartley's project asks two important questions:

1. Can we design a theory of rationality which is non-arbitrary in its choice of commitment?

2. As a corollary to one's choice of commitment, can we can design a theory of rationality which is non-arbitrary in its adherence to a particular set of epistemic principles, standards, and assumptions?

In traditional theories of rationality, Bartley argues an implicit assumption was always made that epistemic *justification* is equated with *criticism*—that to have one we must have the other. Prior to Bartley's work with Popper (twentieth century), it seems the notion that justification be separated from criticism had not been given very much attention in contemporary analytic philosophy. When unpacking Bartley's thesis of *pancritical rationalism*—also called *comprehensively critical rationalism*—it is important to clarify that *justification* is not *criticism*, but rather these concepts

11. Bartley, *The Retreat to Commitment*, 72.

are distinct. Bartley explains, "We may urge the philosophical *criticism* of standards as the main task of the philosopher. *Nothing gets justified; everything gets criticized.*"[12] Moreover, Bartley views this shift from justification to criticism as "a genuine innovation in philosophy whose importance cannot be overemphasized."[13] That being said, Bartley devotes considerable space in his argument toward pointing out how this might be so; Bartley senses that for other philosophers a genuine shift *away from justification and toward criticism* might not be obvious. The following paragraphs serve to unpack the nuances of Bartley's thesis, emphasizing how criticism and justification can be decoupled—how beliefs can be criticized, but, in Bartley's view, need not be justified. In chapters 9 and 10, this aspect of Bartley's thought will serve as Bartley's contribution to my proposal of a religious epistemology, contextualized in a modestly naturalistic epistemology in a modern university.

Criticism, particularly in the wider spectra of the philosophies of science and religion, requires further analysis: In twentieth-century philosophy of science, the concept of *criticism* is essentially Popperian. As considered in detail already, beliefs about states of affairs in the physical world are subject to ruthless, critical tests. As the hallmark of Popper's thought, critical tests are continued even after beliefs have reached high degrees of certitude—even after tested beliefs (objects of cognitive states of knowledge claims) have not failed many previous tests.[14] However, in philosophy of religion, meanings and uses of the concept of *criticism* seem less clear—religious beliefs are seemingly not open to criticism; they are non-tested beliefs (objects of cognitive states of belief claims). In this regard, Bartley points out that, whatever cognitive values do comprise the backbone of a belief (religious) community's epistemology, those values are not really essential to the continued existence of the community. Should, say, a religious community's religious epistemology—e.g., a Christian epistemology—break down, the religious community's identity would probably not suffer too much.[15] A *traditionally faith-based, religious epistemology*, then, seems not really essential to maintaining the religious community's collective identity. On the contrary, such a scenario for a scientific community would likely be disastrous: epistemic standards, cognitive values peculiar to a scientific

---

12. Bartley, *The Retreat to Commitment*, 112.

13. Bartley, *The Retreat to Commitment*, 113.

14. As *H. sapiens sapiens*, we are fallible and imperfect creatures: hence, in accepting the *limitations* of our own cognitive capacities, we acknowledge the Popperian imperative that we continue to test our beliefs even after our beliefs have reached high degrees of certitude—even after our beliefs have not failed many previous tests.

15. Bartley, *The Retreat to Commitment*, 50.

epistemology,[16] and critical testing, are all essential to the day-to-day operation of any scientific project.

Bartley's *non*-justificationary pancritical rationalism is different from typical critical rationalism where notions of both *criticism* and *justification* are included. Rather, pancritical rationalism eschews the supposed requirement that we commit ourselves to an unjustifiable first principle of foundationalism—where notions of *justification* and *criticism* were both required. Instead, we subject *all* of our knowledge claims and belief claims to ruthless, critical tests. Rather than speaking of the *epistemic justification of scientific beliefs*, we shift our attention toward the *epistemic criticism of scientific beliefs* and/or the epistemic criticism of religious beliefs.[17] (Note that, in chapter 2, my analysis was centred already on the suggestion that Popper's ruthless, *critical* tests be applied to scientific beliefs—so, previously, although I applied the common notion of *justification* in my discussion, I was in fact already thinking along the lines of unlimited *criticism* vis-à-vis Bartley.) Pancritical rationalism is also different from what Bartley terms panrationalism[18]—a relativistic framework where there are thought to be many "true" ways to know and interpret the physical world. Nevertheless, when the design of a theory of rationality—seeking to incorporate the aims of both knowledge claims and belief claims—is attempted, suggestions that panrationalism be applied inevitably begin to appear. Indeed, panrationalism is often the motivation for employing the *tu quoque* in either scientific or religious lives. Concerning a relativistic framework, where the *tu quoque* has free rein, Bartley puts well the implications of panrationalism when he

---

16. For example, cognitive values peculiar to a scientific epistemology include recognitions such as (i) we are fallible and imperfect creatures; (ii) that we do possess the perceptual awareness and cognitive capacities necessary for us to collect and test natural experience from brute nature; (iii) that, since we are fallible and imperfect, our interpretations of brute nature are overlaid by our own assumptions and theories. Finally, (iv) most important as a cognitive value peculiar to a scientific epistemology, the notion that, to pursue and accomplish intersubjectively available learning, "we need opportunities to work out inconsistencies and mistakes as we uncover them. This leads us, ultimately, to deeper and more mature understandings of the [physical] world" (Woodward 2014, 57).

17. The notion that epistemic criticism be applied to religious beliefs is perhaps redundant, given especially that, as mentioned already, non-tested, religious beliefs are generated from arguments based on faith: non-tested, religious beliefs *held by faith* convince no one unless one already believes arguments based on faith. Epistemic criticism applied to arguments based on faith is not really a critical endeavour—the faith position undergirding faith-based arguments seems to take epistemic precedence, trumping any epistemic criticism.

18. Bartley, *The Retreat to Commitment*, 85.

describes the "glass house" of the panrationalist, also referred to as the subjective relativist:

> There is a particularly modern irony in the idea of a glass house inhabited by a subjective relativist. Only one kind of glass is suitable for such a building: that ingenious modern one-way window-mirror glass which one sometimes finds fitted in zoo cages, especially in monkey houses. The world can look in at the subjectivist and watch his antics; but when the subjectivist looks outward, he sees only his own face in the mirrors that imprison him . . . Since his world is his mirror image, he is free to create his world. Moreover, if everyone *has* to be a subjectivist, there is a sort of consolation: nobody can look in from the outside. Everyone is alone, inside his own mirror cage, staring at his own face. No wonder the existentialists are bored.[19]

As alluded to previously in chapter 1, in accordance with Bartley's pancritical rationalism, neither an unjustifiable first principle of foundationalism *nor an epistemological tribe in a relativistic framework* provide an intellectual escape hatch for me. Or at least that is my intention—my ideal epistemic situation, including the notion that pancritical rationalism be extended to criticize the philosophy of criticism itself.[20]

That the philosophy of criticism be open to criticism leads me to argue that, in pancritical rationalism, Bartley rightly applies the Popperian principle of *learning from experience* to distinguish a healthy, evolving "knowledge and belief system" from a stagnant ideology. Non-evolving ideologies dismiss new knowledge claims generated from testing new beliefs. To that end, any "knowledge and belief system"—be it a religion, philosophy, or scientific paradigm, etc.—is born with a set of presuppositions and a method to adjudicate beliefs, *but* each "knowledge and belief system" evolves differently: it survives, dies, *or* becomes an ideology. The epistemic criterion, then, for determining whether a "knowledge and belief system" will allow itself to survive, die, or become an ideology, is Bartley's thesis, described most succinctly as *criticizability*. Furthermore, as Wiebe observes, modern

---

19. Bartley, *The Retreat to Commitment*, 82.

20. Pancritical rationalism is logically more basic than other theories of rationality such as panrationalism and critical rationalism; however, a potential argument against pancritical rationalism might be that pancritical rationalism still employs an *assumption* toward a commitment—the *assumption* that we be critical even of the philosophy of criticism itself. (The *tu quoque* reappears!) The radical, critical openness of pancritical rationalism, however, is tied to the Popperian notion of *learning from experience*: I think few would deny that *learning from experience* is an important Western cultural value. (Note also that *experience* in this sense, as in all other areas of this book, is *phenomenal, natural* human experience.)

science has been the only institution to consciously allow *learning from experience* to be its primary goal—an attitude of mind where one is "*not* under an obligation to protect the belief(s) in question."[21] As outlined, religious exercises utilize their own causality, drawing on the actions of CPS-agents. This faith-imbued nature of religious exercises, where non-tested beliefs are placed "epistemically" superior to tested beliefs, means scientific theories (although subject to criticism) are routinely dismissed as counter-productive to mainstream religious life. Be that as it may, such epistemic tension points out why religious exercises appear to be non-rational, hence the problem (generally) of constructing a religious epistemology—the problem of designing a religious epistemology which adheres to (i) faith-based goals in sociocultural institutions and (ii) the apparent aim of theology to provide a rational account of non-tested, religious beliefs.

As mentioned earlier in this chapter, Bartley's project asks two questions:

1. Can we design a theory of rationality which is non-arbitrary in its choice of commitment?
2. As a corollary to one's choice of commitment, can we can design a theory of rationality which is non-arbitrary in its adherence to a particular set of epistemic principles, standards, and assumptions?

With Bartley's pancritical rationalism now unpacked, the following questions—extensions of the preceding two questions—arise:

- Can we apply the rational integrity of a scientific epistemology to religious exercises? In this fashion, can we develop a suitable *model* to construct a religious epistemology?
- In accordance with Bartley's thesis, is the rational integrity of a scientific epistemology—where *learning from experience* is the motivating factor—immune from the *tu quoque*?

About the question of applying the rational integrity of a scientific epistemology to religious exercises (to attempt immunity from the *tu quoque*), it does seem that Bartley does not consider the possibility that a fiduciary component is at play in testing beliefs—the possibility that all theories of rationality presuppose some commitment.[22] That being said, the purpose of Bartley's project is to attempt to avoid the need for a commitment—his emphasis is rather toward *learning from experience*. Moreover, employing

---

21. Wiebe, *The Irony of Theology*, 38.
22. Wiebe, "Comprehensively Critical Rationalism and Commitment," 9, 14.

the *tu quoque* is the very attitude which counteracts a critical mind. As Bartley puts it, "*One gains the right to be irrational at the expense of losing the right to criticize.* One gains immunity from criticism for one's own commitment by making any criticism of commitments impossible."[23] Thus, even if Bartley's pancritical rationalism is construed as just another type of commitment, the epistemic principles and standards inherent to the commitment to pancritical rationalism are such that, in pancritical rationalism, nothing *but* new learning occurs—beliefs are proposed, tested, and then accepted or discarded. Moreover, in the commitment to pancritical rationalism, *criticisms* of other commitments—indeed, *any* other commitments, including the commitment to pancritical rationalism—remain acceptable. For example, about the scientific study of religion, questioning the assumptions (i) that *religion* is a socially isolated phenomenon and (ii) that *religion* as *sui generis* brackets not only the metaphysical reality of religion but also the *scholar* from critical scrutiny,[24] Russell McCutcheon suggests, "Not only the phenomenon one studies (e.g., religion, religious experiences, myths, rituals) but the phenomenon of the study itself (e.g., the science of religion, *Religionswissenschaft*, even scholars of religion as humans authorized to make certain judgements) could, to whatever degree, be said to be the result of one's scale, point of view, theory, or method."[25] While my purpose here is not to critique the method of the scientific study of religion (as McCutcheon implies might be done), it would also be academically naive of me to fail to accept that even the assumptions I employ in this book are open to criticism by way of pancritical rationalism.[26] As a pancritical rationalist, I remain aware of the requirement that I function as a self-critical rationalist. Self-critical awareness cannot sway me from maintaining my own assumptions (nor should it sway other scholars from maintaining their assumptions), but self-critical awareness at least keeps me open to new alternatives—in essence, open to *learning from experience*. Furthermore, Bartley's criticizability thesis suggests that, in being critical of beliefs, critical of criticism itself, *and* in being self-critical, a kind of *consistency* permeates one's learning and testing of beliefs—necessary ingredients to elucidate "knowledge

---

23. Bartley, *The Retreat to Commitment*, 82; emphasis added.
24. McCutcheon, *Manufacturing Religion*, 26.
25. McCutcheon, *Manufacturing Religion*, 8.
26. Recall that the two assumptions I make in this book are as follows: (i) Phenomenal reality provides a standard of observed experiences used for testing beliefs about states of affairs in the physical world. (ii) Religious people's testimonies inform us that religious people possess beliefs about superhuman agents and/or beliefs about trans-empirical worlds.

and belief systems" which critically *survive* (or perhaps simply die) from ones that become stagnant ideologies.

Returning to our central task to articulate the precise role of *experience* in testing beliefs[27] (recall that, for Popper, philosophy of science amounts to a "theory of experience"[28]), Susan Haack, in an unexpected turn, takes Popper to task over his very notion of *experience*: Haack renders Popper a closet skeptic—for Haack, Popper seems not interested in the concept of justified, true belief; Popper seems to deny we have knowledge of the physical world.[29] While similar to Popper, for Haack, a scientific theory is true *just in case*[30] states of affairs in the physical world really are *as* the theory describes those states of affairs to be (so, *true* is not so much substantively, *absolutely true*, but *true* implies an accurate, tested description of states of affairs), Haack is frustrated by Popper's notion that natural human experience cannot support the acceptance of basic statements (observations). Somewhat reluctantly, Haack accepts that, for Popper, "science is, *though only in a negative sense*, rational."[31] In terms of falsification (the "negative sense" in the preceding quotation), Haack is even more alarmed when she finds that Popperian science is not even, negatively, under the control of experience. For Popper, phenomenal experience cannot support the acceptance *or rejection* of basic statements.[32] Rather, for Popper, the acceptance or rejection of basic statements (observations) is a matter of social convention among scientific practitioners.

As explained, Haack's critique of Popper amounts to Popper's claim that basic statements—observations, particular physical events, etc.—cannot be justified by experience; *experience can motivate* a decision to accept or reject a basic statement, but experience itself cannot justify the acceptance or rejection of a basic statement.[33] (Note that we have returned to applying the concept of *justification* in our discussion, which is necessary as Haack applies this concept. Given, however, our previous analysis of critical rationalism and Bartley's pancritical rationalism, the term *justification* could be replaced with the term *criticism*. Finally, justification applied foundationally is covered in my analysis of Haack's basic and derived beliefs at the end of

---

27. As I hope is already clear, articulating the precise role of *experience* in testing beliefs is tied directly to our future, upcoming task of designing a religious epistemology in a modestly naturalistic epistemology.

28. Popper, *The Logic of Scientific Discovery*, 35.

29. Haack, *Evidence and Inquiry*, 143.

30. Haack, *Defending Science—Within Reason*, 25.

31. Haack, *Evidence and Inquiry*, 144; emphasis added.

32. Haack, *Evidence and Inquiry*, 146.

33. Haack, *Evidence and Inquiry*, 145.

this chapter.) Moreover, Haack also takes Popper to task over what she sees to be his denigration of the psychological role in the epistemic justification (criticism) of scientific beliefs. Henceforth, Haack argues persuasively for an *experientialist epistemology*—an antidote to Popper's anti-psychologistic philosophy of science,[34] which exists because Popper separates what he sees to be (i) subjective, psychological human experience and (ii) the objective, logical justification of human beliefs.

Central to any experientialist epistemology are intersubjectively observed experiences of phenomenal reality, used for testing beliefs.[35] To begin with, observations are not propositions, but are physical events.[36] While statements of human beliefs can be expressed propositionally in the forms of either knowledge claims or belief claims, observations themselves are simply physical events. About observations—which undergird an experientialist epistemology—Haack explains, "What is observable depends not only on our perceptual capacities, but also on our ingenuity in devising instruments to extend and improve our powers of detection; the [ontological] boundary of the observable, in other words, like the boundary of the 'purely theoretical,' constantly shifts with advances in instruments of observation."[37] Haack's unpacking of the epistemic factors which contribute to our ability to "observe" the physical world—and, I would add, the *phenomenal*, physical world—highlight some of her motivations in presenting a modestly naturalistic epistemology.[38] Haack clarifies that, in the context of a modest naturalism, *naturalism* contrasts with *apriorism*:[39] as

---

34. Haack, *Evidence and Inquiry*, 148.

35. Indeed, this point represents the first of the two substantive assumptions which I make in this book, namely, that *phenomenal reality provides a standard of observed experiences used for testing beliefs about states of affairs in the physical world.*

36. Haack, *Defending Science—Within Reason*, 128.

37. Haack, *Defending Science—Within Reason*, 129.

38. As outlined, scientific information obtained from disciplines such as psychology or cognitive science helps to point out the *limitations* of the human intellect. Substantive, tested information from science influences epistemology's role in science; pointing out, for example, that human experience is not brute nature, but nature *modified by* our background beliefs, the apparatus and instruments we use to "collect" and test experience (empirical data), fluctuating advances in instrumentation, and one's educational background that persuades one to interpret experience in a particular way. These variables are designed, constructed, and utilized by humans, thus, they are fallible and imperfect. As epistemology is also a human invention, any theory of rationality (an aspect of epistemology) is also fallible and imperfect. At the same time, the ability of natural human experience to serve as a platform through which beliefs are tested is an epistemological question—as are questions about the quality and reliability of the scientific method. Therefore, epistemology itself must not be annexed by science.

39. Haack, *Defending Science—Within Reason*, 307.

considered already, science contributes to epistemology, but epistemology is not subordinate to science either. The phrase *modestly naturalistic*, then, refers to an epistemic position lying somewhere between what Haack suggests is called *traditionalist apriorism* and those more *radical versions of naturalism* which repudiate epistemology altogether.[40] (As examples, radical, "revolutionary" naturalism denies the value of epistemological questions altogether;[41] other versions of scientistic naturalism preserve the notion of an "epistemology," but turn epistemological questions over to science to attempt to resolve completely.[42]) In summary, Haack's philosophical stance of a modestly naturalistic epistemology suggests a modest departure from traditionalist apriorism while also stopping short of replacing epistemology with science.[43]

Beginning in chapter 9—"Designing a New Religious Epistemology for a Scientific Study of Religion"—I propose my own particular experientialist epistemology, a religious epistemology, contextualized in an epistemic stance like Haack's modestly naturalistic epistemology. With this future task in mind, to complete the current chapter, Haack's particular epistemology, foundherentism, is useful in highlighting (a) the role of experience when beliefs are justified foundationally as well as (b) mutual support among beliefs when beliefs are justified in a coherentist sense.[44] In sketching varieties of empirical foundationalism, which elucidate varieties of basic beliefs, Haack distinguishes between *experientialist, extrinsic*, and *intrinsic* versions:[45] Notions of *experientialist* foundationalism—most relevant to the religious epistemology to be presented later—aver that basic beliefs are justified by the subject's own experience, sensory or introspective.[46] In another fashion, in *extrinsic* foundationalism, basic beliefs are justified by a "causal or law-like connection between the subject's having the belief and the state of affairs that makes it true [or makes it testable]."[47] Lastly, *intrinsic* foundationalism contends that basic beliefs are self-justified by their own substantive content.[48] In any case, in the leap from *belief content* (e.g., physical events) to a *propositional claim*, we are concerned primarily with

---

40. Haack, *Evidence and Inquiry*, 169.
41. Haack, *Evidence and Inquiry*, 169.
42. Haack, *Evidence and Inquiry*, 169.
43. Haack, *Evidence and Inquiry*, 169.
44. Haack, *Evidence and Inquiry*, 117.
45. Haack, *Evidence and Inquiry*, 52–53.
46. Haack, *Evidence and Inquiry*, 52.
47. Haack, *Evidence and Inquiry*, 53.
48. Haack, *Evidence and Inquiry*, 53.

the epistemic relationship between the substantive content of the belief and *how* one's propositional claim depends on that content. Moreover, after we express our basic beliefs in a propositional form, derived beliefs can be built from basic beliefs. Analysis of this relationship, between the experiential content of beliefs and how propositional claims depend on content, moves the argument forward in chapter 7 to the use of epistemology in religious life—to the *possibility* of a religious epistemology in contemporary religious life.

7

Philosophical Models in Religious Life

As we surmise from the testimonies of religious devotees, the human mind continues to defer to the actions of CPS-agents. Mythopoeic and CPS-agentic modes of thought continue to permeate the religious epistemic standards of modern religious institutions. Mikael Stenmark and J. Wentzel van Huyssteen have both considered theories of "religious rationality" with persistence. My analysis cannot ignore Stenmark's and van Huyssteen's treatments of the topic. Central to this chapter, then, are assessments of Stenmark's and van Huyssteen's projects vis-à-vis their attempts to epistemically contextualize religious modes of thought in relation to modern scientific thought. In a nutshell, both writers may be thought to represent the postmodernist challenge to modern science: Stenmark articulates a postmodernist rationality, which, similar to the *tu quoque*, permits religious modes of thought to possess their own theories of rationality independent from the rationality of science. Van Huyssteen takes postmodernism as a departure point, then shifting his focus toward a distinctive postfoundationalist rationality, which includes his critique of Haack's foundherentism. In this chapter I also assess the cogency of van Huyssteen's critique of Haack, pointing out where I believe van Huyssteen unfairly points the finger at what he calls Haack's "narrowly individualist and highly idealized,"[1] rational agent.

As mentioned, while both Stenmark's and van Huyssteen's theories of rationality are connected generally with the postmodernist challenge to science, their projects at the same time, then, represent the postmodernist

---

1. Van Huyssteen, *The Shaping of Rationality*, 227.

challenge to the scientific study of religion. Wiebe characterizes the postmodernist challenge to the scientific study of religion as one where the aims of sociology are disputed.[2] Without "an epistemologically grounded account of society,"[3] as he puts it, a science of society and consequently a scientific study of religion remain impossible. Interestingly, Stenmark's and van Huyssteen's projects challenge both the epistemology of modern science as a benchmark for testing beliefs and the notion of a science of society—which includes the scientific study of religion. Stenmark's and van Huyssteen's challenges to these proposals cast their projects—like all science and religion projects—into murky and bumpy waters.

I begin with a summary of Stenmark's project, including a comparison of Stenmark's project vis-à-vis the earlier work of Bartley. In *Rationality in Science, Religion, and Everyday Life* (1995), Stenmark demarcates between: (i) theoretical rationality, (ii) practical rationality, and (iii) axiological rationality.[4] He suggests that theories of rationality are specific to various domains of human knowledges and beliefs. Thus, for Stenmark, there is a model of rationality specific to scientific inquiry; a *different* model of rationality in religious life. Also, in Stenmark's project, different models of rationality ask different questions, including: (i) what should we believe? (theoretical rationality), (ii) what should we do? (practical rationality), and (iii) what should we value? (axiological rationality).[5] Stenmark's motivation for his project—where he presents different models of rationality in different domains of life—is different from Bartley's motivation for his project. Bartley would like to develop a *single* model of rationality, a common epistemic benchmark (immune from the *tu quoque*) for all knowledge claims and belief claims. With this in mind, Stenmark would likely find Bartley's project shortsighted in terms of what Stenmark sees to be the "real-life," faith-imbued component at play in one's perception of the phenomenal, physical world. Stenmark contends, "*Most conceptions of rationality proposed by philosophers have been far too idealized or utopian to apply in an interesting way to actual human agents like you and me. In fact, if taken literally, they imply that human beings are usually irrational in what they do.*"[6] Indeed, when considering the state of current models of rationality in modern research universities, where a scientific epistemology occupies a distinguished role in testing beliefs, Stenmark is unimpressed. Neglecting

2. Wiebe, "Dissolving Rationality," 172.
3. Wiebe, "Dissolving Rationality," 172.
4. Stenmark, *Rationality*, 5.
5. Stenmark, *Rationality*, 5.
6. Stenmark, *Rationality*, 6.

the distinction between *knowledge* and the "*claim to* knowledge," Stenmark embraces the *tu quoque*: as his argument goes, since rationality is about how real people live—their real interests[7]—rationality cannot exclude faith-based aspirations. Stenmark's theory of rationality, then, is faith-imbued in the sense that *a priori* it expects non-tested beliefs to be valued—not just valued aesthetically or socially, but valued *epistemically*.

Moreover, in his *How to Relate Science and Religion* (2004), Stenmark rejects unwavering support for evidentialism. Stenmark argues that judgement-based evidentialism—which he sees as amounting to an attitude of mind whereby beliefs are "*intellectually guilty* until proven innocent"—cannot be applied in *all* aspects of one's practical, religious life.[8] In contrast to judgement-based evidentialism, Stenmark proposes his presumptionism model of rationality:[9] in this model, belief-forming processes (e.g., faith) and belief claims are taken as justified—"*intellectually innocent* until proven guilty"—until such a time as good reasons not to accept one's belief-forming processes and/or belief claims are presented.[10] In addition, Stenmark makes a case that possessing "good reasons" to accept or reject belief-forming processes and/or belief claims involves more practical factors than possessing tested evidence only. Stenmark cites additional factors, such as one being consciously aware of one's evidence, one assessing the quality of one's evidence, and one comparing one's evidence to the evidence of alternative beliefs.[11] Stenmark's concern with judgement-based evidentialism is perhaps understandable—particularly in light of his *a priori* faith-imbued project which epistemically values non-tested beliefs—however, evidentialism is only one aspect of a theory of rationality. To treat the scientific method as a method governed primarily by evidentialism is to limit one's understanding of the scope and purpose of the scientific method. As I have argued in detail, in its wider scope, the scientific method includes inherent capacities to allow intellectual growth, permit new learning, and (if required) modification of existing beliefs. These goals are possible because of evidentialism (which makes testing beliefs possible), but the motivation to apply the scientific method in one's life need not be evidentialism only (or at all), but rather an attitude of mind that is open to the possibility of *new* learning—to the possibility of a more mature understanding of the physical world.

---

7. Stenmark, *Rationality*, 5.
8. Stenmark, *How to Relate Science and Religion*, 89.
9. Stenmark, *How to Relate Science and Religion*, 90.
10. Stenmark, *How to Relate Science and Religion*, 90.
11. Stenmark, *How to Relate Science and Religion*, 91.

Shifting our attention to van Huyssteen's postfoundationalist project, known as *transversal rationality*, van Huyssteen's work appears useful as he attempts to consider the epistemic nuances of scientific and religious exercises. Like Stenmark, van Huyssteen notes that rationality informs "everyday goal-directed actions."[12] Van Huyssteen considers the boundaries between academic disciplines; as he puts it, "within the transversal spaces between disciplines."[13] In his *Alone in the World? Human Uniqueness in Science and Theology* (2006), van Huyssteen outlines how a method centred on such transversal spaces might be useful: "In the kind of multileveled, integrative interdisciplinary conversation that I will argue for, terms like 'transversality' and 'contextuality' will take center stage, and will have the value of identifying shared concerns and points of agreement, and maybe more importantly, of exposing areas of disagreement and putting into perspective specific divisive issues that need to be discussed."[14] Van Huyssteen is to be commended for considering diverse epistemic considerations in his attempt to design a theory of rationality based on overlapping and shared points of contact—"points" whereby we transverse from one academic discipline (e.g., theology) to another (e.g., chemistry). As he suggests, the activity of "problem solving," common to all of religion, theology, and science, is one possibility for actualizing this transversal crossing in practical life.

Though admirable, finding collaborative spaces between academic disciplines is difficult—put simply, various academic disciplines establish their own substantive assumptions and methods. Taking postmodernism as a departure point, van Huyssteen's theory of rationality is characterized *postfoundationalist*. Similar to Haack's foundherentism, in a postfoundationalist model, van Huyssteen argues, neither exclusively overarching metanarratives nor exclusively contextually based modes of rationality are desirable. Thus, between these two contrasting positions, van Huyssteen seeks a middle ground in a postfoundationalist model. Again, like foundherentism, van Huyssteen's postfoundationalist rationality depends on a theory of human experience. Yet this is where van Huyssteen's position becomes ambiguous: For one, van Huyssteen disapproves of theology, as he puts it, formulating "its [theology's] own idea of reason independent of philosophy or the rationality of other reasoning strategies."[15] Yet, in addition, van Huyssteen would like to see theology remain "tied to specific communities of

---

12. Van Huyssteen, *Alone in the World*, 11.
13. Van Huyssteen, *Alone in the World*, 9.
14. Van Huyssteen, *Alone in the World*, 9.
15. Van Huyssteen, *Alone in the World*, 12.

Part 2: Science and Religion Compatibility Systems

faith [albeit] without being trapped by these communities."[16] One of van Huyssteen's solutions to this epistemic conundrum is centred on the tenets of evolutionary epistemology: a consideration of the biological rootedness of rationality, a discipline which van Huyssteen argues has been neglected by contemporary theology.[17]

In keeping with his transversal rationality, van Huyssteen remarks, "evolutionary epistemology will set the interdisciplinary stage, so to speak; create the necessary transversal space for a dialogue between theology and the sciences on human uniqueness."[18] Tenets of evolutionary epistemology include the scientific realization that cognitive capacities are determined by the mechanisms of biological evolution:[19] evolutionary epistemology renders a theory of human evolution a *theory of knowledge*—knowledge is thought to be *produced* through human evolution.[20] Concerning these implications of evolutionary epistemology, van Huyssteen maintains that, from the viewpoint of evolutionary epistemology, the notion that humans possess a subjective, mental state, while physical reality remains independent and objective, becomes untenable. Rather, in evolutionary epistemology, van Huyssteen avers, *knowledge* becomes "an *interactive relationship* between an embodied knower and something that is known."[21] In simple terms, this amounts to a relationship between the knower's evolutionary-based instinct and a "second rationality," the external, symbolic products of the knower's learning and memory.[22]

As the approach seems to go, epistemic tension experienced between universal reasoning strategies and contextually based rationalities is suddenly eluded by the interactive relationship proposed by evolutionary epistemology—the relationship between an embodied knower and an object of knowledge. This *hypothetical realism*—such that our human minds are produced through biological evolution—shifts focus away from the kind of mind humans possess toward the type of physical world that would be necessary to produce a human mind:[23] a *hypothesized* physical world (hypothetical realism) in terms of our *a priori* awareness that we do possess human minds. Finally, in attempting to make a case for the initial plausibility

---

16. Van Huyssteen, *Alone in the World*, 12.
17. Van Huyssteen, *Alone in the World*, 75.
18. Van Huyssteen, *Alone in the World*, 75.
19. Van Huyssteen, *Alone in the World*, 76.
20. Van Huyssteen, *Alone in the World*, 76.
21. Van Huyssteen, *Alone in the World*, 77; emphasis added.
22. Van Huyssteen, *Alone in the World*, 81.
23. Van Huyssteen, *Alone in the World*, 101.

of the assumption that religious belief is *natural*,[24] van Huyssteen makes a faith-imbued "jump," wondering if the hypothetical realism of evolutionary epistemology corresponds with the realist belief claims of religious devotees?[25] While van Huyssteen's application of evolutionary epistemology assists him in temporarily solving the problem of universal and contextually based rationalities,[26] van Huyssteen's faith-imbued "jump," to identify the hypothetical realism of evolutionary epistemology with the realist claims of religion, locates him back in a contextually based rationality. Or, if you like, back in a universal rationality centred on the assumption that hypothetical realism is equated with mythopoeic, religious "realism." In making this faith-imbued move, van Huyssteen renders his transversal rationality a "thin" rationality: epistemic motivations are no longer clear—no reasons are stated for holding particular beliefs. In contrast, notions of a so-called "thick" rationality involve the conscious, intentional stating of motivations for holding the beliefs you hold: a "thick" rationality might encompass multiple domains of human knowledges and beliefs (e.g., empirical and mythopoeic domains), but nevertheless epistemic motivations are *stated* and made clear.

As a corollary to my suggestion that transversal rationality is a "thin" rationality, another concern with transversal rationality is that, in van Huyssteen's project, we are left unsure as to what exactly the term *theology* refers to. Moreover, in attempting to clarify how transversal rationality provides "depth" to a more *useful* understanding of rationality in a postmodernist context, van Huyssteen suggests that *transversal reasoning* replaces *universal reasoning*. In making this theoretical move, in effect, as van Huyssteen puts it, "postmodernism is used against itself."[27] Be that as it may, with transversal rationality now occupying the place of a universal reasoning strategy (ironically transversal rationality now becomes a universal reasoning strategy itself), it seems we no longer have need to consider the question: how does theology even test beliefs about states of affairs in the physical world? Moreover, this question is suddenly placed at the periphery of our "epistemic priority" (my phrase in scare quotes). Transversal rationality is not

---

24. Van Huyssteen, *Alone in the World*, 102.

25. Van Huyssteen, *Alone in the World*, 102.

26. Van Huyssteen's application of evolutionary epistemology assists him in temporarily solving the problem of universal and contextually based rationalities by shifting the problem over to the implications of evolutionary epistemology for human knowledge: the proposal of an interactive relationship between an embodied knower and an object of knowledge recontextualizes (for van Huyssteen's thesis) the problem of universal and contextually based rationalities in biological and evolutionary terms.

27. Van Huyssteen, *Alone in the World*, 23.

so much a typical theory of rationality built around theoretical notions of logic, consistency, and testing beliefs, but rather a rationality directed by the unpredicted, fluctuating experiences of religious (and scientific) lives only. There is no question, then, that van Huyssteen's project, like Stenmark's, is, *a priori*, faith-imbued. Likewise, *theology*, for van Huyssteen, seems a faith-imbued activity, although that is all one can really tell about van Huyssteen's particular conception of *theology* as a mode of thought.[28]

In van Huyssteen's critique of Haack's foundherentism, van Huyssteen locates Haack's foundherentism within the general aims of postfoundationalist theories of rationality.[29] Both van Huyssteen's and Haack's rationalities depend on a theory of experience—*interpreted* experience at that—rendering both projects examples of experientialist epistemologies. Concerning foundherentism, van Huyssteen notes that epistemic fallibilism—a central aspect of all postfoundationalist models—is rightly highlighted in foundherentism.[30] On the other hand, van Huyssteen finds suspicious Haack's tendency toward scientifically construed experience only,[31] leading to van Huyssteen's suggestion that Haack presents us with an idealized rational agent who excludes *religious experience* from the enterprise of epistemology, even implying that Haack's project might be scientistic. About this apparently narrowed scope of the use of personal experience in one's experientialist epistemology,[32] van Huyssteen contends, "Haack's rational agent emerges as narrowly individualist and highly idealized."[33] For example, van Huyssteen questions why existential feelings and attitudes are not permitted in the experiential component of Haack's foundherentism? Indeed, van Huyssteen goes on, Haack permits introspective experience (generally), so why not existentially oriented religious experience?[34]

While it is the case that introspective experience is permitted in Haack's epistemology (basic beliefs are justified by the subject's own experience,

---

28. Note also that van Huyssteen more often cites the academic subject he is addressing as "science *and theology*." This may be personal preference; however, most other authors in the field, including Stenmark, describe the same topic, generally, as "science *and religion*." Given that van Huyssteen contrasts *theology* with *science* in the phrase "science and theology," further supports my observation that theology, for van Huyssteen, is a traditionally faith-imbued, religious activity. Theological thought, for van Huyssteen, seems analogous to mythopoeic religious thought.

29. Van Huyssteen, *The Shaping of Rationality*, 223.
30. Van Huyssteen, *The Shaping of Rationality*, 226.
31. Van Huyssteen, *The Shaping of Rationality*, 226.
32. Van Huyssteen, *The Shaping of Rationality*, 227.
33. Van Huyssteen, *The Shaping of Rationality*, 227.
34. Van Huyssteen, *The Shaping of Rationality*, 227–28.

sensory *or introspective*[35]), van Huyssteen misses the point of what Haack's epistemology, foundherentism, aims to accomplish. (These aims are articulated further in Haack's innocent realism.) For example, when van Huyssteen questions how *interpreted* empirical, introspective, and memory-based experiences, can all be distinguished from other *interpreted* personal experiences—e.g., from *interpreted* religious experiences—van Huyssteen trades on a doubleness in his use of the concept of *interpreted*: Recall that Haack's philosophy of interpretation, so to speak, places her in a two-way dialogue between the enterprises of epistemology and science. Reflecting on the role of *experience* in testing beliefs, questions about the quality and reliability of the scientific method are epistemological questions. Yet scientific information (from psychology or cognitive science) influences epistemology's role in science, pointing out that human experience is not brute nature, but nature modified by our background beliefs, the apparatus and instruments we use to "collect" and test experience (empirical data), and one's particular educational background that persuades one to interpret experience in any one particular way. *Interpretation*, for Haack, is interpretation within the philosophical stance of her modestly naturalistic epistemology—indicating a modest departure from traditionalist apriorism while also stopping short of repudiating epistemology altogether. In contrast, *interpretation*, for van Huyssteen, seems a far more open-ended and ambiguous concept. Indeed, interpretation for van Huyssteen is an intensely personal and existential affair—as would have to be the case if religious experiences were permitted in the source material for an experientialist epistemology. Thus, when van Huyssteen sees existential feelings and attitudes "arbitrarily" removed from Haack's notion of *introspective* experience, and thus critiques this,[36] van Huyssteen in effect critiques a project which is not really Haack's project.

Granted, perhaps the reason van Huyssteen provides the critique of foundherentism that he provides is to point out how Haack's project might be expanded to permit religious experience into the source material for an experientialist epistemology. To permit religious experience, however, would place Haack in an entirely different epistemic stance from what has been referred to as her modestly naturalistic epistemology. Religious experience is entirely *a priori*; even if *introspective* and *interpreted*, introspective and interpreted religious experience is *not* intersubjectively available introspective and interpreted experience.[37] Haack's conception of introspective

---

35. Haack, *Evidence and Inquiry*, 52.

36. Van Huyssteen, *The Shaping of Rationality*, 229.

37. Religious experience is centred on beliefs which are not intersubjectively tested.

experience, while personal, remains open to intersubjective scrutiny. To illustrate this, consider the following remark from Haack about the character of testimonial evidence: "Consider two people both of whom believe that the accused is innocent, one because he saw her himself, a hundred miles away, at the time of the crime, the other because he thinks she has an honest face. The former is more justified than the latter."[38] No doubt the former is more justified than the latter because of the intersubjective realization that to have physically observed the accused (a hundred miles away, at the time of the crime) is a greater warrant for the person's innocence than thinking the accused has an honest face. (Granted, the person claiming to have observed the accused could be lying or be mistaken, but the point is that, intersubjectively, we establish that observed experiences of phenomenal reality possess greater warrant than subjective opinions possess.)

Finally, Haack's modest departure from traditionalist apriorism represents her recognition that humans are fallible and imperfect creatures, thus, some intersubjective scrutiny is required to test beliefs. In a philosophical dialogue with her modest departure from traditionalist apriorism, Haack's stopping short of repudiating epistemology altogether is also her recognition that, since our background beliefs, apparatus and instruments, and educational background are fallible, we require epistemology to assess the quality and reliability of the scientific method. About her experientialist epistemology, which (unlike Popper's epistemology) includes a knowing subject, Haack explains, "With the knowing subject occupying a central place, *epistemology is seen to depend, in part, on presuppositions about human cognitive capacities and limitations.* In other words, the first step has been taken toward a modest kind of meta-epistemological naturalism."[39] In summary, the notion that humans are fallible and imperfect contributes to (i) Haack's modest departure from traditionalist apriorism and (ii) Haack's stopping short of repudiating epistemology altogether.

In conclusion, van Huyssteen's suspicion, that Haack's epistemology tends toward scientifically construed experience only,[40] is misguided. Indeed, Haack is an ontological naturalist, yet Haack's epistemic stance also recognizes our fallible and imperfect nature—rightly acknowledging the importance of intersubjective testing. While advocating for the inclusion of *a priori* religious experience in the source material for an experientialist epistemology, van Huyssteen provides no suggestions as to how such experience would be epistemically measured. Assessing any experience is

---

38. Haack, *Evidence and Inquiry*, 119.
39. Haack, *Evidence and Inquiry*, 164; emphasis added.
40. Van Huyssteen, *The Shaping of Rationality*, 226.

especially crucial given the plethora of shared states of affairs in the physical world described by conflicting claims from both science and religion: e.g., claims about the constitution of physical reality, the origin of human life, the naturalness or unnaturalness of LGBTI identities, free will, or the future course of one's life, etc. In any case, it would be an intellectually inconsistent endeavour to permit non-tested, *a priori* religious experience into the source material for an experientialist epistemology, contextualized in a modern research university. It would also be an intellectually irresponsible endeavour to refrain from intersubjectively testing the observed experiences of phenomenal reality which are permitted.

∽

This concludes part 2. As promised way back in chapter 1, we are now shifting focus—toward a new analysis centred specifically on a scientific study of religion and a religious epistemology. New philosophical—and even theological—horizons await us in part 3.

PART 3

A Scientific Study of Religious Activity and a Religious Epistemology

But the village was very peaceful and quiet, and the light mists were solemnly rising, as if to show me the world, and I had been so innocent and little there, and all beyond was so unknown and great, that in a moment with a strong heave and sob I broke into tears.

—PIP, *GREAT EXPECTATIONS* BY CHARLES DICKENS (1861)

8

A Scientific Study of Religious Activity

COGNITIVE "EXPLANATIONS" FOR RELIGIOUS ACTIVITY

So, WITHOUT WANTING TO sound too melodramatic, for me, Pip's "village" in the preceding epigraph for part 3 (*Great Expectations*) was my adolescent experience with religion . . . the "unknown and great," which Pip alludes to, is modern science. Moreover, the complicated emotions I felt—in navigating my transition from holding religious stories to be descriptions of physical reality to accepting instead that scientific theories are descriptions of physical reality—were not far off from Pip's "strong heave" breaking into tears. What Pip learns, though, in *Great Expectations*,[1] is that, despite the new, unexpected changes one might experience, for better or for worse one is wise to remember one's origins—no matter how starkly those origins might contrast with new beginnings. With this in mind, the balance

---

1. For those unfamiliar with the novel *Great Expectations* (by Charles Dickens), the main character, Pip, receives an inheritance from an unknown benefactor, allowing him to move from his childhood home in the marshes in Kent to a "gentleman's" life in London. In making this transition, Pip, in effect, forgets his family and friends at home—the people who really loved him. Upon discovering that his inheritance was actually the savings of a convict who worked and became rich, Pip finds himself feeling socially and intellectually "dirty"—the "gentleman's" life wasn't all he thought it was. Through a series of tumultuous events, Pip returns to his home in the marshes, learning it is the ties to his place of origin which ultimately ground him in life. At the same time, however, if he hadn't made the move to London, he wouldn't have "grown up" and become his own person—something he also had to do.

of my argument continues to be a delicate one. Entering the third part of this book, I find it meaningful to take a short pause and reflect in the next two paragraphs on the pathways which led me to this juncture as well as my intentions for remaining chapters.

Although I cannot report on the background experiences of others in navigating their own science and religion journeys, I suspect that everyone who reflects on the topic (including possibly those reading this book) will have a story to tell. I hope that, in being honest about parts of my own background, although specific to me, they might encourage others to recognize the great emotional weight attached to science and religion experiences for many people. Firstly, my own run-ins with the social reality of religious life were sometimes conventional and other times quite bizarre. In fairly conventional terms: (i) As a kid and teenager, I wondered *a lot* about God, (ii) as a teenager I made a declaration of faith in the Presbyterian Church, (iii) in my early 20s was confirmed in the Anglican Church, and (iv) in university, studied theology (among other subjects).

Secondly, more "neurotic" experiences with religiosity for me included: (i) My four-year "hiatus" as an undergraduate engineering chemistry student where (looking back) I existed in a kind of intellectual albeit psychologically warped headspace: yes, scientific theories were to be taken "seriously," but then there was that voice in my head—"be *careful*, 'God' is watching"—which permeated my thoughts; (ii) my somewhat humorous experience when, while working as a summer camp counsellor in Europe, I got into a bit of trouble (it seemed) for accompanying Roman Catholic students on a trip to an Anglican "church" (I recall a Muslim student also joining the trip); and (iii) my progression through what will likely remain the most sketchy (and probably most illegal) job interview I will ever attend where as a 24-year-old I was asked by a mainstream Christian church if I had ever had any romantic relationships? This particular religious institution seemed to want to figure out what my genetic sexual orientation is: in real life, I happen to be gay—a fact which (I later learned) would have disqualified me from the particular job I was applying for.[2] So odd!

---

2. In this peculiar job interview, the frustration I felt was rather painful, although I soon realized it was an "artificial" frustration—a "frustration" created by the religious/social institution to serve the institution's own needs (*à la* Berger) to maintain its plausibility structure and to continue to promote its *own* definitions of physical and social realities. Ironically, the experience mentioned was also necessary to my career development—I had to realize the job I was applying for was not the right job for me. To clarify my intention in mentioning this experience, other people in the world suffer psychologically or physically in ways I will never know—so, in the long run, what happened to me here is fairly trivial. My *intention*, though, is to help to point out to others, who might go through a similar experience or a different experience but with similar

So: While I cannot speak for the socially oriented religious experiences of others, for what they're worth, the experiences in the preceding paragraph are *my* experiences with the social reality of religious life . . . I am not embarrassed to share them. If anything, I am *consciously proud* of them: they provided me with first-hand experience of what is the sheer absurdity, unapologetic tenderness, and (sometimes) excruciatingly painful yet by some accounts life-altering aura of the social reality we call "religion" in the modern, Western world. I should also mention that during university I worked as an interim school chaplain and interim church minister—those were positive experiences for me and I cherish those memories (just as I cherish memories of engineering chemistry). The point, however, to be taken away from all of this is that I was *not* led to write this book through a straightforward, predictable, or by any means "easy" intellectual path. That being said, it would also be a shame for me to forget those pivotal experiences which shaped my perspective on the social reality of religious life especially vis-à-vis modern science. All human experiences just happen . . . for the most part I did not choose the experiences which happened to me, but they still happened. And they impacted (in huge ways) my perception of religiosity—especially, too, because they occurred in my early 20s just as I was starting to get exposed to aspects of the world previously unknown to me, including the overall journey of intellectual growth which accompanies higher education. (Other scholars concerned generally with the relationship between science and religion, including William James,[3] are reported to have undergone various bouts of depression, anxiety, or inner turmoil, as they attempted to reconcile their adolescent religious beliefs with a growing *awareness* of modern science.) However, what my seminal experiences in engineering chemistry, religious life, and philosophical theology, provided me with was an impetus to study the *philosophy of* science and religion—to consider seriously the project of compatibility system design while also be-

emotional weight, that ultimately what matters in life is being *honest* about oneself—to yourself and to others. Following the trend of theologians who reflect on death, when I die someday, I want to look back and know that I was honest, that I told the truth. For what it's worth, on this score, see: Blanton, *Radical Honesty*, 1.

3. About William James's early experiences with attempting to reconcile science and religion, Cathy Gutierrez (2011, 600) explains, "Science was still expected to uphold the claims of religion, and when William James was considering his educational options both he and his father assumed a complicity between the two endeavours. As William experimented with a number of vocations ranging from art to medicine, he found himself torn between the purely materialistic explanations he wished to reject and the lure of religion for which he could find little empirical evidence. The seriousness that he applied to this quandary resulted in existential despair and a depression that lasted two years."

coming acutely aware of the limitations of such an endeavour. The remaining chapters of this book, then, will address the following question: *what are the limitations of compatibility system design and, most importantly, do those limitations affect the integrity of the compatibility system project?*

In discussing the character of philosophical problems, Karl Popper does not hesitate to point out that "*we are not students of some subject matter but students of problems. And problems may cut right across the borders of any subject matter or discipline.*"[4] Thus far, my analysis of the problem of constructing a religious epistemology in the modern scientific cosmos has cut across the scholastic borders of epistemology (primarily), sociology of religion, academic theology, and some anthropology: including compatibility system design, CPS-agents rendered institutional facts, my igmythicist approach to myths, and contributory elements from Haack's innocent realism and Bartley's pancritical rationalism. Adding to this eclectic mix,[5] in the discipline of cognitive science of religion, religiosity is understood as embedded in the cultural construct of religion: e.g., social institutions allow metaphysical meaning-making (e.g., mythical projection toward an afterlife) to be socioculturally imprinted over the quotidian capacities of a natural cognitive system. Scientific testing in the area of "experimental theology"[6] seems to provide an empirical basis for the claims of cognitive science of religion. While this work is still quite novel—and, as we shall see, is really an *attempt* to explain religious activity—cognitive science of religion helps to point out some of the experimental work pursued in the scientific study of religion. Furthermore, epistemic assessments of cognitive science of religion (my focus) involve analyses of the *types* of explanations made for religious activity, evaluating whether these "explanations" are epistemically adequate, or not. In other matters, cognitive science of religion (i) seeks to balance religious commitments with scientific investigation (while acknowledging the epistemic values of those enterprises are often contrary to one another), and (ii) considers what the outcomes of experimental theology might imply for the apologetic aims of religious communities; or what experimental theology might imply for compatibility system design.

---

4. Popper, *Conjectures and Refutations*, 88.

5. "Eclectic," given the variety of novel approaches I attempt to utilize, but, of course, methodologically *unified* in the sense that my approaches and the projects of my central philosophers—Popper, Bartley, and Haack—share common themes: (a) they embrace and/or utilize a hypothetico-deductive method, (b) they avoid scientistic tendencies, and (c) for my use, they provide methodological approaches well suited to discussing the epistemic possibility of a religious epistemology contextualized in a modern research university.

6. Boyer, *Religion Explained*, 79.

In a cognitive fashion, religiosity exists, is developed, and is transmitted between individuals *without* the aid of any social institution—*without* any consensus on the truth of belief claims. Applying the meaning of *animism*—"giving a soul"—as its inspiration,[7] cognitive science of religion observes that humans seem compelled to attribute goal-oriented intentionalities toward inanimate objects. As the argument goes, rooted in our evolutionary past, the desire for humans to identify the presence of possible intentional agents in the physical world includes survival benefits. In terms of humans' ordinary cognitive capacity, then, this is the crux of the *hypersensitive agency detection device*, the HADD. With predators (e.g., panthers) nearby, an evolutionary-based, cognitive device in the mind helps humans to detect the presence of predators. So long as effects of false-positives are not too damaging to the human psyche (perhaps false-positives result in overly cautious humans only), a maturationally natural desire to detect predators includes survival benefits. As Robert McCauley observes, "The creature that is inattentive to the movement in the periphery, the shadow passing overhead, or the rustling in the leaves (let alone the sound in the basement) is less prepared to protect itself from predators, competitors, and foes."[8] Thus the evolutionary-based HADD ensures the prevention of fatalities that would result from false-negatives. Justin Barrett explains additional elements of the HADD as follows:

> To summarize, when HADD [hypersensitive agency detection device] perceives an object violating the intuitive assumptions for the movement of ordinary physical objects (such as moving on non-inertial paths, changing direction inexplicably, or launching itself from a standstill) and the object *seems to be moving in a goal-directed manner*, HADD detects agency. Gathering information from other mental tools, HADD searches for any known agents that might account for the self-propelled movement. Finding none, HADD assumes that the object itself is an agent. Until information arrives to say otherwise, HADD registers a nonreflective belief [an automatic, unconscious belief] that the object is an agent, triggering ToM [Theory of Mind tool] to describe the object's activity in terms of beliefs, desires, and other mental states.[9]

In religiosity, CPS-agents (e.g., gods) are thought to possess beliefs, desires, and mental states. As outlined in the preceding quotation, the HADD

---

7. McCauley, *Why Religion Is Natural and Science Is Not*, 81.
8. McCauley, *Why Religion Is Natural and Science Is Not*, 82.
9. Barrett, *Why Would Anyone Believe in God*, 33; emphasis added.

detects apparent "agents" with beliefs, desires, and mental states: in a faith-based manner, then, for some, the HADD is thought to detect goal-oriented CPS-agents, thereby "explaining" religious activity and impacting the cogency of belief about God.

In terms of resources from cognitive science of religion impacting the cogency of belief about God, in *Religion Explained: The Evolutionary Origins of Religious Thought* (2001), Pascal Boyer is careful to distance his work from any apologetic agendas. Boyer explains that, despite scientifically tested cognitive theories about religion, questions such as *is religion in our genes?* or *is religion innate?* remain meaningless questions.[10] What cognitive theories about religion do (potentially) explain is the natural cognitive capacity to *acquire* religious thoughts—a conclusion reached independent of any faith position *per se*. In contrast, Barrett, in his *Why Would Anyone Believe in God?* (2004), attempts to coalesce a substantive faith position with the conclusions of cognitive science of religion. In the following paragraphs, I attempt to show how Boyer and Barrett differ in their methodological approaches concerning whether resources from cognitive science of religion contribute to the cogency of belief about God.

With the apparent aim to equate the HADD (from Barrett's own phrase *hypersensitive agency detection device*) with a proposed cognitive device which detects "God," Barrett, it seems, faithfully "twists" his argument. Barrett presents a thesis that, with an awareness of the existence of the HADD, humans really have no choice *but* to acknowledge the naturalness of belief about God.[11] Moreover, Barrett's work includes an apologetic focus: in a faith-imbued manner, Barrett argues that, since cognitive science of religion suggests belief about God is natural, atheists will have a difficult time in life maintaining their atheism.[12] However, as I see it, Barrett's argument begs the question, outlined as follows:

1. *Barrett's premise*: in one's everyday cognitive capacity, the *HADD* is inborn—a cognitive device one receives for free.

2. *Barrett's conclusion*: through faith-based, apologetic "tweaking," Barrett concludes the HADD detects God, that belief about God is natural—i.e., in a faith-imbued manner, Barrett concludes the HADD is a cognitive device to detect God. (I suppose, by the same line of reasoning, the HADD is also a cognitive device to detect Allah, or to detect Zeus, or to detect any other CPS-agent, etc.)

---

10. Boyer, *Religion Explained*, 3–4.
11. Barrett, *Why Would Anyone Believe in God*, 108.
12. Barrett, *Why Would Anyone Believe in God*, 108–9.

3. *Barrett's premise repeated*: in one's everyday cognitive capacity, a *cognitive device to detect God* is inborn—a cognitive device one receives for free.

As shown in the preceding outline, in *(iii) premise repeated*, the referent *cognitive device to detect God* replaces the referent *HADD* from *(i) premise*. Other than this change, *(i) premise* and *(iii) premise repeated* are the same, while *(ii) conclusion* remains a faith-imbued conclusion.

Barrett's account of cognitive science of religion impacting the cogency of belief about God is not scientifically persuasive. Like the epistemically centred projects of other faith-imbued science and religion scholars (including Drees, Stenmark, and van Huyssteen), Barrett's science and religion project, centred on cognitive science of religion, attempts to combine an assumption without initial plausibility (i.e., that the CPS-agent, "God," is an ontological reality) with falsifiable belief testing in modern science. The intriguing aspect of Barrett's project is that, while Barrett maintains religious motivations in the form of an assumption without initial plausibility, Barrett's project also requires falsifiable beliefs. If Barrett did not allow falsifiable beliefs from cognitive science of religion to influence the substantive content of his project—for example, his acknowledgement of the neurophysiological rootedness of cognitive science—Barrett's project would not *appear* nearly as persuasive as it does. In this sense, Barrett's project functions as a legitimation strategy similar to those legitimation strategies presented in chapter 2: by aligning his work vis-à-vis falsifiable belief testing, Barrett attempts to "justify" his apologetic motivations relative to the distinguished (albeit, following Haack's lead, not uncriticized) epistemology and method of modern science. Secondly, Barrett's project is an example of a faith-imbued compatibility system: science and religion—analyzed through the lens of cognitive science of religion—are seemingly combined at the substantive level. Be that as it may (and acknowledging that for faith-imbued observers this would be an emotionally appealing compatibility system), Barrett's conclusion—that, with an awareness of the existence of the HADD, belief about God is natural—is not a tested conclusion. Nor does Barrett's conclusion elucidate a tested causal connection between the scientific theory of the HADD and the cogency of belief about God.

In contrast to Barrett's approach, Boyer's methodological approach toward resources from cognitive science of religion is more modest. Boyer assesses conclusions from experimental theology, formulating tested conjectures about how cognitive science of religion might explain a natural cognitive capacity to *acquire* religious thoughts. (Similar to the notion that humans possess a capacity to catch a seasonal cold—they possess the vulnerabilities of a respiratory system—Boyer presents a thesis that humans possess a cognitive capacity to acquire "religion."[13]) Boyer's work, however, stops short of making a faith-imbued "jump" toward relating this natural cognitive capacity to the cogency of belief about God. Despite the differing methodological approaches of Barrett and Boyer, I suggest that, so long as one remains aware of how the approaches differ, both Barrett's and Boyer's projects in experimental theology make a useful contribution to my design of a religious epistemology—as well as to a compatibility system between a scientific study of religion and a religious epistemology. While my upcoming proposal of a religious epistemology (starting in chapter 9) will not specifically utilize content from experimental theology (my project is centred on epistemology and compatibility system design rather than on cognitive science of religion), conclusions from experimental theology support my claim in this book that the human mind continues to defer to the actions of CPS-agents: to that end, mythopoeic and CPS-agentic modes of thought continue to permeate the religious epistemic standards of modern religious institutions. This particular claim is important to my igmythicist approach to myths, whereby, in a representational fashion, myths are neither mere delusions nor reflections of an ontological reality for the gods, but myths are the application of meaning-enclaves (human values) enclosed in the sociocultural world of natural human experience. For my purposes, then, experimental theology helps to point out the following:

- The neurophysiological reality behind the simple deference of the human mind to the actions of CPS-agents.
- My philosophical proposal that, since this simple deference of the human mind to the actions of purported agents *is* an intersubjectively tested, neurophysiological reality,[14] our conception of myths is rightly *shifted*: We mentally transition from believing that myths are either mere delusions or reflections of an ontological reality for the gods, *toward* our *practical use* of the neurophysiological reality behind myths—*toward* our formulating of a new religious epistemic framework whereby we participate in symbolically oriented, human-sourced projects of world-construction and meaning-making in a postmetaphysical, academic setting!

∼

13. Boyer, *Religion Explained*, 4.
14. Barrett, *Why Would Anyone Believe in God*, 32–33.

Boyer describes the cultural trappings of religiosity—including religious concepts, myths, and values—in terms of meme theory ("copy-me" programs) and meme-transmission.[15] About this, Boyer notes, "Religious ontologies surprise people by describing things and events they could not possibly encounter in actual experience."[16] Counter-ontological (counter-intuitive) representations of a superhuman agent include an ontological category (e.g., categories of *person, animal, tool, natural object,* etc.) and a violation of that category within a catalogue of culturally oriented, supernatural templates for religious concepts.[17] As the argument goes, for cognitive reasons pertaining to outcomes from our evolutionary heritage, the human mind is predisposed to be prepared to acquire counter-ontological variations of certain mental concepts. Variations of these mental concepts seem to coalesce well with the nature of religious thought. In Boyer's and Barrett's experimental theology, controlled experiments are performed whereby concepts which correspond to supernatural templates are tested for their ease of memory recall compared to other concepts which do not correspond to supernatural templates.[18] As Boyer explains, "Barrett and I designed fairly coherent stories in which we inserted various new violations of ontological expectations as well as episodes that were compatible with [default] ontological expectations. The difference in recall between the two kinds of information would give us an idea of the advantage of violations in individual memory."[19]

Boyer outlines how long-term memory recall suggests that ontological violations are better preserved in one's individual memory than other concepts which do not include violations.[20] Moreover, violations of ontological expectations are better recalled than what Boyer terms "mere oddities."[21] For example, in experiments performed, Boyer explains that violation of the ontological category of *person*, as in the statement "a man who walked through a wall,"[22] was recalled better than *no* violation of the ontological category of *person*, but violation of default expectations only,[23] as in the

---

15. Boyer, *Religion Explained*, 35.
16. Boyer, *Religion Explained*, 55.
17. Boyer, *Religion Explained*, 78.
18. Boyer, *Religion Explained*, 79.
19. Boyer, *Religion Explained*, 79.
20. Boyer, *Religion Explained*, 80.
21. Boyer, *Religion Explained*, 80.
22. Boyer, *Religion Explained*, 80.
23. Boyer, *Religion Explained*, 80.

statement "a man with six fingers"[24] (a mere oddity only). About these experiments, Boyer concludes, "The memory effects—we find better recall for ontological violations than for oddities or for standard associations—seem to explain *the anthropological observation that oddities are not found at the core of supernatural concepts, and ontological violations are.*"[25] To that end, as alluded to in chapter 2, relying on and testifying to the activities of CPS-agents in one's life does not require that one have a "religion" or a "god," as examples from various cultures illustrate. Examples include: (i) beliefs about aliens, ghosts, spirits, or witches; (ii) beliefs about dead human ancestors to which animals are sacrificed;[26] (iii) from Boyer's fieldwork in Cameroon, the belief that invisible dead people are a menace to non-dead people;[27] (iv) also from Boyer's fieldwork, the belief among the Fang people that the power of witches (belief of witches is another belief) always trumps anti-witchcraft power;[28] and (v) in some human groups, beliefs about initiation rituals whereby adolescents must undergo complex rituals (as though rituals were kinds of "CPS-agents" themselves) in order to acquire the "secret" knowledge of adulthood.[29]

In conclusion, about relying on and testifying to the activities of CPS-agents in one's life, Boyer notes, "One group's unimportant religious concepts can become another's religion, and vice versa."[30] In addition, Boyer points out how explicit, "theologically correct"[31] conceptions of God as a non-standard, superhuman agent are "stored," if you will, in verbal, propositional form: e.g., the explicit statement "God is omnipresent." These explicit concepts contrast with implicit, "theologically incorrect" conceptions of God as a more standard, anthropomorphic agent, "housed" in one's intuitive psychology.[32] However, Boyer is careful to point out that "you do not need to have theologians around in order to think in [so-called] 'theologically correct' ways."[33] For example, Boyer maintains that in societies with no explicit theological frameworks, even possibly in non-literate societies, explicit,

24. Boyer, *Religion Explained*, 80.
25. Boyer, *Religion Explained*, 81; emphasis added.
26. Boyer, *Religion Explained*, 242–43.
27. Boyer, *Religion Explained*, 90.
28. Boyer, *Religion Explained*, 20.
29. Boyer, *Religion Explained*, 243.
30. Boyer, *Religion Explained*, 91.
31. In experimental theology, the concepts of *theological correctness* and explicit, "theologically correct" conceptions of God were formulated by Justin L. Barrett (Boyer, *Religion Explained*, 88).
32. Boyer, *Religion Explained*, 89.
33. Boyer, *Religion Explained*, 89.

"theologically correct" versions of non-standard, superhuman agents still exist:[34] e.g., the explicit statement "spirits are invisible." In those societies, concepts are easily acquired via tacit expectations about the physical world, possibly leading to formulations of other beliefs such that invisible spirits are like human beings, because spirits are thought to have minds that work like human minds.[35]

A NOTE ON NATURAL COGNITIVE SYSTEMS AND UNNATURAL COGNITIVE SYSTEMS

In other aspects of cognitive science of religion, in his *Why Religion Is Natural and Science Is Not*, Robert McCauley provides an additional methodological perspective on the intellectual landscape of science and religion—a *cognitive*, comparative analysis grounded in the cognitive naturalness of religiosity and cognitive unnaturalness of scientific thought. McCauley's thesis is that religious exercises are derived from a maturationally natural cognitive system—in the popular sense of "being *religious*," which, for McCauley, is the spontaneous transmission of *religiosity* between individuals. (The production of technology, too, is thought to be cognitively natural.) In contrast, scientific exercises are grounded in an unnatural cognitive system, characterized by deliberate reflection and critical thought. Moreover, McCauley's thesis supports the realization that theological exercises are not religious *per se*, but are exercises of investigation and inquiry which *attempt* to be "science."

McCauley distinguishes between (i) practiced naturalness and (ii) maturationally natural cognition.[36] Practiced naturalness is based on human experience in a particular domain of knowledge—e.g., observed experiences which lead one to obtain expert knowledge in a particular field. *Maturationally natural cognition*, or *maturational naturalness*, is not based on any human experience, but rather is derived from one's innate and intuitive understanding of the physical world—e.g., perennial techniques of chewing and walking—knowledge one receives "for free." Maturational naturalness requires small amounts of effort only to be understood (without reflection), despite the fact that the information involved might be complex. In addition, techniques of maturational naturalness are easily grasped: with minimal effort, techniques are spontaneously transferred between individuals. McCauley summarizes this unexpected realization

---

34. Boyer, *Religion Explained*, 89.
35. Boyer, *Religion Explained*, 89.
36. McCauley, *Why Religion Is Natural and Science Is Not*, 5.

as follows: "Their maturationally natural systems equip human minds to readily generate, retain, deploy, and transmit religious representations. *By contrast, the prominence of those maturationally natural systems is mostly an obstacle to the invention and the investigation of alternative causal conceptions.* Broadly speaking, this is why science is so hard to learn and why it is so hard to do."[37] Moreover, McCauley goes on, "The deepest source of science's cognitive unnaturalness is the ever-growing disparity between our maturationally natural perceptions and intuitions about things and the very different picture of the world that science discloses."[38] Modern scientific thought, then, being outsourced from an unnatural cognitive system, leads to counterintuitive representations of physical reality. Theology, too, being systematic and polemical, is less easily transmitted between individuals than maturationally natural "agentic thinking" is transmitted.

Counterintuitive representations of physical reality are not inaccurate descriptions of physical reality, but they are not as easily formulated, understood, or transmitted between humans as are the agentic representations of physical reality found in religiosity and permeating modern religious institutions and ritual systems.[39] McCauley's perspective on these fronts is that the continued existence of modern science may be fragile.[40] McCauley points out the vulnerability of science relative to other powerful political and social institutions, suggesting science is a sociologically fragile enterprise—science is an exercise misunderstood by the general public to be an

---

37. McCauley, *Why Religion Is Natural and Science Is Not*, 82; emphasis added.

38. McCauley, *Why Religion Is Natural and Science Is Not*, 106.

39. McCauley and Lawson, in their *Bringing Ritual to Mind: Psychological Foundations of Cultural Forms*, discuss a theory of religious ritual form. As a theory of actions, a theory of religious ritual form, McCauley and Lawson argue, can be used in the scientific study of religion to define or conceptualize the category "religion." Being careful not to conceptualize *religion* in such a way that the framework is so broad that *any* human action might count as religion (e.g., people participating in communal cheering at a sports game could be construed by some to be "religion"), McCauley and Lawson (9) defend their theory of actions by demonstrating how a theory of actions relates actions specifically to the actions of CPS-agents. The components of religious rituals include a CPS-agent, an act (usually via an instrument, e.g., water), and a patient (the person receiving the action of the ritual). Interactions between a CPS-agent and a patient (and sometimes via an intermediary) are thought to bring about ontological changes in the physical world which are either temporary or permanent. In the context of religious institutions, religious rituals are thought to possess an insider criterion—religious rituals are open to religious initiates only (for instance, baptism, circumcision, circling the Kaaba, etc.). Whereas religious actions (generally) are described by an outsider criterion—religious actions are open to anyone (e.g., anyone—including the non-religious—can claim to have a mystical experience).

40. McCauley, *Why Religion Is Natural and Science Is Not*, 279.

activity about "truths-to-be-memorized."[41] On this score, I agree with Mc-Cauley—the notion that science is actually composed of beliefs subject to ruthless, critical tests (and possible modification or even complete refutation) seems not well understood by the public. However, to be honest, I find it difficult to appreciate McCauley's position that the continued existence of modern science, then, is fragile: *does not the realization that science allows for improvement and modification of one's beliefs—and how this makes learning possible—mean that science is a human activity with much potential for future existence?* My new igmythicist approach to myth (presented initially in chapter 4; to be unpacked further) provides a solution to the proposed, ever-growing problem that science and academic versions of theology, vis-à-vis a quotidian religiosity, are sociologically *fragile*. The new igmythicist approach, as well as its solution to the problem that science seems sociologically fragile, are articulated further and presented throughout the next two chapters—*Designing a New Religious Epistemology for a Scientific Study of Religion* (chapter 9), followed by *What About the "Beyond"? Two Pathways Moving Ahead: Ultimism and an Inductive Faith* (chapter 10). Many of the ideas I have hinted at throughout this book "come full circle" in these next two chapters.

---

41. McCauley, *Why Religion Is Natural and Science Is Not*, 281.

9

Designing a New Religious Epistemology for a Scientific Study of Religion

WHAT TYPE OF RATIONALITY?

IN THE RATHER OBSCURE, yet brilliant, film *The Night of the Hunter* (1955), the adolescent character, John Harper, helps himself and his younger sister, Pearl, escape in a rowboat down a *river* after a fraudulent preacher (Robert Mitchum) murders their mother (Shelley Winters) all the while convincing the gullible townspeople he is a prophet. In the film, while escaping with his sister, John courageously says to himself, "*There's still the river!*"[1] The film's unusual plot and dialogue are rich with religious themes, including allusions to escaping from bondage (in this case, the biblical image of a *river*[2] is apropos), being (unwittingly) cared for, and, in the end, embracing the qualities of a pure heart. Moreover, this theologically oriented *Bildungsroman* is especially intriguing if one considers that, while John and Pearl experience a coming of age which includes religious dimensions, the townspeople acclimatize themselves to the religious teachings of the preacher: he *reassures* them—no doubt his presence (on the "surface" at least) matches their impression of what a religious life ought to be. At the

---

1. *The Night of the Hunter*, directed by Charles Laughton (MGM, 1955), iTunes (2015). Screenplay by James Agee. Featuring Robert Mitchum and Shelley Winters.

2. See the biblical narrative in Exodus 2.

end of the film, the townspeople undergo a kind of existential crisis: they discover the preacher's fraudulent nature, and, having fallen for him, their perceptions of themselves and their own lives are acutely questioned. On the other hand, the characters, John and Pearl, having undergone a crisis of their own, find unconventional solace within a group of misplaced children and adolescents, mentored by an older woman, Miss Cooper, who fills the role of advocate and guide; unashamedly, she describes herself as a strong (mustard seed) tree with branches for many birds.[3] All in all, it's a highly interesting film, because it highlights the psychological interplay of innocence, fear, and endurance—facing whatever obstacles life throws your way and evolving to become a more mature, a more *human*, person because of those obstacles.

Intellectual and emotional dilemmas centred on the question of science and religion are, for many, academic and personal obstacles: the obstacle is (i) for some, an epistemic complication in Western, intellectual achievement; (ii) for others, an emotional red herring in the struggle for faith. Whatever the contexts for various individuals, these academic and personal obstacles seem to materialize themselves as fairly intense psychological dilemmas: epistemic complications in intellectual life or emotional distractions in one's struggle for faith might cause one to question one's assumptions, background experiences, future life goals, and, perhaps most importantly, one's sociocultural identity. As Peter Berger brilliantly puts it, "The difficulty of keeping a world going expresses itself psychologically in the difficulty of keeping this world subjectively plausible."[4] As considered in great detail in this book, both scientific and religious exercises aim to describe shared states of affairs in one, physical world: the projects of science and religion (for either scientific or religious practitioners) are included in Berger's suggestion that sociocultural enterprises possess the task of maintaining the world's subjective plausibility. Moreover, social worlds are heavily structured by conversations between individuals and significant others. As examples of significant others, Berger cites parents, teachers, and peers,[5] and, following Berger's lead, we could extend *significant others* to include scientists, theologians, professors, and writers. Consider what happens, though, when a significant other dies, moves away, or how the subjective plausibility of a social world is affected when, say, an individual makes a conscious decision to reject a significant other? In the contexts of scientific and faith-imbued lives specifically, what happens when, for example, (i) new

---

3. See the biblical narrative in Mark 4:30–32.
4. Berger, *The Sacred Canopy*, 16.
5. Berger, *The Sacred Canopy*, 16.

scientific theories are tested, suggesting life did not all at once come into being as religion claims it did or that, at death, brain activity most surely ceases forever; or (ii) when a mostly non-religious person, whose friends have all died, finds it difficult to locate any meaning in life and becomes severely depressed; or (iii) when a person who grew up in a religious community realizes he or she is not heterosexual and is told to keep that information secret?[6] In short, from Berger's terminology, "the world begins to totter, to lose its subjective plausibility."[7] And, given any of the preceding examples (and there are many, many others), to pretend that the world has not begun to totter, that the world has not started to lose its subjective plausibility, would be a kind of denial of the *human condition* and/or a fairly intense psychological dilemma. (In applying the phrase *human condition*, I am thinking about this phrase's typical usage to point out human reflection about various phases of human life, including birth, childhood, adolescence, adulthood, and death, as well as human reflection about common emotional states, including hope, fear, and love, etc.)

About the epistemic interfaces of science and religion, and our academic and social location in the new, disenchanted cosmos of science, perhaps what is most unsettling (for some) is that our acclimatized expectations of what a religious life *ought* to be are suddenly questioned. Like the townspeople in *The Night of the Hunter*, who acclimatize themselves to the religious teachings of the fraudulent preacher, although they have definite expectations of what religion *is*, they also prevent themselves from recognizing and evaluating new, radically different modes of thought when they arise, leading eventually to psychological distress about the "plausibility" of their own plausibility structures. (Although the example from *The Night of the Hunter* is an extreme, fictional example, centred on a fraudulent preacher who is a murderer and a brother and sister who escape down a river, the existential implications I describe here—portrayed brilliantly in the film—are applicable to the intense psychological dilemmas of science and religion.[8])

---

6. In these examples—from possible scenarios in scientific and faith-imbued lives specifically—"significant others" are the human enterprises of science and religion themselves, which exist in relationships with individuals: how subjective individuals perceive, utilize, and assess the epistemic and/or social merits of these enterprises.

7. Berger, *The Sacred Canopy*, 17.

8. Moreover, the notion of psychological "escaping" has its place in personal science and religion dilemmas. From examples already mentioned: (i) New scientific theories which suggest life did not all at once come into being as religion claims it did or that, at death, brain activity most surely ceases forever, might psychologically cause one to want to "escape" the non-tested, mythopoeic worldview of religion. Or, (ii) concerning a mostly non-religious person, whose friends have all died and who finds it difficult to

Designing a New Religious Epistemology for a Scientific Study of Religion   165

Thus, in light of the new scientific cosmos, formulating new perceptions of what a religious life *is* or *isn't* becomes necessary—in a sense, "theologizing" (or meaning-making) in this new cosmos which is represented epistemically by a modestly naturalistic epistemology. For us, that "there's still the river"[9] implies that there's still work to do; that it's still premature to give up on attempting to recontextualize (replace) *myth* and non-tested, religious beliefs in a modern research university. (Unpacked further in this chapter, the recontextualizing of *myth* occurs in an epistemic stance like Haack's modestly naturalistic epistemology.) Moreover, that "there's still the river" implies that I haven't given up yet; that I'm not bogged down

---

locate any meaning in life and becomes severely depressed, that person might discover that he or she wants to "escape" the purely materialistic life he or she previously sought. Or, (iii) concerning a person who grew up in a religious community and realizes he or she is not heterosexual and is told to keep that information secret, that person might find that he or she wants to (for psychological reasons, as fast as is possible) "escape" the psychological confines of a *final, fixed, and substantive* religious life—or at least *reinterpret* religious life vis-à-vis the substantive, tested beliefs of modern science.

9. As is hopefully apparent, I have chosen the image of a *river*, because of the powerful symbolism of rivers in religious narratives: e.g., themes of escaping from bondage, crossing over to new beginnings, or finding refuge, etc.

by former innocence or fear,[10] but I'm pushed forward by new, intellectual stamina.[11]

Metaphorically, one's travelling down a river to escape past oppression, or one's crossing over a river to begin a new phase of life, are symbols of one's new beginning; of one's fresh start. *In well-known biblical narratives, think of the infant Moses who travels (unwittingly) by way of the Nile River to escape oppression;*[12] *or Joshua who leads his people across the Jordan River to begin a new phase of life!*[13] *Or even think of the lesser-known narrative of the prophet Elisha who crosses over the Jordan River as he succeeds his mentor Elijah—who himself had just previously crossed over the same river.*[14] Throughout this book, I've often referred to the assumption that religious people's testimonies inform us that religious people possess beliefs about superhuman agents and/or beliefs about trans-empirical worlds.[15] When

---

10. To be honest, the potential *fear* of the existential implications of either science *or* religion in one's life, and/or the naive *innocence* that either enterprise might bring. Put simply, this refers to facing up to the emotional and psychological frustrations that come with attempting to balance (i) the cognitive values characteristic of a scientific epistemology with (ii) the peculiar nature of belief claims (with their corresponding non-tested beliefs) included in a religious epistemology. As outlined in this book, any theory of rationality which allows intellectual space for the presence of belief claims at the same time begins to sacrifice the cognitive values characteristic of a scientific epistemology. As cognitive values are lost, the question arises of whether we still possess an "epistemology"? Alternatively, if we remove belief claims from our religious epistemology, but consequently preserve the cognitive values of science, have we missed the point of what a religious epistemology was supposed to accomplish? What a religious epistemology "was supposed to accomplish" is the mental recognition, for the religious devotee, that traditional religious life does include non-tested beliefs, which are supposed to differ epistemically from tested beliefs in science. Moreover, the *a priori* recognition (again, for the religious devotee) that these non-tested beliefs will not diminish the existential value or faith-based aims of a religious epistemology. At any rate, the epistemic issues raised by questions about science and religion can be emotionally and psychologically daunting, especially as one undergoes a process of *intellectual maturation*; as one begins to rationally question the "plausibility" of one's own plausibility structures. As a kind of psychological escape hatch, it might seem far easier to just believe that science and religion will just "take care" of themselves—the naive innocence of either science or religion. So, a *willingness* to honestly and openly approach the question of science and religion does require some intellectual stamina.

11. And, for what it's worth, in the mythopoeic story of the Garden of Eden, the gods—*elohim*—bestow human beings with faculties of intellect and reason when the gods create human beings in their image. (See the biblical narrative in Genesis 1:26–27.)

12. See the biblical narrative in Exodus 2.

13. See the biblical narrative in Joshua 3.

14. See the biblical narrative in 2 Kings 2.

15. Indeed, this is the second of the two substantive assumptions that I make in this book.

Designing a New Religious Epistemology for a Scientific Study of Religion 167

assessing the initial plausibility of that assumption in chapter 1, I pointed out how that assumption itself did not include the faith-imbued tenets that superhuman agents or trans-empirical worlds, about which religious people express beliefs, are metaphysical realities. However, what that assumption did include was the sociological observation that, given a population of people (speaking generally), some of those people, when asked about their religious commitments, will provide *testimonies about superhuman agents and trans-empirical worlds—or testimonies about religious narratives, symbols, and existentially relevant metaphors*. As it happens, these testimonies provide us with a look into religious individuals' mindsets—as those mindsets are understood by the individuals who are testifying about (reporting) their belief experiences. In this way, superhuman agents and trans-empirical worlds, about which religious people testify, amount to kinds of cultural postulations—belief claims arising from within the cultural construct of religion and, physiologically, from the predilections of a maturationally natural cognitive system.[16]

In keeping with this theme of *human testimonies*, and the possible emotional and psychological roles of testimonies in a scientific study of religion, I, too, possess my own testimony, which helps to relay my motivations in moving forward: Expressed metaphorically, my sense that "there's still the river"—in literal terms, *that there's still valuable work to do; that I haven't given up yet*—is, in effect, my own particular testimony. As an igmythicist,[17] my testimony is not falsifiable: I *cannot* test (from intersubjectively observed experiences of phenomenal reality) whether my conjecture—that there's still valuable work to do; that I needn't give up yet—reaches a high degree of certitude, or whether my conjecture is false. And while it is very possible that my desire to *keep on trying*,[18] so to speak, is a testimony arising from my own particular sociocultural and intellectual background, as well as even physiologically from the predilections of my maturationally natural cognitive system,[19] this particular human testimony is my *practical* expression of what it means to "theologize" in a modern university.

16. See the description and outline of a maturationally natural cognitive system—from McCauley's thesis of the naturalness of popular religion and the unnaturalness of modern science—in chapter 8.

17. My igmythicist approach to conceptualize *myth* in the modern scientific cosmos was presented in chapter 4.

18. That is, *keep on trying* to attempt to recontextualize (replace) *myth* and non-tested, religious beliefs in a modern research university; in a modestly naturalistic epistemology.

19. Possibly arising physiologically from the predilections of a maturationally natural cognitive system, because if my testimony—*to keep on trying to recontextualize myth and non-tested, religious beliefs in a modern research university*—is in fact an emotional

It might be surprising (even perplexing), to some, that I suddenly introduce the term *theologizing* into my scientific study of religion, which (explained in chapter 1) seeks to explain, using tested, scientific beliefs, rather than theologize by way of non-tested CPS-agents. As an igmythicist, my use of the term "theologizing"—recontextualizing *myth* in a modestly naturalistic epistemology—is assessed in the remainder of this book. Note that I do place the preceding terms *theologizing* and *theologize* in scare quotes to point out how their usages in my context are not typical theistic, faith-imbued usages whereby CPS-agents are invoked to know and interpret the physical world. Moreover, as Wiebe notes, the final chapters of many books in the scientific study of religion seem to undergo what he terms the *last chapter syndrome*:[20] in the scientific study of religion, for nearly the entire duration of one's analysis, ontological realities for CPS-agents were bracketed, but then, suddenly, in one's final chapter, CPS-agents ("gods") appear as explanatory forces. Falling victim to the last chapter syndrome is not my intention either. In accordance with Berger's methodological atheism, ontological realities for CPS-agents *remain* bracketed in these final chapters, which means chapters 9 and 10 remain my contribution to a genuine scientific study of religion. Despite my insistence that CPS-agents remain bracketed, what are not bracketed (nor have they been throughout this book) are *subjective, human testimonies*, including my own, outlined in the preceding paragraph.[21]

Nevertheless, in bracketing ontological realities for CPS-agents, I do realize that, for some, what I have done is, in effect, "pulled the plug" on the entire tradition of faith-imbued theology, both past and present. *However*, as outlined in chapter 1, in my analysis, what I also bracketed was the ontological

---

and psychological remnant of my adolescent religious background and those theological career interests I pursued in my early 20s, then my testimony is still, in some sense, "faith-imbued" with the actions of CPS-agents, arising from the predilections of my maturationally natural cognitive system.

20. Donald Wiebe, interview by Christopher R. Cotter, The Religious Studies Project, February 6, 2012, http://www.religiousstudiesproject.com/podcast/podcast-donald-wiebe-on-theology-and-religious-studies/.

21. Of course, although testimonies, including my own, are not bracketed, *non-tested* testimonies themselves cannot serve as explanatory forces in one's academic work. In accordance with the first of the two substantive assumptions which I make in this book—*phenomenal reality provides a standard of observed experiences used for testing beliefs about states of affairs in the physical world*—only those beliefs which *are* tested by way of intersubjectively observed experiences of phenomenal reality are permitted as possible explanatory forces. Nevertheless, subjective testimonies can help to point out one's emotional and psychological motivations in pursuing a particular academic question or problem; or the personal, background experiences one brings to a particular question or problem.

status of the external, physical world. Similar to the methodological atheism adopted in the academic study of religion, the particular philosophy of science I advocated for was a "methodological atheism" about the truth of scientific statements (as with religious statements)—a "methodological atheism" about the ability of scientific statements to correspond in a foolproof manner with the truth of the external, physical world.[22] It would not be inaccurate, then, to classify my philosophy of science (generally) as a philosophy of science which brackets the ontological status of the external, physical world. So, all in all, while bracketing ontological realities for CPS-agents, I have also tried to distance myself, as far as is possible, from an absolutist conception of science whereby the truth of the external, physical world is affirmed to correspond with the statements of science; where the statements of science are thought to be infallible. Thus, in my analysis, intersubjectively observed experiences of phenomenal reality make the testing of beliefs possible; however, objects of tested beliefs are not assumed to be necessarily equated, substantively,[23] with the truth of the external, physical world.

About the personal, psychological dilemmas of science and religion, while I suppose there remains the possibility that one merely states one is "not interested in science and religion," or that one believes "science and religion will just 'take care' of themselves" (possible responses whether one originates from a predominately religious *or* mostly scientific mindset), it seems most individuals adopt one of the following more explicit responses or a variant of one of the following:[24]

1. Reject the modern scientific enterprise.
2. Attempt to make religion "fit" science.
3. Attempt to make science "fit" religion.
4. Place science and religion in separate "compartments."
5. Reject the non-tested beliefs of religious life.

---

22. As mentioned, the assumptions underlying my philosophy of science are similar to the assumptions employed in Nancy Cartwright's instrumentalism: Cartwright remarks, "The fundamental laws of the theory are true of the objects in the model [constructed model to fit observed phenomenon into a theory], and they are used to derive a specific account of how these objects behave. But the objects of the model have only *'the form or appearance of things'* and, *in a very strong sense, not their 'substance or proper qualities'*" (Cartwright, *How the Laws of Physics Lie*, 17; emphasis added).

23. *Substantive* realities of objects of tested beliefs—realities thought to exist "behind" appearances—contrast with observable, *phenomenal* realities of objects of tested beliefs.

24. These five possible responses to the question of science and religion (inspired by Smart) were considered initially in chapter 4.

I note that *variants* of the preceding responses are quite possible, because, as discussed, *various brands* of religiosity are compared and contrasted with modern science. As McCauley candidly notes in the following two summary questions: "The pressing questions are: (1) Who gets to say whose religiosity is or is not true or whose version of Islam (or any other religion) is the right one? and (2) On what rationally convincing basis do they get to say it?"[25] Ironically, the epistemic implications of McCauley's summary questions are unexpected byproducts of the post-Kuhnian compatibility system. While science is argued to be no more rational than religion, at the same time, this application of the *tu quoque* renders particular belief communities (religions) themselves irrational. Bartley rightly noted how employing the *tu quoque* is the very attitude of mind which counteracts the critical mindset of the pancritical rationalist. In a modern university, while the *tu quoque* might render one's particular belief community temporarily immune from criticism, this temporary immunity means that the criticisms of other belief communities by other religions become impossible.[26]

Following the argument of post-Kuhnian compatibility system enthusiasts, then, not only is science no more rational than religion, but now (though post-Kuhnian compatibility system enthusiasts were not anticipating this) every religion is seen to be no more rational than any other religion. In addition, this realization points out how the post-Kuhnian compatibility system (like the demythologized compatibility system) attempted to rule *prima facie* in favour of one, particular belief community. However, as epistemically *neutral* reasons were never stated for committing to a particular religion or brand of religiosity through which the comparison of science and religion was made, particular religions cannot claim to be more rational than other religions. When analyzed in this fashion, Bartley's caution—that application of the *tu quoque* leads to an outright irrationalism for any commitment—is not some melodramatic, epistemic paranoia, but is an honest acknowledgement that the *tu quoque* leads to an outright postmodernism in the modern university. This emphasizes further how arguments held by faith, which inevitably crop up in the post-Kuhnian compatibility system by way of one's *choice* of religion, convince no one *unless* one already believes arguments based on particular brands of faith.

To that end, as examples, consider (a) a mythologized variant of Christianity which makes belief claims about metaphysical objects or (b) a demythologized variant of Christianity regarding the Christian worldview more as an ethical system or a way of life. Indeed, depending on which brands of

---

25. McCauley, *Why Religion Is Natural and Science Is Not*, 227.
26. Bartley, *The Retreat to Commitment*, 82.

Christian religiosity are compared and contrasted with science, the natures of any of the preceding five responses to science and religion would be quite different. When applying a demythologized brand of Christianity, none of the preceding five responses really apply since a demythologized Christianity does not seem to require the building of a compatibility system that would attempt to logically permit tested, scientific beliefs and non-tested, religious beliefs to exist on the same intellectual turf. On the other hand, in applying a brand of Christianity which makes belief claims about metaphysical objects, all of the preceding five responses are possible, leading some to (i) reject the modern scientific enterprise, (ii) attempt to make religion "fit" science or (iii) science "fit" religion, (iv) place science and religion in separate "compartments," or (v) reject the non-tested beliefs of religious life. Moreover, as considered, various definitions and conceptualizations for the concepts *God* or *myth*[27]—whether applied by theists, atheists, agnostics, or igtheists—render various types of comparisons and contrasts of science and religion. My comparison and contrast of "science and religiosity *simpliciter*" situates this book in the scientific study of religion, oriented by my two substantive assumptions: (i) that phenomenal reality provides a standard of observed experiences used for testing beliefs about states of affairs in the physical world, and (ii) that religious people's testimonies inform us that religious people possess beliefs about superhuman agents and/or beliefs about trans-empirical worlds. The type of comparison and contrast of science and religion I defend, then, is linked directly to the *type* of rationality I propose, involving (a) an ontology grounded in Haack's innocent realism as well as (b) an epistemic stance suitable for a modern university like Haack's modestly naturalistic epistemology. My application of Haack's arguments is then supported by Bartley's criticizability thesis, suggesting that, in being critical of beliefs, critical of criticism itself, *and* in being self-critical, a kind of *consistency* permeates one's learning and testing of beliefs. As mentioned, these are necessary ingredients to elucidate "knowledge and belief systems" which critically *survive* (or perhaps simply die) from ones that become stagnant ideologies.

As outlined, the crux of Haack's modestly naturalistic epistemology is that *naturalism* contrasts with *apriorism*:[28] science contributes to epistemology, but epistemology is not subordinate to science either. In a scientific study of religion, where various conceptions of the *relationship* between

---

27. For example, (i) *God* as *substantive reality* or as *institutional fact*, or (ii) *myths* as *substantive descriptions of physical reality* or as *symbolic, human-sourced representations of physical reality*.

28. Haack, *Defending Science—Within Reason*, 307.

epistemology and science are possible,[29] Haack's philosophical model—a modest departure from traditionalist apriorism while also stopping short of replacing epistemology with science—*supports* my thesis: In this book, while CPS-agents remain bracketed, human testimonies—types of "epistemologies"—help to point out emotional and psychological motivations at play in a scientific study of religion: i.e., subjective motivations at play in pursuing academic questions about *science and religion*, *myth*, and *religious life* in the modern university. For example, subjective motivations perhaps prompted by universal feelings of wondering about death . . . or of speculating on the purpose of human life. Thus, subjective, human testimonies are not replaced by science, yet scientific theories—in this case, theories from cognitive science of religion—influence the *role* (*function*) of human testimonies in a scientific study of religion. For example, cognitive science of religion suggests that human testimonies are *sociocultural byproducts* of physiological processes, such as the HADD and a maturationally natural cognitive system.

So: Similar to the *science-influenced epistemology* of Haack's modestly naturalistic epistemology, in dialogue with her *epistemology-influenced science*, I propose an ongoing dialogue between *science-influenced human testimony* and *human-testimony-influenced science*. That being said, Haack, herself, might be surprised by my application of her projects in this fashion toward a scientific study of religion.[30] Haack, whose work does not centrally address theological-type or religious-type matters, comments that "it is incomprehensible why anyone would seriously engage in theological inquiry if he didn't think the deity is knowable to some extent by creatures with powers such as ours."[31] By a similar token, Haack suggests it would be incomprehensible for a person to engage in scientific inquiry *unless* he or she thought the physical world was in fact knowable.[32] Haack's realist intents, undergirding her philosophy of science centred on everyday investigation and inquiry, are demonstrated clearly in her realist insistence that scientific inquiry presupposes a knowable physical world; likewise, from my reading of Haack, that theological inquiry presupposes God is an onto-

---

29. As mentioned, other possibilities to conceptualize the relationship between epistemology and science include: (i) radical, "revolutionary" naturalism which denies the value of epistemological questions altogether (Haack 2009, 169); or (ii) versions of scientistic naturalism which preserve the notion of an "epistemology," but turn epistemological questions over to science to attempt to resolve completely (Haack, *Evidence and Inquiry*, 169).

30. I think Haack might be interested, but quite possibly surprised.

31. Haack, *Defending Science—Within Reason*, 139–40.

32. Haack, *Defending Science—Within Reason*, 139.

logical reality. Haack's perception of theological inquiry (no doubt) is that theology is a faith-imbued exercise: in terms of mainstream theology, then, Haack makes a fair observation that (faith-imbued) theologians presume a CPS-agent-based, religious ontology, thereby presuming God is knowable in the framework of such an ontology. Haack's perception of theology, however (although no oversight of her own), is limited to these mainstream, faith-imbued, and what I call *non-academic*,[33] versions of theology. In contrast, an alternative, *constructive* version of theology is possible, including a new science and religion discourse, outlined in the following paragraphs.

From Paul Kurtz's igtheism, as well as from my thesis of igmythicism, conceptions of *God* as an *institutional fact* and *myths* as *symbolic, human-sourced representations of physical reality*, creatively call to mind a new, alternative, and refreshing conception of theology in the modern university—the formulation of a *constructive theology* in settings of unpredicted, fluctuating, experiential, and *tested learning* in the scientific cosmos of the twenty-first century. Igmythicism—an extension of the tenets of Kurtz's igtheism—"opens the mind," so to speak, to the possibility of a new science and religion discourse, centred on a new conception of *myth*: As in *igtheism*, the prefix *ig*, from *ig-mythicism*, is derived from the word *ignorant*, although *ignorant* does not imply a negative attitude *per se* toward *myth*. Rather the "ignorance" of igmythicism (like the "ignorance" of igtheism directed at theism) refers to the realization that the statement "*myths are descriptions of physical reality*" is a nonsensical statement. Yet, in a creative, practical move, igmythicism provides an opportunity to clarify—that is, to eliminate—the "ignorance" of traditional myth by suggesting a new, alternative conception of myths vis-à-vis the distinguished epistemology of knowledge claims . . . *myths* as *symbolic, human-sourced representations of physical reality*. Moreover, this new conception of myths supports a constructive theology—one centred on symbolically oriented, human-inspired projects of meaning-making, in the modern research university. Quite appropriate to the goals of igmythicism, a constructive theology is an *open-minded* and *open-ended* academic exercise—an academic theology in a dialogue with other academic disciplines, such as the natural sciences or the social sciences. Even just etymologically, a *constructive* theology suggests that theology contains a *useful*, beneficial purpose for humans. (Keep these ideas in mind; there's more to this in the following section.)

The core principles of Haack's innocent realism lend themselves well to this new science and religion discourse. As discussed, innocent realism

---

33. *Non-academic* in contrast to Wiebe's *academic* theology (Wiebe, *The Irony of Theology*, 12).

permits the *a priori* assumption that "something" exists independent from you or me, but this version of realism appears "innocent" in the sense that the "something" which exists is about the phenomenal world as perceived and constructed by *us*: how *we*—as fallible and imperfect, yet rational and sophisticated creatures—know, interpret, and construct the phenomenal world to be. Thus, from innocent realism, we get the best of both worlds: (a) we are not forced to sacrifice the cognitive values of our scientific epistemology—our explanations for human experiences and testimonies are indeed derived from observed experiences of phenomenal reality only, *and* (b) we are left still with intellectual space to identify our human experiences and testimonies within the meaning-structures of sociocultural institutions, including religions. In the style of Habermas's postmetaphysical thinking, statements of subjective, human testimonies—like moral, artistic, and emotional statements—need not be reduced to natural, causal interactions only. In accordance with our three-fold characterization to *realize, identify*, and *explain* beliefs about the physical world, *human testimonies—types of belief claims*,[34] along with their corresponding non-tested beliefs—might be explained (or be explained in the future) using tested, scientific theories about states of affairs in the physical world. Yet religious-type, human testimonies are *humanly* identified—indeed, testimonies are contextualized; are made sense of—in faith-based, sociocultural institutions. In summary, the contribution of innocent realism to my assessment of a possible compatibility system between a scientific study of religion and a religious epistemology is that subjective, human testimonies *do* have a role to play in a scientific study of religion. Inspired by innocent realism—where human beings, and their mental activities, are indeed *part of* the intersubjectively available world—human testimonies might play a role in the scientific study of religion by helping to construct a *human-inspired*, sociocultural/philosophical framework for constructive theological reflection. That is, similar in style to human-inspired myths, a *human-inspired* framework used to identify emotional and psychological contexts whereby one is *motivated* to design a religious epistemology in a modern university, or to attempt science and religion compatibility system design, etc.

My philosophical approach, then, outlined using the parameters I have stipulated, is different from yet similar to all of Wiebe's, Drees's, Stenmark's, and van Huyssteen's methodologies—which are also all different from one another. For additional clarity, I highlight these differences and similarities as follows:

34. Here, *human testimonies* could be thought of as *belief claims*: human testimonies as *belief claims* would then include non-tested beliefs as the objects of the cognitive states of testimonial claims.

- *Wiebe's* assumptions recognize the critical method of the sciences as setting an epistemic benchmark for testing beliefs, leading to Wiebe's suggestion that theology is neither a religious activity nor a scientific one, but, in a faith-based manner, *faith-imbued theology* attempts to function both religiously *and* scientifically. This contrasts with Wiebe's foundationalist "academic theology," which functions scientifically only, and thus is *ironic* as it suggests that theology can be inimical to faith-based aspirations. While my project is certainly grounded in Wiebe's arguments, concerning the nature of theology as a mode of thought in relation to modern science, my project considers how academic theology might be extended, *à la* postmetaphysical thinking, toward some practical, real-life applications by way of my igmythicist approach to myth. Like Wiebe, I bracket ontological realities for CPS-agents. However, unlike Wiebe, I consider in greater detail (applying ideas from innocent realism) the role of *human testimony* in academic theology—to provide a human-inspired framework to identify emotional and psychological motivations at play in one's academic work.

- *Drees's* assumptions, to a point, recognize the critical method of the sciences as setting a benchmark for testing beliefs (Drees is an ontological naturalist). However, in a faith-based manner, Drees allows the possibility that objects of belief be identified/located in trans-empirical worlds, rendering Drees's method a method which attempts the inclusion of both assumptions with initial plausibility and assumptions without initial plausibility. Like Drees, I function as an ontological naturalist. However, unlike Drees, my project is oriented such that, *à la* innocent realism, objects of human belief are identified in sociocultural institutions only; not in presumed trans-empirical worlds.

- *Stenmark's* assumptions allow a model of rationality specific to scientific inquiry and a different model of rationality in religious life. As argued in this book, neglecting the Popperian distinction between *knowledge* and the *"claim to* knowledge," Stenmark embraces the *tu quoque*: as his postmodernist argument goes, since rationality is about how real people live, rationality cannot exclude faith-based aspirations. Stenmark's theory of rationality, then, is faith-imbued in the sense that *a priori* it expects non-tested beliefs to be valued epistemically. Like Stenmark, I accept that rationality (generally) is about how real people[35] live. However, unlike Stenmark, *à la* pancritical rationalism, I

---

35. Here, *real people* as in those individuals who actively seek to learn from natural human experience—from testing their beliefs by way of the intersubjectively available, phenomenal, physical world, etc.

view the principles of a theory of rationality as centred on a *disengaged* worldview—in being critical of beliefs, critical of criticism itself, *and* in being self-critical, some consistency is allowed to permeate one's testing of beliefs.

- *Van Huyssteen's* assumptions recognize that theology cannot just employ reasoning strategies different from those of other academic disciplines. However, van Huyssteen's postfoundationalist model includes the suggestion that, as "problem solving" is common to all of religion, theology, and science, overlapping and shared points of contact exist between these disciplines—in a seemingly faith-based manner, one "transverses" from the tenets of one mode of thought (e.g., mythopoeic thought) to the tenets of another (e.g., scientific thought). Like van Huyssteen, I argue theology cannot just employ reasoning strategies different from those of other academic disciplines. However, unlike van Huyssteen, *à la* innocent realism, I view the activity of problem solving in a modern university as undergirded by tested beliefs in a naturalistic ontology. At the same time, *motivations* toward problem solving are supported by notions of postmetaphysical thinking, permitting statements not reducible to causal interactions only to inhabit "levels" of socially constructed realities of their own.

If the four preceding summaries point out anything (and I do hope they point out something), it is that *Scientific Models for Religious Knowledge* (the title of this book) are complicated, eclectic, and often perplexing models. Let us take up these complications in the following section.

POSSIBLE COMPLICATIONS FOR A RELIGIOUS EPISTEMOLOGY IN A MODERN UNIVERSITY SETTING—WHAT DOES THIS COMPATIBILITY SYSTEM BETWEEN A SCIENTIFIC STUDY OF RELIGION AND A RELIGIOUS EPISTEMOLOGY REALLY LOOK LIKE?

It is my sense that some objections may arise at this stage or have arisen throughout the preceding analysis. Even if not so, these hypothetical objections—as well as my replies to them—help to situate the penultimate sections of this book vis-à-vis my preceding analysis. In my context, what does "theologizing" mean—indeed, in my context, does this concept have *any* significance? For example, Ninian Smart, if he were living, might question (or be concerned about) aspects of my thesis.[36] As Smart put it, "If we assume, more generally, that there is no Ultimate, no Beyond, then we assume that religion is false. Religion, then, is a finger that points, but at nothing. There is no moon for it to point to."[37] Furthermore, others might be concerned that, in appealing to Haack's innocent realism and modestly naturalistic epistemology, I have attempted to make religion "fit" a naturalistic ontology; that in doing so I have disregarded what is, for many, the personal, existential integrity of traditional faith-based aspirations. Further still, for those who believe the continued existence of modern science is sociologically fragile, a new compatibility system between a scientific study of religion and a religious epistemology may seem like a futile idea. Here, and in chapter 10, I shall reply to all of these possible objections: my replies will serve to "bring full circle" the philosophical design of a religious epistemology, alluded to throughout this book. Until the end, we are looking toward a new compatibility system between a religious epistemology and a scientific study of religion—and what this elusive structure might look like. In addition, analyses of possible objections, and my replies to them, capture potential benefits and limitations (from various perspectives) for the proposed compatibility system along with its new religious epistemology.

A Possible Objection

In my context, what does "theologizing" mean—indeed, in my context, does "theologizing" have *any* significance?

Reply

This book includes an extension of the postmetaphysical project—our realization that potential compatibility systems are attempts to actualize some of the aims of a postsecular society. At the same time, in a disengaged theory of rationality, a scientific explanation reveals a cause for *how* a state of affairs in the physical world occurred. When applying *scientific models to religious knowledge*, then, epistemic care must be taken to ensure (i) that natural causality is not mixed with CPS-agentic causality, with supernormal aims, or with purported "higher" level truths, (ii) that experiential source material

---

36. Not that I think Smart (for example) would outright part company with my project, but, if he were living, Smart might *question* (be concerned about) some aspects of my project. In my replies to possible objections (in chapters 9 and 10), I take up these hypothetical matters.

37. Smart, *Worldviews*, 135.

is tested, and (iii) that intersubjective scrutiny is maintained. Otherwise, *no epistemic considerations are ever made* about those shared states of affairs in the physical world which are the epistemic territory of both science and religion: e.g., claims about the constitution of physical reality, the origin of human life, the naturalness or unnaturalness of LGBTI identities, free will, or the future course of one's life, etc., etc.

Notions of experientialist foundationalism aver that basic beliefs are justified by the subject's own experience, sensory or introspective. *Subjective, human testimonies*—types of *introspective* experience, because testimonies require examination of one's own emotional and psychological constitutions—are relevant to "theologizing" in the scientific study of religion. Firstly, while natural causality is strictly maintained, emotional and psychological motivations are required to contextualize and make sense of the academic questions which are pursued in the scientific study of religion. This particular application of human testimonies is, at first, wholly *a priori*: we possess *no* tested beliefs suggesting that human testimonies *should* play a role in testing other beliefs. Popper, too, was adamant that the justification and criticism of beliefs is a logical matter only, occurring apart from the emotional or psychological genesis of a belief. So, while Popper acknowledges the possibility that subjective, human factors might influence the formulation of a proposed belief, he emphasizes how those factors play no role in testing the belief; nor are there any tested beliefs suggesting that subjective, human factors should have a role to play in the methodological process of testing in general.

Secondly, similar to Haack's modest departure from epistemology as wholly *a priori*, my application of human testimonies—to contextualize and make sense of academic questions pursued (in the scientific study of religion)—includes a modest departure from human testimonies as wholly *a priori*.[38] So, my application of subjective, human testimonies is not such that the sciences of cognition cannot also provide options for how these

---

38. Modest, methodological departures from *human testimonies* or *academic disciplines* classified as forms of *traditionalist apriorism* include modest departures from traditionally *a priori* academic disciplines such as epistemology or theology, or, a modest departure from *a priori* subjective, human testimonies. As outlined, *modest departures* refer to the fact that the sciences of cognition influence our perception and application of *a priori* human testimonies and/or academic disciplines: So, while we refrain from repudiating categories of *a priori* human testimonies or *a priori* academic disciplines altogether, I argue we implement two-way philosophical dialogues between *a priori* human testimonies and science and/or *a priori* academic disciplines and science. Similarly, in postmetaphysical thinking, two-way dialogues between scientific statements and those moral, religious, artistic, or emotional statements not reducible to natural, causal interactions only.

human testimonies are realized, identified, or explained. Rather, scientific theories from cognitive science of religion provide opportunities for us to make *informed*, conscious efforts (a) to explain—in this case, to explain *religious testimonies* centred on the *actions of CPS-agents*; and (b) to point out how testimonies are realized physiologically and/or psychologically by our evolved human species. From here, cognitive science of religion also helps suggest how testimonies about objects of belief might be identified in sociocultural institutions. The point about sociocultural institutions is that, as cognitive science of religion (a) explains CPS-agent-based testimonies by way of the HADD and (b) points out how CPS-agent-based testimonies are realized physiologically through a maturationally natural cognitive system, options to identify objects of belief in trans-empirical worlds become *less plausible*.[39] However, in light of the possibility of a natural explanation by way of the HADD and an awareness of a physiological realization by way of a maturationally natural cognitive system, the *identification* of objects of belief in sociocultural institutions is a *plausible alternative*.

In terms of "theologizing," then, I present a new, alternative conception of twenty-first-century theology—a *constructive theology* centred on the following three characteristics:

1. Objects of non-tested beliefs *realized* physiologically through a maturationally natural cognitive system.

2. Objects of non-tested beliefs *identified* (*located*) in sociocultural institutions, including religions.

3. Objects of non-tested beliefs (e.g., CPS-agents) that we attempt to *explain* by way of the HADD.[40] Or, *testimonies about* these objects of non-tested beliefs that we attempt to explain.

---

39. That, by way of the HADD and a maturationally natural cognitive system, it becomes less plausible to identify objects of belief in purported trans-empirical worlds, refers to the fact that, in a naturalistic ontology, one's substantive assumptions already do not include assumptions that trans-empirical worlds are ontological realities. Moreover, when employing scientific theories such as the HADD and a maturationally natural cognitive system in one's framework, it would be intellectually inconsistent to suddenly include trans-empirical worlds in a pre-established framework centred already on intersubjectively observed experiences of phenomenal reality only.

40. Here I say *attempt to explain by way of the HADD*, because, while the HADD does explain one's proclivity toward detecting apparent agents in the natural world, the HADD does not demonstrate an explicit causal connection between what the HADD apparently "detects" *and* the specific cultural construct of "God." Nevertheless, the scientific theory of the HADD does explain proclivity toward detecting agency, in general, in the natural world.

Notice that my framework in entirely *natural*: trans-empirical worlds are never directly included; CPS-agents never invoked. Yet, at the same time, *à la* postmetaphysical thinking, my framework is not dismissive of *a priori* subjective, human testimonies altogether—just as Haack's modestly naturalistic epistemology is not dismissive of *a priori* epistemology altogether, but situates a science-influenced epistemology vis-à-vis the complex, eclectic web of all other human knowledges and beliefs. Similarly, we are now contemplating the possibility of science-influenced human testimonies—amounting to a new, academically more fruitful, constructive theology—vis-à-vis the complex, eclectic web of all other human knowledges and beliefs.

About the *meaning-making*, which occurs in this new conception of twenty-first-century, constructive "theologizing," Smart's separation of religious "brute" facts from human products directed us toward the influence that myths continue to have on perceptions and mental states of humans who live in the modern world (as testimonies of religious devotees informed us). As discussed in chapter 4, if the physical world is not really subjectivized at all, then myths must be entirely human creations (projected onto a neutral, physical world) whose origins must be either mere delusions, or, alternatively, reflections of what is an ontological reality for the gods. From these two contrasting positions, I proposed what I called the igmythicist approach to myths—whereby myths are newly conceived as *symbolic, human-sourced representations of physical reality*. As Smart also pointed out, the myth-maker picks out contingent features of the universe and then arranges those features in a particular symbolic fashion.[41] Thus, what is most important is the role myths play—i.e., mythopoesis—in formulating a symbolic reality for the religious observer. That being said, Smart's concern with my project (if he were living) might be that my proposal of meaning-making in the twenty-first-century scientific cosmos does not require a metaphysical "ultimate," a metaphysical "beyond"—in short, does not depend on the assumption that trans-empirical worlds *are* ontological realities. For Smart, this might amount to the inappropriate presupposition that religion is false (although Smart does not assume religion is necessarily true, either).[42]

Smart's hypothetical concern with my project would be centred on the presupposition that *prima facie* religion requires a metaphysical reality to which religion (on the physical earth) corresponds. With this presupposition included, no doubt my project cannot be seen to "point" to a metaphysical "ultimate." In response to this possible objection, in terms of my arguments about CPS-agents rendered institutional facts and compatibility systems

---

41. Smart, *The Science of Religion*, 79.
42. Smart, *Worldviews*, 135.

Designing a New Religious Epistemology for a Scientific Study of Religion 181

rendering the symbol element of a myth as *social* rather than substantive, it is my contention that there really are no compelling motives to uphold the *prima facie* assumption that religion requires a metaphysical reality to which religion corresponds.[43] (Just as I see no compelling reasons to make the *prima facie* assumption that statements of science must correspond in a foolproof manner with the truth of the external, physical world.) Instead, with CPS-agents rendered institutional facts, and in light of subjective, human testimonies about superhuman agents (which continue to permeate modern societies), the so-called "ultimate," to which religion corresponds, is related to the *collective and social recognition of the existence of CPS-agents in the natural world*. Again, as argued in chapter 4, the existence of CPS-agents is reported in a collective fashion: from testimonies of religious devotees, we find a collective recognition of the existence of CPS-agents. Likewise, Berger and his colleagues were drawn to study the phenomenon of religion as a human enterprise, one that originates from the products of collective human activity and human consciousness. In a sense, *a scientific study of religion becomes a scientific study of collective human activity and consciousness—a scientific study of the human condition*. Finally, what is so useful about current scientific theories, like the *HADD* and a *maturationally natural cognitive system*, is that these scientific theories help to explain *how* there is a collective and social recognition of the existence of CPS-agents in the natural world. Finally, informed by Haack's innocent realism, these (possible) scientific explanations need not erase all *meaning* or *social significance* from natural human experiences and testimonies. As we've considered, innocent realism inspires us to develop a sort of philosophical framework which identifies and locates human experiences and testimonies within the meaning-structures of sociocultural, religious institutions. In other words, we are developing a sort of compatibility system between a scientific study of religion and a religious epistemology—which, in actuality, could amount to a compatibility system between a scientific study of the human condition and a *human-inspired*, religious epistemology. (More to this in chapter 10!)

~

---

43. Indeed, it could be argued that this presupposition—that *prima facie* religion requires a metaphysical reality to which religion corresponds—is what has caused much of the science and religion debate over the past 150 years in particular. Forgoing this *prima facie* assumption (which does not possess a very high initial plausibility anyway) does not necessarily dismiss faith-based, religious motivations, but recasts the science and religion problem in a new, alternative perspective—a new constructive theology in the modern scientific cosmos—as presented in this book.

At this juncture, I anticipate two upcoming, *potential* pathways—*Pathway #1* or *Pathway #2*—that readers might be drawn to follow: In what follows, *Pathway #1* might help to reduce or even eliminate the existential tension or angst felt because of Smart's hypothetical concern with my project. Readers who find themselves objecting in the same manner that Smart might object will likely be drawn to *Pathway #1*—which delves into J. L. Schellenberg's concept called *ultimism*. In what follows in *Pathway #2*, one continues moving forward with an analysis which continues to methodologically bracket ontological realities for trans-empirical worlds. *Pathway #2* explores the possibility of an alternative religious life along with our new constructive theology, contextualized (exclusively) in the sociocultural world of natural human experience—what might be called an *inductive faith* in *Pathway #2*. In the following pages, in chapter 10, I try to provide some attention to both *Pathway #1* and *Pathway #2*, attempting to deal with what readers might perceive to be the benefits and/or limitations of each pathway. For some readers, both pathways might even intermingle together; however, my primary motivation here is that, with Smart's hypothetical concern in mind, we now have two pathways to consider—two potential solutions to the objection that my project (thus far) cannot be seen to "point" to a metaphysical "ultimate" or "beyond."

10

What about the "Beyond"?
Two Pathways Moving Ahead: Ultimism and an Inductive Faith

PATHWAY #1: ULTIMISM POINTS TO THE METAPHYSICAL "BEYOND"—PROBLEM SOLVED!

J. L. SCHELLENBERG'S PROPOSAL for an *evolutionary religious thought* is an interesting contribution to contemporary philosophy of religion—especially because his proposal already exists outside of the cultural baggage of sectarian religions. However, in one important respect, Schellenberg's scientifically non-tested proposition, known as *ultimism*, which undergirds his evolutionary religious thought, is still "traditional" in the sense that ultimism is entirely *a priori*. Moreover, since ultimism's specific details, e.g., its cultural trappings, are not clear, ultimism exists *a priori* on its own, without any substantive contributions from the natural or social sciences. The curious manner in which ultimism is different from sectarian religions, yet also "traditional" at its "religious" core, is best summed up by Schellenberg in the following statement:

> Ultimism is a broader idea than theism (though, like it, opposed to philosophical naturalism), referring quite generally to the accessibility of an ultimate good springing from something ultimate in reality and value, rather than specifically to salvation found in a personal relationship with a perfect creator who loves

us like a parent, or to any other extant religious details. Given its breadth and our immaturity, we must admit that ultimism may well be true, even if we think that many existing attempts to fill it out, including traditional theism, are provably false. (In part this is because many *other* detailed ways of filling it out may well remain undiscovered.)[1]

Schellenberg argues that ultimism, like traditional theism, is opposed to philosophical naturalism:[2] Is ultimism, though, in an epistemic dialogue with some *versions* of naturalism? Is ultimism, like igmythicism, compatible with a modest naturalism—compatible with a modestly naturalistic epistemology? Given the information contained in the preceding quotation, it would seem the answer to these questions is that ultimism is not compatible even with a modestly naturalistic epistemology like Haack's. However, what ultimism provides is a possible solution to the concern that Western society requires a metaphysical "ultimate" to which religion (on the physical earth) corresponds. Let us look into this possible solution.

In *The Wisdom to Doubt: A Justification of Religious Skepticism* (2007), Schellenberg maintains that natural reason requires us to be skeptical about traditional religion[3]—but also skeptical about typical disbelief in religion, too.[4] As Schellenberg puts it, "According to a religious disbeliever, *no* religious claim, that is, no claim entailing that there is an ultimate salvific reality, is true. That is how a religious disbeliever sees the world."[5] Unlike most "skeptics," Schellenberg wishes to avoid absolutist claims about absolute disbelief in religion. In a supportive manner, looking ahead to new forms of religious thinking, Schellenberg encourages us to think about new possibilities for a future religious life, through the lens of a diachronic conception of religion.[6] In a diachronic conception of religion, religious attitudes are fluid, spread out over time, rather than with a synchronic conception of religion,[7] where religious attitudes are static, fixed at a single moment in time. (In fact, Schellenberg's diachronic conception of religion will be quite important to my development of an inductive faith in *Pathway #2*.) *In summary, Schellenberg encourages us to ask whether we have even come close to encompassing all of the alternatives for what a future sociocultural, religious*

1. Schellenberg, "Philosophy of Religion," 105.
2. Schellenberg, "Philosophy of Religion," 105.
3. Schellenberg, *The Wisdom to Doubt*, 1, Kindle.
4. Schellenberg, *The Wisdom to Doubt*, 2, Kindle.
5. Schellenberg, *The Wisdom to Doubt*, 2, Kindle.
6. Schellenberg, *Evolutionary Religion*, 53.
7. Schellenberg, *Evolutionary Religion*, 53.

*life might look like?*⁸ So, without wishing to put an end to one's religious investigation into possible, future religious modes of thought (which would put an end to ultimism), Schellenberg remarks, "If our concern is not just for *an* understanding but for *understanding*, then we will resist the temptation to foreclose such investigation."⁹ Schellenberg appears to speak about a complete and overall understanding of the physical world, and, probably, an overall understanding of all of what reality *might* encompass, including possible trans-empirical worlds.¹⁰ In this fashion, Schellenberg's methodology, as it pertains to ultimism, does not only *not* bracket an ontological reality for ultimism, but also keeps itself open to the possibility that a complete understanding of all of what reality might encompass could include some understanding about an ontological reality for ultimism. In this scheme, then, maybe religion on earth, after all, "points" to a metaphysical "beyond" (*maybe*).

Concerning possible belief about ultimism, mentally experiencing an involuntary, non-tested belief about ultimism would affirm ultimism (for the ultimistic believer). Conversely, mentally experiencing disbelief about ultimism would deny ultimism (for the ultimistic disbeliever).¹¹ Schellenberg argues that neither of those options—neither religious belief nor religious disbelief—seem rationally justified. So, with this epistemic complication in mind, and with a current lack of other options, Schellenberg calls for a new, *belief-less* form of evolutionary religion—one more appropriate to our current moment in time.¹² Also, he argues, a form of evolutionary religion compatible with natural reason and compatible with our current lack of evidence for non-tested, religious beliefs. Moving toward a belief-less form of evolutionary religion, two important philosophical shifts occur in Schellenberg's evolutionary religious thought:¹³ (i) a shift from involuntary belief to voluntary faith, and (ii) a shift from theism to ultimism as the object of a voluntary, imaginative faith. With these two philosophical shifts

---

8. Schellenberg, *Evolutionary Religion*, 50–51.

9. Schellenberg, *The Wisdom to Doubt*, 144, Kindle.

10. Note that, in this context, complete and overall understanding does not seem to refer to a so-called non-gnostic conception of *understanding*—i.e., *understanding* as requiring tested, empirical beliefs and evidence. Rather, complete and overall understanding here seems to imply a religious connotation for understanding—that complete and overall understanding would potentially require more than tested beliefs only or not even require any tested beliefs at all (for advocates of this religious conception of understanding).

11. Schellenberg, *The Wisdom to Doubt*, 2, Kindle.

12. Schellenberg, *Evolutionary Religion*, 82.

13. Schellenberg, *The Will to Imagine*, 14, Kindle.

complete, what ultimism exactly is, and how a faith response to ultimism could be practically applied in one's life, become more apparent, outlined in the following paragraph.

In *The Will to Imagine: A Justification of Skeptical Religion* (2009), Schellenberg describes, practically, what a voluntary assent to his ultimism would look like: In the pursuit of a religious goal, a faith directed toward a religious goal—called an operational faith[14]—might act on a propositional belief or on a propositional faith. When operational faith acts on a propositional faith—on a "faith *that* . . ."—the propositional faith, on which operational faith acts, could be a *belief-less* propositional faith. In this case, as Schellenberg's argument goes, when an operational faith acts on a belief-less propositional faith, the result is an individual who mentally endorses an *imagined representation* about the physical world: a propositional, faith-based response to ultimism—a voluntary assent to ultimism.[15] About this, Schellenberg notes:

> What ultimistic religion means, one might say, is lending one's imagination and will to this possibility of a religious dimension to life. And if you do so, and if more transcendent experiences result, and if in them you are indeed objectively related to the Ultimate, then even if at the time you remain uncertain as to whether that's so (as you must if your state is one of [imaginative] faith instead of belief), the value of your life has surely been increased.[16]

The *imaginative* element[17] of one's faith-based response to ultimism is indeed curious: followers of ultimism, in a way, are *skeptics who adopt an imaginative faith response to ultimism*, but who nevertheless remain skeptical about ultimism.[18] Followers of ultimism cannot know how the physical

---

14. Schellenberg, *The Will to Imagine*, 2, Kindle.
15. Schellenberg, *The Will to Imagine*, 2, Kindle.
16. Schellenberg, *The Will to Imagine*, 180, Kindle.
17. Schellenberg, *The Will to Imagine*, 77, Kindle.
18. As outlined, when an operational faith acts on a belief-less propositional faith, what we might experience is a voluntary, faith-based response to ultimism—the religious goal in this new, alternative religious approach. In Schellenberg's thesis, then, an imaginative faith response to ultimism presents itself as a new religious attitude, capable of being analyzed alongside other typical believing, disbelieving, and purely skeptical worldviews (Schellenberg 2009, 2, Kindle). As Schellenberg sees it, in the purely skeptical worldview referenced here, one would adopt the view that there is no good evidence available to support neither involuntary belief about ultimism, nor its denial, but in this case one would also experience no imaginative faith response to ultimism. Ironically, followers of ultimism, in a way, are *skeptics who adopt an imaginative faith response to ultimism*, but who nevertheless remain skeptical about ultimism—just

world is in terms of ultimism; they cannot know if the tenets of ultimism accurately describe the physical world—whether ultimism is a brute fact, or not. However, more to the point of Schellenberg's thesis about ultimism, followers of ultimism can *imagine* that ultimism accurately describes the physical world—and then voluntarily assent to that possibility.[19]

Furthermore, about a still culturally unspecific, simple ultimism, Schellenberg notes, "One who has faith of this sort, while recognizing that religious belief is unjustified [that non-tested, religious beliefs are unjustified], voluntarily assents to simple ultimism alone (propositional faith) and acts on her assent (operational faith), seeking to do what it is appropriate to do given the truth of that claim [given the perceived truth of simple ultimism]."[20] Despite its culturally unspecific form, Schellenberg suggests the tenets of ultimism form a kind of *triple transcendence* which followers of ultimism can make some substantive assumptions about.[21] Schellenberg theorizes (assumes) that ultimism includes the following ontological pieces: (i) a *metaphysically* ultimate reality, which is the deepest fact about the physical world and all of reality (whatever "all of reality" is); (ii) an *axiologically* ultimate reality, which is a collection of the greatest possible existential values of human life (e.g., values of splendour or excellence); and (iii) a *soteriologically* ultimate reality, which is, for humans, the greatest possible good, well-being, and wholeness in life—*beyond what nature alone could provide*.[22] (Thus, a soteriologically ultimate reality is certainly not compatible even with a modest naturalism like Haack's.)

What does *Pathway #1* look like? To start, *Pathway #1* helps to reduce and perhaps, for some, even eliminate the existential angst felt because of Smart's hypothetical concern with my project. But, would *Pathway #1* really work for you? For example, if you are reading this book as a Christian, or a Muslim, or a Jew, or a Buddhist, or a Hindu, or a Confucianist, or maybe a Spiritualist who holds séances, does *Pathway #1* really work for you? If you do identify with one of the preceding labels, my guess is that, at first glance, *Pathway #1* doesn't really work for you, but I still think you might like to read a bit further. Similarly, if you are reading this book as an atheist or an agnostic, does *Pathway #1* really work for you? Again, if you do identify with one of the two preceding labels, my guess is that, at first glance,

---

not purely skeptical. So, while still being skeptical about ultimism, followers of ultimism can imagine that ultimism accurately describes the physical world—and then voluntarily assent to that possibility.

19. Schellenberg, *The Will to Imagine*, 77, Kindle.
20. Schellenberg, *The Will to Imagine*, 16, Kindle.
21. Schellenberg, *Evolutionary Religion*, 94.
22. Schellenberg, *Evolutionary Religion*, 94.

Pathway #1 doesn't really work for you, but I still think you might like to read a bit further.

Religiously minded individuals could be forgiven for thinking that ultimism doesn't really fulfill their personal requirements when it comes to belief about a real-life, metaphysical "beyond" (no offense to Schellenberg's concept of ultimism intended). After all, ultimism, thus far conceived, is a culturally unspecific, non-detailed description of a metaphysical "beyond"—one that doesn't even presume the cultural trappings of theism, where a personal CPS-agent (e.g., a personal god) would be included in one's own belief system. At the same time, atheists and agnostics are probably left wondering if ultimism is supposing *too much* about whatever a metaphysical "beyond" might be, or wondering if ultimism is supposing, inappropriately, that a metaphysical "beyond" is an ontological reality. Agnostics, in particular, seem to prefer to hold off on any personal, non-scientific answers about what a metaphysical "beyond" is or isn't; however, ultimism *is* suggesting a personal, non-scientific answer to the specific nature of a metaphysical "beyond," albeit a culturally unspecific answer. What *Pathway #1* looks like in terms of either its metaphysical nature, its perceived ontological components, or its possibilities for a new, alternative religious life, is fairly self-explanatory from Schellenberg's presentation of ultimism (which I summarized in the preceding pages). In other words, about ultimism—construed as a possible answer to the dilemma that Western society requires a metaphysical "ultimate" to which religion corresponds—I really can't say anymore. In short, in *Pathway #1*, ultimism points to the metaphysical "beyond" that Western society seems to require—problem solved! However, in the following paragraphs, I shall consider briefly how ultimism could engage itself more explicitly with some substantive contributions from the natural or social sciences—this approach would support the aims of the particular constructive theology envisioned in this book.

As presented, Schellenberg's *a priori* ultimism is epistemically and practically incompatible with general philosophical naturalism,[23] thereby (it would seem) also incompatible with tested beliefs from modern science. While it is the case that ultimism is culturally unspecific (free from the constraints of current sectarian religions), so long as ultimism remains wholly *a priori*, we have no ground rules—no cultural bearings, as it were—for deciding the cultural direction(s) in which any future religious life, centred on ultimism, could go. Wholly *a priori* ultimism, with no substantive contributions from the natural or social sciences, could be too disorienting—too vulnerable to the wrong kinds of cultural conditioning. To put it bluntly, if

---

23. Schellenberg, "Philosophy of Religion," 105.

all that is required to adopt an imaginative faith response to ultimism is to adopt an imaginative faith response to ultimism's triple transcendence—and then to acknowledge that, from there, unlimited religious ways of life centred on ultimism are possible—what would prevent the formulation of culturally inappropriate instantiations of ultimism? To be specific, what would prevent the formulation of ideological, religious ways of life, centred on ultimism, *which are also centred on inappropriate cultural values*, such as, say, sexism or homophobia? Obviously, it's not that ultimism as presented thus far promotes culturally inappropriate worldviews, but it's a dangerous world: what would prevent someone else, or some other social institution, from arguing that, since ultimism is culturally unspecific, ultimism is open for appropriation toward the metaphysical development of just *any* worldview?[24] (I suppose the same concern could be applied to agnosticism and atheism, too, but at least these worldviews, being as they are (ideally) in dialogue with the intersubjectively available natural or social sciences, can try to avoid appropriation toward inappropriate cultural values.)

The argument here—important to *Pathway #1*—is a fine one: Ultimism is not a bad solution—indeed, we are very much indebted to Schellenberg for pointing us toward this unique solution, free from current sectarian religious baggage (which is so liberating). However, ultimism construed so far as wholly *a priori*, requires, I argue, some intersubjectively available *ground rules* arising from within the sociocultural world of natural human experience. That is, ultimism requires some substantive contributions from the natural or social sciences, provided the natural or social sciences are intersubjectively available enterprises. Thus, a *science-influenced ultimism*, in a two-way dialogue with an *ultimism-influenced science*, would situate ultimism within the wider academic context of a scientific epistemology while also preserving the triple transcendence which undergirds ultimism. If my arguments in this book have been clear, you will notice that once again I am returning (for philosophical inspiration) to Haack's model of a modestly naturalistic epistemology—to her proposed dialogue (in her book *Evidence and Inquiry*) between a *science-influenced epistemology* and an *epistemology-influenced science*. (This was the same philosophical model which I applied

---

24. Similarly, typical theistic religions, such as, say, Christianity or Islam, when conceived as wholly *a priori*, have been vastly interpreted, misinterpreted, and then misappropriated in all kinds of various ways. Nothing stops some social institutions from arguing that Christianity or Islam support culturally inappropriate values; likewise I am concerned that ultimism as wholly *a priori* could fall victim to the same fate. A *science-influenced ultimism*, in a two-way philosophical dialogue with an *ultimism-influenced science*, could help address this concern.

previously to formulate my two-way dialogue between *science-influenced human testimony* and *human-testimony-influenced science*!)

Now, in Pathway #1, such a two-way dialogue, between *science-influenced ultimism* and *ultimism-influenced science*, would *not* be modestly naturalistic—instead, it would be a sort of ontological blend of naturalistic elements from science with *transcendent* components from ultimism. However, in this two-way dialogue, since both science and ultimism would be in philosophical conversation with the other, *neither one would be completely immune from having to be aware of the other's substantive contributions toward the new religious life being proposed*. In this fashion, tested beliefs from the natural sciences might explain states of affairs in the physical world. Moreover, in the social sciences, the culturally conditioned responses, that in modern society no one's rights be infringed and no one be harmed, would also be promoted. Then, at the same time, ultimism's triple transcendence would come into play—providing to the dialogue (between science and ultimism) some ultimistically attuned ideas about, say, the greatest possible existential values for human life (e.g., values of splendour or excellence), or, say, some ultimistic suggestions about how humans might achieve the greatest possible good, well-being, or wholeness in life.

About ultimism providing metaphysical information about the deepest fact about the physical world and all of reality, I have my reservations about whether that task really belongs to ultimism *or*, rather, belongs to the epistemic territory of the tested beliefs of science. It is the case that tested beliefs in science already attempt to uncover information about the deepest fact(s) about the physical world. However, since tested beliefs from science are focused on facts about the physical world only, in a two-way dialogue between *science-influenced ultimism* and *ultimism-influenced science*, I suppose that, for the ultimistically inclined individual, ultimism, too, could make a metaphysical contribution toward uncovering the deepest fact(s) about all of reality, assuming that "all of reality" is meant to include both the physical world *as well as* possible trans-empirical worlds—in this case, possible ultimistic worlds.

The preceding sketch completes our look into *Pathway #1*—a possible solution to the concern that society requires a metaphysical "beyond" to which religion corresponds. Although ultimism (developed by Schellenberg) is culturally unspecific, and so may not appeal to theistically inclined individuals, and although ultimism makes substantive assumptions about a triple transcendence, and so may not appeal to atheistically inclined or agnostically inclined individuals, ultimism, to use Smart's metaphor,[25] could

---

25. Smart, *Worldviews*, 135.

direct us to the "moon," which religion on earth is supposed to correspond with. Moreover, the new religious life envisioned by ultimism might be academically supported by a *science-influenced ultimism* in conversation with an *ultimism-influenced science*. Ultimism as wholly *a priori* just seems too vulnerable to the wrong kinds of cultural conditioning—just as, say, Christianity or Islam as wholly *a priori* have been so vastly interpreted, *misinterpreted*, and then misappropriated in all kinds of various ways. Yet if ultimism could acknowledge some intersubjectively available, substantive contributions from the natural or social sciences, and if the natural and social sciences could acknowledge possible substantive contributions from ultimism's triple transcendence, then there is a new, attractive possibility vis-à-vis ultimism: A new religious life—centred on both ultimism *and* modern science—could help to reduce and perhaps eliminate any existential angst felt because my project (thus far) has not explicitly pointed to a metaphysical "ultimate." As stated, in *Pathway #1*, ultimism points to the metaphysical "beyond" that Western society requires—problem solved!

Moving ahead, *Pathway #2* will take us in a different direction, but one that is more in keeping with the particular assumptions and methodological approach that I have employed throughout this book. Readers will have to decide for themselves how the following *Pathway #2* compares or contrasts with *Pathway #1*, and which pathway they themselves prefer. In what follows, igmythicism returns too, since igmythicism *is* the methodological means through which our new constructive theology gets to be realized, articulated, and enjoyed. Without delay, enter *Pathway #2*.

PATHWAY #2: THE "BEYOND" IS A SOCIOCULTURAL OUTCOME OF AN INDUCTIVE FAITH—BUT A HIGHLY VALUABLE OUTCOME!

Peter Berger, whose analysis of the empirically observable and researchable phenomenon of religion has been useful to us thus far, returns now in this chapter with his compelling thesis of an *inductive faith*[26]—an intriguing idea that helps to solidify and support possible outcomes of my (still nascent but evolving) igmythicism. Some initial orientation on Berger's inductive faith needs to be sketched. As mentioned in chapter 1, I take *faith* generally to be a *life stance*, centred on one's own sociocultural environment, including one's subjective background experiences and/or future life goals. Also, as mentioned, in this book, when I speak about a physical or social reality as *faith-*

---

26. Berger, *A Rumor of Angels*, 57.

imbued, I am speaking about a physical or social reality which is conceived and interpreted under the auspices of one's sociocultural environment, including one's subjective background experiences and/or future life goals. For some, this will amount to the auspices of a typically religious worldview (including whatever background experiences and/or future life goals contribute to and perpetuate that religious worldview). For others, interpreting a physical or social reality as *faith-imbued* might amount to interpreting those realities through the lens of an alternative, postmetaphysical mode of thought—one that is not traditionally religious, but nevertheless one that is *interpretive*, often drawing on one's private emotional and psychological constitutions. Most generally, then, *faith* refers to any life stance which, in a non-scientific fashion, contributes to and buttresses one's conceptions of physical and social realities.

So far as I am aware, Berger's *inductive faith* is unique among philosophical and theological schools of thought. Using the empirically observable phenomenon of religion and the language of *observable* as his departure points, Berger contends, "In the *observable* human propensity to order reality, there is an intrinsic impulse to give cosmic scope to this order, an impulse that implies not only that human order in some way corresponds to an order that transcends it, but that this transcendent order is of such a character that man can trust himself and his destiny to it."[27] Following Berger's argument, the observable phenomenon of what seems to be humans' *intrinsic impulse* to find order—to find and maintain an ordered, meaningful existence, in spite of natural chaos—is a signal of transcendence.[28] However, important in my analysis, a signal of transcendence as transcendence *is understood by* the individual reporting the experience of a cosmic order—transcendence in the *mindset* of the reporting individual. In my analysis, then, a signal of a *perceived transcendence*, of a perceived cosmic order. I admit it is perplexing to me that Berger does not seem to resolve this issue in a way consistent with his own promotion of a methodological atheism about the ontological statuses of religious concepts: A *transcendent, cosmic order* refers to a trans-empirical world; for Berger to speak of signals of any trans-empirical world is odd, given especially that trans-empirical worlds are neither empirically observable nor researchable phenomena. Granted, one might contend that what Berger is really concerned about are the *signals of*, not the reported *transcendent, cosmic order* itself. If this is indeed the case—and I propose it is—some unpacking of what these signals *actually are* will be required.

---

27. Berger, *A Rumor of Angels*, 56; emphasis added.
28. Berger, *A Rumor of Angels*, 57.

As we shall soon see, Berger's *inductive faith* and his perplexing *signals* are intimately connected.

As the philosophical term *inductive* suggests, *inductive faith*[29] begins—and, in some sense, *ends*—in the sociocultural world of *natural human experience*. Whether inductive faith "points" to, or is the reflection of, an independent, superhuman reality is a methodological issue that we cannot resolve. However, as Berger notes, for the individual who publicly reports a private experience of a transcendent, cosmic order, inductive faith is "the ultimately true vindication of human order."[30] Indeed, what is important is that, *in the mindset* of the reporting individual and thus *for that individual*, inductive faith *is* a *reflection* of an independent, superhuman reality, reported to be "on display" in the phenomenal, physical world.

However, reassuringly for you and me, Berger's conception of his signals does rely on an empirically observable phenomenon—specifically, what appears to be humans' *ludic constitution*, a sociologically researchable human behaviour. Drawing on the interesting work of cultural theorist, Johan Huizinga, in *Homo Ludens: A Study of the Play-Element in Culture* (1955),[31] Berger's *argument from play*,[32] as he calls it, brings to our attention the seemingly ludic element—i.e., *playful* element—existing innately in the mental constitutions of humans. In Berger's thesis of signals, this innate element of *human play* is thought to help to construct an *enclave* of *meaning* in the social world of everyday human life, whether a play whose qualities are perceived as "joyful" or sometimes as "painful." In this instance, Berger's conception of *human play* (by way of Huizinga's work) provides a framework to intimate how a perceived transcendent, cosmic order can momentarily be thought to exist outside the natural, "serious" world (a.k.a. outside the physical world). Moreover, how such a transcendent, cosmic order can be perceived to be temporally distinct—perhaps even perceived to be ontologically distinct—from the natural, "serious" world.[33] For example, with human experiences perceived as "joyful," about this temporary suspending of the (sometimes frightening) natural, "serious" world, Berger remarks, "It is this curious quality, which belongs to all joyful play, that explains the liberation and peace such play provides. In early childhood, of course, the suspension is unconscious, since there is as yet no consciousness of death. In later life

---

29. Berger, *A Rumor of Angels*, 57.
30. Berger, *A Rumor of Angels*, 57.
31. Huizinga, *Homo Ludens*, 1.
32. Berger, *A Rumor of Angels*, 57.
33. Berger, *A Rumor of Angels*, 58.

play brings about a beatific reiteration of childhood."[34] Furthermore, inductive faith, being outsourced from the world of natural human experience, "does not rest on a mysterious revelation, but rather on *what we experience in our common, ordinary lives*."[35] Consequently, then, the human realization of joyful play, experienced in common, ordinary life, could be perceived to be a signal of transcendence—again, a signal of transcendence as transcendence is understood by the individual reporting the experience of joyful play. Still, any reported experiences of transcendence, Berger reminds us, cannot be empirically tested.[36] However, sociologically researchable signals (of a perceived transcendence) in the natural world contribute to the *source material* for an inductive faith. Along with human play, in Berger's scheme, additional human gestures—e.g., perceived qualities of *order, hope, humour*; even *horrors* and *expressions of damnation*[37]—also serve as signals of a perceived transcendence; serving, too, as source material for an inductive faith.

Human experiences collectively identified as *joyful, orderly, hopeful*, or even *horror-stricken*, etc., could also be seen as pointing to (or psychologically supporting) the sociocultural reality of CPS-agents—supporting the notion that CPS-agents are *institutional facts* (to use Searle's terminology), considered already in chapter 4. At any rate, so-called signals of transcendence are pointers to a religious interpretation of the human condition.[38] In this book, a religious interpretation of the human condition as contemporary religious life is recontextualized in a modestly naturalistic epistemology. Overall, Berger encourages us to look toward regaining an appropriate metaphysical perception of these everyday human experiences[39]—a *new* metaphysics for these so-called signals of transcendence—*rooted in* the everyday experiential content of an inductive faith. What we need to do, then, is to create a new metaphysical option: *In this book, a new metaphysics for contemporary religious life and for our new constructive theology—a new metaphysics made possible through igmythicism as well as situated in terms of a modest naturalism*.

We no longer can just accept the two usual, polarized choices of theism or scientistic naturalism. So, our new metaphysical choice cannot fall victim (i) to traditional, *a priori* theism, which maintains that CPS-agents are ontological realities, or (ii) to a radical, scientistic naturalism, which would

---

34. Berger, *A Rumor of Angels*, 59.
35. Berger, *A Rumor of Angels*, 60; emphasis added.
36. Berger, *A Rumor of Angels*, 60.
37. Berger, *A Rumor of Angels*, 60–72.
38. Berger, *A Rumor of Angels*, 62.
39. Berger, *A Rumor of Angels*, 75.

turn the typical questions of *a priori* theology over to cognitive science and evolutionary psychology to attempt to resolve completely. In our new metaphysical option (made possible through igmythicism), the existential integrity of faith-based aspirations is preserved, but is recast in new lights. That "integrity" is now *emotional* and *psychological*—that is, the existential integrity of one's subjective faith is reconfigured in emotional and psychological terms, including my proposal of commonsense, human-sourced myths and beliefs, also by way of igmythicism. Moreover, these igmythicistic maneuvers support our constructive theology—an open-ended exercise where an academic theology participates in a philosophical dialogue with other academic disciplines, such as the natural sciences or social sciences. As mentioned previously, even just etymologically, a *constructive* theology suggests that theology contains a *useful*, beneficial purpose for humans. For example, the particular constructive theology proposed here (again, made possible through igmythicism) recognizes the need for social solidarity with others, but this time, provocatively, *without* the need to theorize or assume that CPS-agents are ontological realities.

What does *Pathway #2* look like? Well, for one, with any type of inductive reasoning, we see an attempt to derive "stronger" conclusions from "weaker" premises. This is the temptation in *Pathway #2*. As David Stove succinctly puts it, "In an inductive argument, the premises are simply reports of something which has been (or could have been) observed; *the conclusion is a contingent proposition about what has not been (and perhaps could not be) observed.*"[40] Following Berger's lead, we have sociologically (and intersubjectively!) observed signals of joy, order, or hope, etc., in the sociocultural world of natural human experience. What we have *not* observed—and perhaps cannot ever observe—is a perceived trans-empirical "beyond." So we *cannot* make a shift, inductively, from the sociologically observed *signals of* to the unobserved conclusion that a perceived trans-empirical "beyond" is an ontological reality (thought to correspond with the signals). A temptation with *Pathway #2* might be to think of *Pathway #2* as really providing us with more information than it can provide. For example, thinking that Berger's signals really are providing us with metaphysical information about an ontological reality for a perceived transcendent order. However, as inductive faith begins, and also really *ends*, in the world of natural human experience, our premises for an inductive faith—our sociologically researchable signals—are all that we have to work with. Any attempt to derive "stronger" conclusions from these modest premises would be a traditionally

---

40. Stove, *Scientific Irrationalism*, 111–12; emphasis added.

faith-based activity—but one that doesn't need to take place for the merits of *Pathway #2* to really shine through.

Though, to be sure, for some, this would also be the limitation of *Pathway #2*: Since it is the case that, with an inductive faith, ontological realities for trans-empirical worlds and CPS-agents remain bracketed, those with traditional religious proclivities might not really know where to even begin to get their "religious" or "spiritual" bearings from, should they decide to try out an inductive faith. Indeed, as McCauley reminds us, the conscious removal of agentic causality from science can leave humans "floundering and incredulous."[41] And, with *Pathway #2*, we are not even dealing with science *per se*, but we are dealing with an inductive faith, outsourced from the world of natural human experience. So, if the removal of agentic causality from science can leave humans confused (when culturally science is not even concerned with agentic causality to begin with), then it's no surprise that the conscious removal of agentic causality from the source material for an inductive faith might leave religiously minded humans quite upset—even atheists confused. *We are all so culturally conditioned to think that any kind of "faith" is supposed to be centred on superhuman agents and/or "other worlds." Not necessarily so!*

Options for a sociocultural, inductive faith are conceived through the lens of alternative, postmetaphysical thinking—a kind of *interpretive* thinking about the human condition, which draws on one's private emotional and psychological constitutions. As mentioned in chapter 5, postmetaphysical thinking avoids a devaluation of those statements—moral, religious, artistic, or emotional, etc.—which seem to resist reduction to natural, causal interactions only. Moral, religious, artistic, and emotional statements, etc., take on *social significances* of their own, while ontological claims about CPS-agents, which are not easily resolved, remain bracketed. So often, it seems, these intriguing types of "postmetaphysical faiths" get shoved aside as not really "faiths," or as just not worth pursuing. Yet, our inductive, postmetaphysical faith in *Pathway #2* serves some very special, interpretive functions for a twenty-first-century, constructive theology: (a) Our inductive faith discovers traces of what might be called *meaning*—by way of perceived signals of joy, order, and hope. Moreover, (b) our inductive faith allows us to consciously construct and impose *human-sourced (human-inspired) meaning* and *social significance* onto the physical world—inspired through perceived signals of joy, order, and hope. Theorized in this fashion, the conscious, human construction and imposition of meaning and social significance onto the physical world is an entirely human activity, which, nevertheless,

---

41. McCauley, *Why Religion Is Natural and Science Is Not*, 224.

is initiated by humans' *a priori* awareness of perceived signals of joy, order, and hope—realized and found in the world of natural human experience. In the inductive faith of *Pathway #2*, the difference from traditional religious versions of faith is that we're just not going any "further"—to put it bluntly, in *Pathway #2*, we just don't see any reason to go any further. Rather, here's what's important: What matters in *Pathway #2* is that *social solidarity*—with its related matters of human bonding and the emotional integrity of human relationships—is pursued and strengthened *because of* the human construction and imposition of meaning onto the physical world. This imposition of meaning occurs by way of an inductive faith—which, in turn, was made possible by way of igmythicism. So, through the unique methodological turns of igmythicism, traditional *myth* no longer must depend on any one particular definition or conceptualization. As igmythicists, accepting that the statement "*myths are descriptions of physical reality*" is a nonsensical statement, we are presented with the opportunity to reconfigure, to recontextualize, *myths* for application in a modern university setting—*myths as symbolic, human-sourced representations of physical reality.*

~

We've considered already how igmythicism brings to our awareness the realization that traditional, *a priori* religious concepts, like *myth*, no longer must depend on any one particular definition or conceptualization. Instead, the realization of concepts like myth now occurs in a two-way dialogue between subjective, human testimony and the sciences of cognition. Informed by humans' awareness of perceived signals of joy, order, and hope, in the world of natural human experience, the origins of myths are "*human*"—hence my emphasis, by way of igmythicism, that myths operate as symbolic, *human-sourced* representations of physical reality. Whether or not myths are mere delusions is perhaps still arguable. However, since myths are *informed by* the source material for an inductive faith—are *informed by* perceived signals of joy, order, and hope—the emphasis about what myths *are* is rightly shifted toward *myths as human in origin, but as informed by an inductive faith*, rather than myths as just mere delusions. As noted in chapter 4, myths are articulations of human values—joy, order, or hope, etc.—when these values are realized and identified in a modestly naturalistic epistemology. But still, like an inductive faith, the origins of myths begin, and also end, in the sociocultural world of natural human experience. There are no non-tested, perceived trans-empirical worlds involved here! Furthermore, if the origins of myths are "human," yet informed by an inductive faith, then perhaps now, in a startling, creative move, *CPS-agents* are even recast as *reflections of ourselves—CPS-agents* as our own *human-sourced representations of physical reality*. Symbolic, human-sourced representations that recognize the distinguished epistemology of knowledge claims (in science), but human-sourced representations which nevertheless are not entirely annexed by the epistemology of knowledge claims either.

The preceding analysis leads me to argue—somewhat courageously—that the *initiation* of so-called *religious experiences*, into a religious epistemology, amounts to the following two human activities:

1. The *initiation*, of human life experiences and testimonies—the initiation of the *human condition* itself[42]—*into* the meaning-structures of sociocultural institutions.

2. Next, those same human experiences and testimonies—that same human condition—*expressed*, metaphorically, *by* the symbolic trappings of sociocultural institutions, whether the trappings of religions, universities, or any other culturally aware human enterprises.

Furthermore, as discussed, symbols express the "ultimate" by implying their own lack of ultimacy: the most important aspect of symbols is the ultimate reality to which they point. In addition, symbols allow societies to move beyond typical space-time perspectives, serving as cultural mediums through which the testimonies of religious devotees can be relayed to those not privy to experiences reported by religious devotees. The "beyond," or the ultimate reality, then, to which symbols point, need not be some nonsensical, ineffable, inaccessible, final, fixed, substantive, trans-empirical world. In conclusion, the ultimate "beyond," to which symbols point, *is* the subjective, unpredicted, and fluctuating *human condition* itself—*realized* physiologically and/or psychologically, *identified* in sociocultural institutions, and *explained* using tested, scientific theories about states of affairs in the physical world. In addition, van Huyssteen rightly points out that "[religious] traditions are, among other things, long-established testimonial chains."[43] Germane to our project, the role of *testimonial chains* or *testimonial experience* is to subjectively uncover—that is, uncover in emotional and psychological terms—those human motivations at play in (a) pursuing various academic questions in the scientific study of religion or (b) pursuing a

---

42. As mentioned, in applying the phrase *human condition* in this context, I am thinking along the lines of this phrase's typical usage to point out human reflection about various phases of human life, including birth, childhood, adolescence, adulthood, and death, etc., and human reflection about common emotional states, including hope, fear, and love, etc.

43. van Huyssteen, *The Shaping of Rationality*, 230.

diachronically oriented "religious" life inside the academic context of the modern university.

As examples of testimonial experience, we have emotional and psychological motivations expressed by the symbolic theme in chapter 9 that "*there's still the river*," or those socially bonded realities, initiated into belief communities by reflection about culturally conditioned concepts like *blest are the pure in heart*[44]—where, perhaps, *being pure in heart* is being honest, being true to oneself, and being genuine with others. Or, consider Peter Berger's notion of "a rumor of angels," from the title of his book *A Rumor of Angels: Modern Society and the Rediscovery of the Supernatural*, mentioned previously. In this instance, Berger, too, seems to be directing us toward the possibility that subjective, human testimonies can point out emotional and psychological motivations through which questions are asked or problems analyzed (whether one is aware of the physiological or sociocultural *sources* of testimonies, or not). When considered in these fashions, the philosophical ground rules of knowledge claims provide an epistemic benchmark for testing beliefs—establishing, for instance, epistemic principles, standards, and assumptions, through which all of our beliefs are tested. However, the social, *postmetaphysical* realities of belief claims are not entirely dismissed either: while the tested beliefs of knowledge claims explain causal connections, the non-tested beliefs of belief claims (like the symbol element of a myth in a compatibility system) take on *sociocultural* realities, rather than substantive ones. In summary, belief claims as socially bonded, emotional and psychological meaning-structures—located in belief communities which are, in turn, situated *in* a web of knowledge claims in the modern scientific cosmos.

Some might wonder what business I have in proposing what might be (on first glance) such a strange, but *new, sociocultural approach for "religion" in the twenty-first-century university*? But my proposal, at least in so far as operating as a new, alternative look at what "religion" *could be*, is neither entirely unexpected nor academically naive. To support my claim—that my desire, to academically seek out a new religiosity and consequently a new constructive theology, is not that far-fetched—I appeal to Schellenberg's diachronic conception of religion. Another short turn back to Schellenberg's ideas is required: To begin with, Schellenberg advocates for a philosophical notion of *deep time*,[45] centred on the *deep future*.[46] While science provides us with many new, counterintuitive, and tested beliefs, Schellen-

---

44. See the biblical narrative in Matthew 5:8.
45. Schellenberg, *Evolutionary Religion*, 9.
46. Schellenberg, *Evolutionary Religion*, 32.

berg reminds us that it can be difficult to displace our previous, "seemingly intuitive ideas"[47] with new, tested beliefs—a process made easier only *after* new evidence used for testing beliefs becomes available. Contributing toward our sense of deep time, with an emphasis toward the possible *future* development of our human species (instead of past developments only), Schellenberg notes that we might be wise to reorient ourselves with a direction toward the vast timescales of biological as well as sociocultural evolutionary developments. Moreover, this would help us to put into perspective how far human intelligence has come and yet *how much further still human intelligence might have to go*. In a nutshell, Schellenberg calls this interesting concept, about the possibility of a deep time centred on the deep future, the *great disparity*.[48] As twenty-first-century philosophers of science and religion, the implications of Schellenberg's great disparity—and its related ideas—are important in supporting the argument made here for *Pathway #2*. I consider these implications in the following paragraphs.

The *great disparity*[49] is one of three sociocultural evolutionary shifts,[50] proposed by Schellenberg, contributing toward Schellenberg's evolutionary approach to a contemporary philosophy of religion.[51] Operating as a possible mechanism of sociocultural evolutionary change in the contemporary religious situation, the great disparity aims to help us to reorient our limited perceptions of deep time and the vast timescales of evolutionary change. Significant evolutionary thinking is usually centred on the deep past, yet, as Schellenberg points out, since earth may remain inhabitable for another billion years,[52] much of our *future* sociocultural, religious thought—whatever that may be—is yet to come. At any rate, the past 50,000 years or so of human cultural activity (since the "cultural explosion" of *H. sapiens sapiens* between sixty thousand and thirty thousand years ago[53]) appears to be a much shorter period of time than the period of time yet to come—possibly a billion years compared to just 50,000 years—for humans to be alive and living on earth *in the years of the deep future* down the road.

Important to our development of an inductive faith in *Pathway #2*, Schellenberg's second evolutionary shift, the *diachronic conception of*

---

47. Schellenberg, *Evolutionary Religion*, 10.
48. Schellenberg, *Evolutionary Religion*, 18.
49. Schellenberg, "Philosophy of Religion," 104.
50. Schellenberg, "Philosophy of Religion," 104.
51. Schellenberg, "Philosophy of Religion," 103.
52. About this figure of a *billion years*, Schellenberg cites a well-known paper: Schröder and Smith, "Distant Future of the Sun and Earth Revisited."
53. Mithen, *The Prehistory of the Mind*, 15.

religion,⁵⁴ is a proposed sociocultural mechanism which conceives "religion" as a human enterprise socially *spread out over time*.⁵⁵ Diachronically, we observe various possibilities for what a social religious life *is* or what it *could be*. A diachronic conception of religion contrasts with a synchronic conception of religion⁵⁶—where religious life is thought *not* to socially evolve over time, but rather current instantiations of religion are seen to be static and unchanging. However, the evolutionary shift made possible through a diachronic conception of religion, which is rooted in our newly found sense of a deep future, raises the possibility that current examples of religion—as well as past religious expressions—are not the only sociocultural possibilities for what a future "religious life" could look like. As I, too, have argued, "religion," in its broadest sense, is an *evolving* sociocultural, human enterprise. As considered already in *Pathway #1*, in Schellenberg's thesis of an evolutionary approach to philosophy of religion, Schellenberg's own diachronic conception of religion calls for an *imagination*-based, non-detailed faith⁵⁷—i.e., a faith response to ultimism. In other words, a religious "investigation" into various possibilities for a future religious life—a future beyond this early stage of what Schellenberg identifies as our current evolutionary religious development and our current "imaginative ultimistic faith."⁵⁸

Lastly, the third evolutionary shift included in Schellenberg's scheme for an evolutionary approach to philosophy of religion is his *temporal relativity of religious assessment*⁵⁹—brilliantly, human religiosity is now honestly and openly thought to be *dependent on* one's sociocultural location and, in a related sense, *dependent on* one's particular moment in time and history. The temporal relativity of religious assessment speaks well, then, to our twenty-first-century project of constructing a *new* religious epistemology, and, consequently, a *new* philosophy of science and religion.⁶⁰ Furthermore, to adequately speak about any constructive theology, or any form of religious life, is to speak about *and assess* what types of theologies or forms of religious life are most suited to the moment in time and history we humans currently inhabit. For example, (i) theologies or forms of religious life most

---

54. Schellenberg, "Philosophy of Religion," 104.
55. Schellenberg, *Evolutionary Religion*, 53.
56. Schellenberg, "Philosophy of Religion," 104.
57. Schellenberg, "Philosophy of Religion," 106.
58. Schellenberg, "Philosophy of Religion," 106.
59. Schellenberg, "Philosophy of Religion," 105.
60. We require a *new philosophy of science and religion* to help us to academically contextualize our attempted design of a compatibility system between a scientific study of religion and a religious epistemology.

suited to our current moment in time in the modern scientific cosmos (e.g., a constructive theology made possible by way of igmythicism), or (ii) in terms of science and religion compatibility system design, our current attempts at that project within the context of contemporary postmetaphysical thinking.

Interestingly, Schellenberg's third evolutionary shift, the temporal relativity of religious assessment, contrasts with the controversial notion that William Warren Bartley calls taking a "Gestalt approach"[61] toward religious texts: for example, following what might be called a *biblical Weltanschauung*, where one views the Bible as a single, *uniform* text, as though the Bible could provide a religious interpretation of natural history and human history, applicable to all times and all places.[62] Of course, my arguments in this book point out that any such "Gestalt approaches" toward religious texts, or toward religious attitudes and practices for that matter, epistemically fall apart, because they fail to live up to the aim of intellectual integrity desired in the modern university: The *non*-temporally relative status of any religious *Weltanschauung*, which views religious life as static and unchanging, *cannot* respond to any of the epistemic issues raised by our current awareness of conflicting claims made by science and by religion about shared states of affairs in one, physical world. Furthermore, the apparent inability of an unchanging religious worldview to be self-critical—or the inability of its followers to employ any critical thought about their own traditionally faith-based, religious epistemology—means any epistemic progress made in current compatibility system design will go unnoticed (or simply be unappreciated) by a temporally insensitive religious community centred on a static religious worldview. In summary, unlike so-called "Gestalt approaches," Schellenberg's evolutionary religion is (i) willing to reinterpret religious attitudes and ideas for our own time and/or possible future times, (ii) is less concerned with the religious past or dependent on religious authority figures or past founders of religions, and (iii) encompasses a forward looking view, focused on the *redesign* of religious life.[63] As Schellenberg astutely remarks, "How many more 'axial ages'[64] may yet lie ahead? (A synchronic conception of religion obscures this thought from us, but a more appropri-

---

61. Bartley, *The Retreat to Commitment*, 50.
62. Bartley, *The Retreat to Commitment*, 50.
63. Schellenberg, *Evolutionary Religion*, 75.
64. The phrase *axial ages* is taken from the so-called "Axial Age," a period of time from about 2,900 to 2,200 years ago, when religions such as Taoism, Confucianism, and Buddhism appeared (Schellenberg 2013, 56). Schellenberg uses this phrase, then, to ask whether other "axial ages"—encompassing new religions or new forms of religiosity—might appear in the deep future? The idea is intriguing.

ate diachronic one will bring it into view.)"⁶⁵ Indeed, the provocative twist for *Pathway #2* is that, while the inductive faith developed and employed in *Pathway #2* could be thought of as contributing toward another so-called "axial age," this inductive faith (made possible by way of igmythicism) *operates exclusively in the sociocultural world of natural human experience.* Maybe somewhat controversial, I realize, but I don't believe it really has to be that upsetting. Let's look into this a bit more.

~

To recap: In *Pathway #2*, we're envisioning, and working to formulate, a new, innovative religiosity, re-conceived outside of temporally insensitive, doctrinal religions—now, "religiosity" as a cultural construct, epistemically in a two-way dialogue with the cultural construct of modern science. This innovative religiosity maintains what might be called a "religious" orientation (the scare quotes around "*religious*" are intentional) in that beliefs about the human condition—including related matters of social bonding and human emotions, etc.—are the *focal points* of one's contemporary "religious" experiences. However, unlike temporally insensitive religions, our current formulation deliberately recasts the traditional theological concepts of *God* and *myth* in entirely new lights, recontextualizing those concepts outside of doctrinal faith traditions and then situating them in the framework of a scientifically oriented, yet emotionally charged, twenty-first-century university. This reconfiguring of the concepts of *God* and *myth* allows for an eclectic mixture of (a) testimonies about religious experiences and (b) modern science—all the while maintaining careful attention toward the delicate interfaces of these diverse modes of human thought. Remember, though, at the forefront of all of these scholastic maneuvers are igtheism and igmythicism: it's igtheism and igmythicism that are (even if just rhetorically) bringing to our attention the possibility—if not the contemporary academic need—to recast the traditional theological concepts of *God* and *myth* in the modern university.

To that end, igmythicism helps to generate awareness in religious studies about the cognitive proclivity of the human mind to defer to claims about the actions of CPS-agents—as explanations for states of affairs in the physical world. In this sense, igmythicism assists in pointing out how such cognitive proclivity can render a constructive theology, modern science, and critical thinking as types of *counterintuitive* human exercises. Yet, the curious twist is that, through new and alternative instantiations of religious concepts (by way of igmythicism), these human exercises *need not* be so counterintuitive

65. Schellenberg, *Evolutionary Religion*, 68.

after all! *Supporting a diachronic conception of religion, igmythicism is placed in a strategic position to help to expand and reinterpret the natures and roles of religious values, all the while preserving the cultural construct of modern science (a web of knowledge claims) as an epistemic benchmark for testing beliefs.* Moreover, the potential attractiveness of igmythicism, for theists, atheists, agnostics, or igtheists alike, is that commonsense human values, and other human-inspired religious concepts, are now embraced *outside of* temporally insensitive, doctrinal religious communities. *In a refreshing move, commonsense, human-sourced values—e.g., hopes, fears, or loves—are actualized in the postmetaphysical stances of the empirically observable phenomena of contemporary scientific lives and religious lives.* This diachronic shift, toward a *temporally sensitive* look at contemporary scientific and religious lives, allows us to more openly *and honestly* assess the epistemic and postmetaphysical interfaces of human religiosity, a constructive theology, and modern science—as these modes of human thought exist, are perpetuated, and are deployed, in our modern universities.

To form a mental picture of it all, it's as though, metaphorically, *modern science* is the structural foundation "down below," and the *cultural shaping of religiosity* is the high-rise building "up top." On top of our *bedrock foundation of tested, scientific beliefs*, we can see a kind of empirically observable cultural medium that flows over top—where *human experiences* and *human testimonies about those experiences* get to be realized, shared, and then perhaps constructed some more. In the scheme I propose, this "top layer" is the cultural home of our various religions and also the cultural platform, if you will, where we communicate our religious experiences if and how we choose to. In terms of a relationship, then, between *science* and *religiosity*, the cultural sharing of various forms of religiosity has not "forgotten" about modern science "down below," nor does the science "down below" have the right to completely annex the cultural shaping of religiosity "up top." So, science is not getting the "final word" on what human life *is*, but nor do the meaning-making projects of religiosity get to be sociologically immune from having to be *aware of* current scientific theories or recent empirical developments in science either—say, for example, recent empirical developments in cognitive science of religion or evolutionary psychology.

Moving forward from the preceding argument, if a constructive theology and its cultural shaping of religiosity were conceived as types of *social sciences*, our preceding mental picture becomes even clearer: About the interrelation between the natural sciences and the social sciences, as Susan Haack puts it, "The natural sciences draw a contour map of the biological determinants of human nature and the biological roots of human culture, *on which the social sciences superimpose a road map.*"[66] On the one hand, the emotionally and psychologically rooted human activities behind our constructive theology are situated by the neurophysiological rootedness of the cognitive science of religion, including the biological determinants of the HADD (Barrett's thesis),[67] as well as a maturationally natural cognitive system (McCauley's thesis).[68] At the same time, both our constructive theology and its cultural shaping of religiosity take on sociocultural realities of their own, *which, as argued, are best expressed as directing us toward the subjective and fluctuating human condition itself.* In the scientific study of religion, back once again to our three-fold characterization to identify a belief about "something" in the physical world (this time, beliefs about what we're calling the *human condition*), beliefs about the human condition are: (i) *realized* physiologically and/or psychologically, (ii) *identified*—even *described*—using sociocultural, intentional language, and (iii) *explained* using tested, scientific theories about states of affairs in the physical world.

Advocates for the scientific study of religion, Luther H. Martin and Don Wiebe, share an interesting view about the use of sociocultural, intentional language (an intentionality) in the scientific study of religion.[69] In their recent *Conversations and Controversies in the Scientific Study of Religion* (2016), Martin and Wiebe (eds.) argue that (a) to *describe* human religious activity requires intentional language, but (b) this does not preclude attempts to *explain* that same intentionality at a "different level of reality."[70] Indeed, as I, too, have hinted at throughout this book, human testimonies—about beliefs, fears, and desires—can be reported and *described*, often by way of intentional language about those beliefs, fears, and desires. Then, in addition, attempts can be made to *explain* reported experiences of beliefs, fears, and desires, by attempting to *explain* the mental intentionalities which are employed when these various human testimonies are subjectively realized, then publicly reported, by humans.

Perhaps similar to Haack's preceding position, about the social sciences superimposing a "road map" onto the biological roots of human nature and culture, Martin and Wiebe summarize their position as follows: "What exists at one scale of reality, in other words, is built from material at a lower scale of reality."[71] In the preceding quotation, Martin's and Wiebe's specific

---

66. Haack, *Defending Science—Within Reason*, 161; emphasis added.
67. Barrett, *Why Would Anyone Believe in God*, 33.
68. McCauley, *Why Religion Is Natural and Science Is Not*, 224.
69. Martin and Wiebe, "Why the Possible Is Not Impossible But Is Unlikely," 283.
70. Martin and Wiebe, "Why the Possible Is Not Impossible But Is Unlikely," 283.
71. Martin and Wiebe, "Why the Possible Is Not Impossible But Is Unlikely," 283.

choice of words—*built from material*[72]—suggests that Martin and Wiebe are reductionist in their account—at least more reductionist than Haack claims to be. For Martin and Wiebe, intentional language about beliefs, fears, and desires has the potential to be explained entirely by causal connections between physical particles, built (potentially) from the most basic level of physical reality. Haack's account, about the social sciences superimposing a "road map" onto the biological roots of human nature and culture, is *perhaps just similar* to Martin's and Wiebe's position, because Haack claims to reject reductionism or at least maintains that her position should not be classified as reductionist *per se*.[73] Instead, Haack advocates for an integration of the natural sciences and the social sciences, using her road map analogy.[74] Let us consider further how Haack's curious scheme of integrating the natural sciences and the social sciences can help us to fortify our growing notions of an inductive faith and a constructive theology.

Following Haack's scheme, descriptions of objects of human beliefs, as well as descriptions of human fears and desires, would take on *sociocultural existences of their own*. While these sociocultural existences may depend first on the existence of a basic level of physical reality, sociocultural existences are not fully realized or identified—*in terms of their meaning, social significance, or instrumental purpose*—by causal interactions alone. Consequently, what we have then is (i) a possible neurophysiological account of beliefs *in addition to* (ii) some reference to everyday human conventions in an intersubjectively available, sociocultural environment—which supplies *meaningful content* and some *social significance* to beliefs.[75] As mentioned in chapter 9, the characteristics of our new constructive theology include objects of non-tested beliefs realized physiologically through a maturationally natural cognitive system; then those same objects of non-tested beliefs identified in sociocultural institutions, like religions.

What we have here is probably the most controversial—and maybe the most confusing—aspect of the inductive faith I present in *Pathway #2*. Throughout this book, I never once as your author told you what to think, nor did I ever tell you to necessarily agree with me or with the arguments I was making (although if you did agree, then that's awesome). However, to fully appreciate the provocative nature of our inductive faith, which "metaphysically" anchors our constructive theology, you and I must accept that, in *Pathway #2*, CPS-agents are not ontological realities—*thus, in Pathway*

---

72. Martin and Wiebe, "Why the Possible Is Not Impossible But Is Unlikely," 283.
73. Haack, *Defending Science—Within Reason*, 157–61.
74. Haack, *Defending Science—Within Reason*, 161.
75. Haack, *Defending Science—Within Reason*, 160.

#2, *God is not an ontological reality*. Once that is established, the provocative twist in *Pathway #2* is that CPS-agents and God are still real, but their *meaningful content* and *social significance* are apparent and real only when CPS-agents and God (or any other objects of non-tested beliefs) are identified and located *inside of* sociocultural, religious institutions. Outside of those institutions, CPS-agents and God are not real. (Full stop.)

Is this so surprising intellectually? After all, consider the law, the elected government, or the modern university—none of these social institutions possess any ontological realities which correspond to their physical or social "incarnations" on earth. Instead, they are entirely *human-sourced*. And, moreover, if any of these social institutions ceased to exist, their objects of experience would just as quickly cease to exist—or at least would cease to be real outside of their respective institutional structures. In *Pathway #2*, religious institutions are viewed no differently—CPS-agents and God cease to be real outside of the sociocultural contexts of religious institutions. However, what does not cease—and this is where it might get confusing—are those emotionally and psychologically rich *human testimonies about* CPS-agents, such as *human testimonies about* God, or *about* Allah, etc. The preceding point, about emotional and psychological testimonies, is why our constructive theology is very careful to emphasize that it *does recognize* objects of non-tested beliefs as *realized* physiologically—emotionally and psychologically—by way of the cognitive underpinnings of a maturationally natural cognitive system. Our constructive theology might also attempt to explain objects of non-tested beliefs (say, by way of the HADD), but that is still a separate matter from humans' *a priori* awareness of perceived objects of non-tested beliefs; for example, humans' *a priori* awareness of perceived signals of joy, order, and hope, in the sociocultural world of natural human experience.

We might wonder then: Does *Pathway #2* just amount to a bit of rhetorical tap dancing? Are human testimonies about CPS-agents just mere delusions that we think are something else and as a society we just can't accept that? The answer is *no*, human testimonies about CPS-agents are not just mere delusions any more than symbolic, human-sourced myths, conceived by way of igmythicism, are mere delusions. Human testimonies about CPS-agents—e.g., testimonies about the gods—just don't originate from any ontological reality for the gods. But, like myths, testimonies about the gods are *informed by*—and *originate from*—the source material for an inductive faith, which means they are *informed by* (for instance) perceived signals of joy, order, and hope. In this manner, the metaphysical "beyond" (to which religion on earth corresponds) is a sociocultural outcome of an inductive faith—and, in terms of structuring and maintaining social solidarity, is a highly valuable outcome! In *Pathway #2*, social solidarity is achieved through perceived, human-inspired qualities of joy, order, and hope—by way of these meaning-enclaves, which are located in the world of natural human experience. Indeed, in *Pathway #2*, not all is lost—there's still an emotionally and psychologically rich human nature; there are still new possibilities to appreciate and construct meaning and significance. Metaphorically, "there's still the river!"

Recapitulation

To wrap up our analysis of *Pathway #2*—its proposed solution to the possible objection that my project (thus far) did not "point" to a metaphysical "beyond"—the following ideas and conclusions are important:

- Following a Schellenbergian, *diachronic* look at religion, an inductive, postmetaphysical faith helps to point out how our newly formed conception of myths is informed by perceived signals of joy, order, and hope. Igtheism and igmythicism had already provided us with the methodological means (even if just rhetorically) to allow us to recast the traditional theological concepts of *God* and *myth* in the modern university. Then, from our unpacking of what an inductive faith is, we achieved a clearer picture of what it means for myths to be *newly* conceived as symbolic, human-sourced representations of physical reality: temporally sensitive myths are *human-sourced*, yet myths as articulations of human values (in a modestly naturalistic epistemology) means that myths are informed by intersubjectively available, perceived signals of joy, order, and hope.

- Following Berger's lead,[76] an inductive, postmetaphysical faith ushers in a new "metaphysics." On the one hand, this new "metaphysics" is "postmetaphysical" in the sense that ontological claims about CPS-agents remain bracketed. At the same time, this new "metaphysics" (inspired by a Haackian innocent realism) is sensitive to the day-to-day realities of contemporary scientific lives and religious lives—is informed by these sociologically and intersubjectively observable phenomena. Yet this *new* "metaphysics," which grounds our constructive theology, means that our constructive theology is also similar to a Wiebian academic theology: since our new "metaphysics" recognizes the critical method of the sciences as setting an epistemic benchmark for testing beliefs, our constructive theology ends up being inimi-

---

76. Berger, *A Rumor of Angels*, 75.

cal to traditional religious life—in Wiebian terms, *the "irony of" our constructive theology*. However, our constructive theology, being anchored by an inductive, postmetaphysical faith, ushers in a new version of "faith"—a collective, interpretive outlook on the human condition, centred on our *a priori* awareness of signals of joy, order, and hope, realized and found in the sociocultural world of natural human experience.

- *Lastly, remember our discussion of cognitive intentionalities for science and religion back in chapter 4?* Conveniently, the particular cognitive intentionality employed in our inductive faith and new constructive theology is like the *conscious* intentionality employed in modern science. As argued in chapter 4, in modern scientific thought there is an explicit desire to test beliefs—a conscious, indeed self-proclaimed, interest to know and interpret the physical world. Likewise, our inductive faith and constructive theology appeal to modern science to set the epistemic benchmark for testing beliefs. *Yes, our inductive faith and constructive theology also appeal to the emotional and psychological roles of testimonies in a scientific study of religion*. However, these testimonies operate in a two-way dialogue with modern science, functioning rather as *personal motivations* for the questions and problems that we pursue in the scientific study of religion. In a two-way dialogue, between *science-influenced human testimony* and *human-testimony-influenced science*, the sciences *continue* to set the epistemic benchmark for actually testing our beliefs. Since our inductive faith and constructive theology appeal to modern science, our inductive faith and constructive theology, like science, employ a *conscious* intentionality to attempt to know and interpret the physical world. Thus, quite conveniently, modern science, our inductive faith, and our new constructive theology, are all *commensurable* human enterprises—very helpful in the analysis that follows: what our compatibility system between a scientific study of religion and a religious epistemology *really looks like*.

A Possible Objection

Some readers might be concerned that, in appealing to Haack's innocent realism and modestly naturalistic epistemology, I have attempted to make religion "fit" a naturalistic ontology; that in doing so I have disregarded what is, for many, the personal, existential integrity of traditional faith-based aspirations.

Reply

In accordance with igmythicism, the recontextualizing of *myth* occurs in an epistemic stance like Haack's modestly naturalistic epistemology. *Subjective, human testimonies*—themselves types of "epistemologies," because human testimonies are thought to contribute to one's beliefs about the external, physical world and one's interpretation of the world—are influenced by scientific theories from the sciences of cognition. In the type of rationality we are employing, a two-way dialogue, between *science-influenced human testimony* and *human-testimony-influenced science*, helps to render the *myths* of human testimonies as *symbolic*; as *representational*. The *myths* of human testimonies are now compatible, on a *practical level*, with those cognitive values peculiar to a scientific epistemology. For example, cognitive values such as the following:

1. As humans, we are fallible and imperfect creatures.

2. Yet, as humans, we do possess the perceptual awareness and cognitive capacities necessary for us to collect and test natural experience from brute nature.

3. Since we are fallible and imperfect creatures, our interpretations of brute nature are overlaid by our own assumptions and theories.

4. Most important as a cognitive value peculiar to a scientific epistemology, the notion that, to pursue and accomplish intersubjectively available learning, as humans, "we need opportunities to work out inconsistencies and mistakes as we uncover them. This leads us, ultimately, to deeper and more mature understandings of the [physical] world."[77]

A temporally sensitive constructive theology, like symbolically oriented myths, need not be thought to test beliefs about states of affairs in the physical world. Indeed, the role of our twenty-first-century, constructive theology is *not* to test beliefs about states of affairs in the physical world. Rather, the role of this constructive theology is to outline those *emotional* and *psychological* motivations at play in pursuing academic questions and problems in the scientific study of religion. Thus, one of the most important take-home points here is that, although testimonies about emotional and psychological motivations cannot be tested (as scientific beliefs can be tested), emotional and psychological motivations—in the styles of Haackian innocent realism or Habermasian postmetaphysical thinking—still take

---

77. Woodward, *Adventure*, 57.

on sociocultural existences of their own. *Socioculturally, testimonies about emotional and psychological motivations operate as the methodological form of a religious epistemology, in the scientific study of religion.* Even if they operate in an instrumentalist fashion only (in our religious epistemology), testimonies about emotional and psychological motivations don't just get eliminated. Testimonies about emotional and psychological motivations are *real*, but they're not really supported by tested, scientific theories either. Although, as discussed, perhaps the HADD and a maturationally natural cognitive system are beginning to provide us with some tested information about how human cognitive processes operate, contributing to our scientific understanding of the nature of religious thought.

As I see it, by conceptualizing religious thought and theological thought within a modestly naturalistic framework, my goal is not to make religion "fit" science. If that was my goal, I would likely continue to assume (i) that religious and theological exercises can elucidate causal connections about states of affairs in the physical world, and (ii) that religiosity and theology provide accurate descriptions of the physical world—two tenets I openly reject, supported by arguments made in this book. As neither of these two tenets are my goals, my project is not to make religion "fit" science, but to evaluate how religious life, theology, or myth, etc., might play *new*, alternative *roles* in the modern scientific cosmos—where science *already* provides us with tested beliefs about (accurate descriptions of) the physical world.

To recap: How different is the methodological form of our religious epistemology from that of a scientific epistemology? The short answer: *quite different*. To unpack the answer to this question in more detail, we look toward our evolving compatibility system between a scientific study of religion and our new religious epistemology: Firstly, recall that a *scientific study of religion* itself—by virtue of its intrinsic critical methodology and corresponding tested beliefs—is a kind of knowledge claim in modern science. A scientific study of religion is a kind of knowledge claim in modern science, because to claim that one possesses a critical methodology suited to a scientific study of religion (and to advocate for such a study) involves the *four conceptual components of knowledge claims*, presented initially in chapter 1, and outlined here as follows:

1. A cognitive state, encompassing the knowledge claimant's attempt to know the physical world—in this case, the knowledge claimant's attempt to possess a critical methodology suited to a scientific study of religion, which epistemically includes tested beliefs about the physical world.

2. A specially certified proposition—in this case, the critical methodology intrinsic to a scientific study of religion—which is the object of the preceding cognitive state.
3. A verbal statement made by the knowledge claimant that he or she mentally possesses (in this case) a methodology suited to a scientific study of religion. Moreover, that this methodology is open to external analysis by outside parties.
4. Some reasons, provided by the knowledge claimant, which are used to attempt to convince (and ideally assure) outside parties that the claimant's methodology suited to a scientific study of religion in fact constitutes and provides access to justified, human knowledge.

Secondly, keep in mind that a *religious epistemology* itself is a kind of belief claim in religious life. A religious epistemology is a kind of belief claim in religious life, because to claim that one possesses a religious epistemology involves the *two conceptual components of belief claims*, presented initially in chapter 1, and outlined here as follows:

1. A cognitive state, encompassing the belief claimant's attempt to know the physical world—in this case, the belief claimant's attempt to possess a religious epistemology which includes non-tested beliefs about the physical world.
2. A verbal statement made by the belief claimant that he or she mentally possesses (in this case) a religious epistemology—which itself is a non-tested belief, including a collection of other, corresponding non-tested beliefs, all of which are assented to by the belief claimant.

In summary, a science and religion compatibility system—specifically between a scientific study of religion and our new religious epistemology—fits neatly into our overall exploration in this book of an epistemology of belief claims in religious life relative to an epistemology of knowledge claims in scientific practice.

As Ninian Smart pointed out, the splitting of a myth into its component parts of *fact* and *symbol*, and the attempted rejoining of *fact* and *symbol* in the modern scientific cosmos, is what a compatibility system (generally) amounts to. Following the splitting of *fact* and *symbol*, and their attempted rejoining in a modern compatibility system, *symbol* takes precedence, recovering and representing whatever notions of "ultimacy" were intended by the original myth. Finally, from my argument in chapter 4, in the compatibility system, *fact* is rendered an *institutional fact*—which may have always been the case; however, in the modern scientific cosmos, the realization of mythological facts *as* institutional facts becomes possible. With Smart's formulation in mind, for a compatibility system, specifically between a scientific study of religion and our new religious epistemology, the following events occur consecutively:

1. In the *scientific study of religion*, the splitting of pre-scientific myths—and their corresponding *religious epistemologies*—into component parts of alleged *mythological facts* and related *mythological symbols*. Then, by way of igtheism, our provocative realization that mythological facts (e.g., "God") are actually institutional facts. Next, by way of igmythicism, our realization that mythological symbols are in fact human-sourced or human-inspired symbols, informed by our *a priori* awareness of signals of joy, order, and hope, in the sociocultural world of natural human experience.

2. In the *scientific study of religion*, the attempted rejoining of (a) the institutional facts of a *religious epistemology* with (b) the human-sourced symbols of a *religious epistemology*. This attempted rejoining helps to point out some diachronically oriented, religious motivations for the work that we do in a scientific study of religion. Arising from out of our religious epistemology, we identify and locate testimonies about emotional and psychological motivations for the questions and problems we pursue in the scientific study of religion. All the while we also maintain the cultural construct of modern science (knowledge claims) as our epistemic benchmark for testing all of our beliefs.

It is important to emphasize again that our religious epistemology is connected with our inductive, postmetaphysical faith as well as with our constructive theology. Moreover, our religious epistemology is *compatible with* our scientific study of religion *because of* our diachronically oriented realizations that mythological facts *are* institutional facts and that mythological symbols *are* human-sourced symbols. As this book set out to argue, if a theory of rationality refers to (i) a philosophical system for testing the propositional beliefs of knowledge claims and (ii) if it were possible, testing the propositional beliefs of belief claims, then we have certainly met the *first* requirement: an epistemology of knowledge claims in scientific practice establishes, for us, epistemic principles, standards, and assumptions, through which the propositional beliefs of knowledge claims are consistently tested. We have also considered how the propositional beliefs of belief claims cannot be tested as the propositional beliefs of knowledge claims can be tested, but this observation is what has allowed us to maintain some consistency in what we *can* test—that is, the propositional beliefs of knowledge claims.

Yes, the argument here is a delicate one: the propositional beliefs of belief claims cannot be tested as the propositional beliefs of knowledge claims can be tested. (Full stop.) But this realization is what allows us to design a completely *new* compatibility system (by way of igtheism and igmythicism), specifically between a scientific study of religion and a religious epistemology. This new compatibility system *maintains consistency* in the testing *of all of* our propositional beliefs. Importantly, those shared states of affairs in the one, physical world, described by conflicting claims from both science and religion,[78] no longer epistemically fall apart, but are consistently tested by the principles of an epistemology of knowledge claims as applied in scientific practice—that is, tested by way of our intersubjectively observed experiences of phenomenal reality. Finally, what isn't lost either, or completely annexed by science either, are those emotional and psychological motivations for the questions and problems we pursue in the scientific study of religion. Those *subjective, human testimonies are the methodological form of our new religious epistemology,* as well as related to our inductive faith and constructive theology.

~

Those who feel unconvinced by my formulation—whether religious devotees, scientists, or those who claim to be both scientific and religious—are perhaps justified in wondering why these emotional and psychological motivations, which make up the methodological core of our religious epistemology, are even important? Or wondering, what is the point of these motivations? Or concluding, simply, who cares? In response to these objections, I offer up the following thoughts: The limitations of modern compatibility system design—indeed, if there really are any limitations—exist only when religious life, theology, or myth, etc., are conceptualized outside of the new igmythicist approach I propose in this book. If the philosophical and theological nuances of igmythicism can be appreciated, the existential integrity of faith-based aspirations is not lost, but is recontextualized, is made sense of personally, in face of modern science—a goal alluded to throughout this book. When I mentioned near the start of this book that I rarely find *honesty* about epistemic matters in contemporary science and religion literature, I was referring to this point, now unpacked, that the integrity of the compatibility system project need not be affected when religious life, theology, or myth, etc., are conceptualized by way of the methodological

---

78. For example, claims about the constitution of physical reality, the origin of human life, the naturalness or unnaturalness of LGBTI identities, free will, or the future course of one's life, etc.

maneuvers that an igmythicist uses. In a nutshell, for the igmythicist, modern science already provides us with tested beliefs about the physical world; this fact should not worry us—in short, this *is* what science does. At the same time, for the igmythicist, *religiosity, human testimonies,* and *subjective, introspective experience* (generally), accomplish other goals. Namely, natural phenomena behind those cultural constructs are thought to initiate emotional and psychological meaning-structures *into* belief communities, which are, in turn, located *in* the modern scientific cosmos.

A word about *honesty*: Smart, too, was aware that the proposed task to design any compatibility system would be difficult. He noted, "*It does not matter particularly for my argument here whether compatibility systems fully work*, in the sense of correctly handling the relationship between religion and science. *What is important is that they provide an account which intelligent and honest people can accept.*"[79] Perhaps, in purely logical terms, our new compatibility system does not fully work—it deliberately recasts the theological concept of *myth* (which traditionally was purely mythopoeic in nature, presuming that El, God, and Allah are ontological realities) into a new fashion to attempt to achieve a sort of "compatibility," but a "compatibility" which is more *practical* rather than purely logical. However, following Schellenberg's notion of a diachronic conception of religion, if this recasting of *myth* results in our ideal instantiation of *myth*, as *myth* is contextualized in the modern university, then the following could also be argued: it's not so much that we have deliberately recast *myth* outside of its mythopoeic roots to just easily achieve some sort of compatibility between a scientific study of religion and a religious epistemology, but rather this recasting of *myth* in the modern university results in, well, just what myth *is* or what myth *should be* in the modern university.

Finally, when epistemic distinctions between knowledge claims and belief claims are not acknowledged, or when both science and religion are thought to provide accurate descriptions of states of affairs in the physical world, it is no wonder that all of these options to maintain an absolutist "conflict" thesis, a faith-imbued "non-conflict" thesis, or a "place science and religion in separate 'compartments'" thesis, or reject science, or reject religion, etc., etc., arise. Once the distinction is made that modern science provides us with tested beliefs, while religious life, theology, or myth, etc., provide us with *socially bonded meaning*—emotional and psychological motivations for the work we accomplish and the academic questions we pursue—epistemic tension between science and religion falls away. Moreover,

---

79. Smart, *The Science of Religion*, 83; emphasis added.

the need for legitimation strategies disappears; the need for traditional (purely logical) compatibility systems evaporates.

My approach, outlined in the preceding paragraphs, may seem, to some, too jaded or too disenchanting. Given those personal aspects from my own life I opened up about in chapter 8, some may even be inclined to wonder if my own background—in particular, my negative experiences with some aspects of mainstream religious life—have prompted me to defend the particular thesis I propose. While that may be one motivating factor (and, if so, it does point out the relevance of one's own emotional and psychological testimonies in pursuing an academic question!), another more *liberating*, more *important*, motivation I possess in defending the thesis in this book is that theists, atheists, agnostics, and igtheists alike might be drawn to aspects of the new constructive theology and the new philosophy of science and religion which follows. In that sense, my target audience and readership for this book exceed the internal confines of any one particular knowledge community *or* belief community, addressed rather to our *Homo sapiens sapiens* species itself! Indeed, this was my focus previously when, considering the *role* of a religious epistemology in the modern scientific cosmos, I connected human life experiences and testimonies with the unpredicted and fluctuating human condition itself. This was followed by my suggestion that subjective, human testimonies are initiated into sociocultural frameworks whereby human testimonies are then experienced—in a representational fashion—by the symbolic trappings of human institutions.

Indeed, our religious epistemology is unlike any traditionally faith-based, religious epistemologies that I am aware of. For example, our religious epistemology is certainly not a Spiritualist epistemology, a psychical epistemology, or a Christian epistemology, etc. But at the same time our religious epistemology certainly is *interpretive*, drawing on our own private emotional and psychological constitutions. Thus, our religious epistemology is rightly associated with an *inductive, postmetaphysical faith*. To clarify that our religious epistemology is neither traditionally faith-based, nor scientific, we could even place our phrase *religious epistemology* in scare quotes as "religious epistemology"—to help to point out the epistemic quandary that we have been attempting to solve. Furthermore, although the "cognitive values" of our "religious epistemology" still might deviate (somewhat) from the cognitive values of a scientific epistemology, analyzing the *social, emotional*, and *psychological* importance of our "religious epistemology" in the twenty-first century is an academic question still worthy of consideration.

Heading toward the Book's End ... Yet Again, Another Possible Objection

But, as hinted at toward the end of chapter 8, what if the continued existence of modern science is sociologically *fragile*—what if science is *vulnerable to* powerful political and social institutions? If you do believe the future of science is at risk, you may be wondering whether our new compatibility system, between a scientific study of religion and a religious epistemology, could even survive in the modern university?

Reply

To respond to this hypothetical objection, allow me to draw us back to the issues we set out to address when considering (in chapter 6) how a scientific epistemology might operate as a *model for* religious knowledge: So, to that end, have we been successful in applying the rational integrity of a scientific epistemology *to* religious exercises? In that fashion, have we developed a suitable model to construct a religious epistemology? For one, about *provisional* as opposed to *essential* parameters as they relate to religious mythologies, the demythologizing of any religion, i.e., the removing of traditional metaphysical claims, recasts the category of "religion" in the modern world. With *any* religion demythologized, the highlighting of socially bonded meaning—social solidarity—a goal and outcome of contemporary religious life, helps to ease concerns that faith-based aspirations might have been completely eliminated. *However*, and I feel compelled to clarify this point further, that *symbolically oriented*, faith-based aspirations were not eliminated was possible only because of my epistemic separation between knowledge claims and belief claims in a modern scientific cosmos—where science *already* provides us with tested beliefs about the physical world! Moreover, William Bartley's thought, which contributes to my proposed religious epistemology in a modern university, emphasized the importance of consistency in testing beliefs: as *learning from experience* is intrinsic to modern science, in being critical of beliefs, critical of criticism itself, *and* in being self-critical, some *consistency* permeates one's testing of beliefs.

Thus, in the formulation I propose, with the principles and assumptions of a scientific epistemology operating collectively as our stabilizing model (or force) for a religious epistemology, epistemic consistency in the testing of all of our beliefs is indeed maintained. Since humans seem to possess a natural cognitive proclivity to just defer to claims about the actions of purported CPS-agents in the physical world, epistemic consistency helps to maintain a careful balance between (a) these CPS-agent-based representations of the physical world and (b) radically counterintuitive representations of the physical world. As mentioned, counterintuitive representations of the physical world,[80] presented by way of tested, scientific theories, are at odds with those everyday, maturationally natural representations of the physical world, presented by way of modern religions and other non-institutionalized versions of religiosity. Unlike counterintuitive representations of the physical world, CPS-agentic thinking seems to continue to permeate modern religious thought. For example, religious devotees' *innate motivations*—for desiring to construct a religious epistemology which maintains that CPS-agents are ontological realities—*result in* mental impediments to the theory of rationality I propose as well as impediments to practicing igmythicism. Ironically, these impediments may also lead to the formulations of objections to the overall project explored throughout this book.

About the preceding point, that CPS-agentic thinking could generate cognitive impediments toward the formulation of alternative, critical modes of thought—and thus cognitive impediments toward the arguments made in this book, including impediments toward our new compatibility system between a scientific study of religion and a religious epistemology—we need to be aware of this academic quagmire. However, I also think that we can, psychologically, attempt to get away from its potentially impeding effects. For one, Radek Kundt, who works on the cognitive science of religion, reminds us that within the human mind various unconscious mental processes operate at different unconscious levels.[81] However, despite unconscious mental processes, Kundt suggests, "Given time and effort one might be able to consciously process knowledge about how unconscious levels operate, trace those mechanisms, make them (or their results) explicit and, in a manner of speaking, 'throw them away' on a formal conscious level."[82]

Intriguingly, then, igmythicism provides a response to the proposed, ever-growing problem that science and academic versions of theology (vis-à-vis a quotidian religiosity) are sociologically fragile: From Robert McCauley's thesis that science provides counterintuitive representations of the physical world, the view, that the continued existence of science is fragile, is somewhat alarming. Although science does allow for improvement and modification of beliefs (and although this does make learning possible), scientific thought, in competition so to speak with everyday, CPS-agentic thought, is at risk (or so goes McCauley's claim). Yet, through acknowledging

80. McCauley, *Why Religion Is Natural and Science Is Not*, 117.
81. Kundt, "A Scientific Discipline," 257.
82. Kundt, "A Scientific Discipline," 257.

the idea that human knowledge possesses a moral character—a *morality of knowledge*,[83] to use Wiebe's phrase—the possibility to recontextualize *myth* in the modern scientific cosmos includes our project to formulate a new constructive theology in the modern university. In this new constructive theology, to achieve an adequate morality of knowledge, tested beliefs from modern science are *preserved through* our critically oriented *"claims to* knowledge." Further still, igmythicism includes a methodology whereby traditional, *a priori* religious concepts, like *myth*, no longer must depend on any one particular definition or conceptualization. Instead, the realization of concepts like myth now exists in a two-way dialogue between subjective, human testimony and the sciences of cognition—*myth* reinterpreted and replaced for application in a scientifically oriented, yet emotionally charged, twenty-first-century university.

So, in responding to the concerns of those who believe the future of science is at risk, the igmythicist—through learning about tested beliefs from cognitive science of religion—becomes psychologically *aware* that various unconscious mental processes, such as the HADD and a maturationally natural cognitive system, operate within the human mind. Then, becoming aware of those unconscious mental processes, as well as becoming *aware of* the overall epistemic conflict between knowledge claims and belief claims, the igmythicist begins to evaluate new definitions for religious concepts: new definitions which help the igmythicist to still participate in the meaning-making projects of an inductive faith and a constructive theology, but this time without falling victim to those cognitive proclivities which seem to cause other humans to just defer to claims about the actions of purported CPS-agents.

Our new religious epistemology, formulated by way of igmythicism, still includes further benefits: Post-Kuhnian compatibility system enthusiasts had argued that empirical experience in scientific practice is theory-laden and interpreted, but they neglected that *so is the apprehension of symbols and subjective experience* in other human enterprises,[84] including religions. Bartley rightly points out that symbols, like other components of human experiences, are dependent on interpretational rules. Furthermore, for the igmythicist, with various conceptualizations of *myth* now possible, interpretational rules for symbols and subjective experience are now especially subjectivized *no less* than empirical experience in scientific practice might be subjectivized. In other matters, the igmythicist's formulation also helps to avoid existential identity crises, described by Bartley as exchanging "I am

83. Wiebe, "Comprehensively Critical Rationalism and Commitment," 1.
84. Bartley, *The Retreat to Commitment*, 61.

confused,"[85] for "I am a member of a confused tradition [a confused faith community]."[86] In a liberating manner, for the igmythicist, crises of identity no longer need exist: Undergirded by this book's two substantive assumptions—*(i) that phenomenal reality provides a standard of observed experiences used for testing beliefs about states of affairs in the physical world, and (ii) that religious people's testimonies inform us that religious people possess beliefs about superhuman agents and/or beliefs about trans-empirical worlds*—the igmythicist enjoys some unique freedom to reinterpret religious concepts as they are emotionally or psychologically relevant to academic questions pursued in the scientific study of religion. The liberation experienced by this kind of approach is indeed refreshing: while the igmythicist accepts that knowledge claims provide an epistemic benchmark for testing beliefs, the igmythicist also acknowledges emotional and psychological values located in belief communities *in* the modern scientific cosmos. For theists, atheists, agnostics, or igtheists—*now turned igmythicists!*—this unique combination of knowledge claims and socially bonded belief claims has much potential for application in the science and religion debate of the twenty-first century—a *new philosophy of science and religion*!

Note, too, that our new igmythicist approach to the science and religion debate is also *different* from Gould's well-known, non-overlapping magisteria (NOMA) approach: *Unlike* NOMA, in our scheme, science and religion are not just on different turfs, where they just don't have to "know" that the other exists. Instead, what's important for us is a constructive engagement—a constructive theology!—between science and religion, along with an inductive faith which recognizes the cultural and human underpinnings of both science and religion. In our scheme, this constructive engagement is further emphasized by an ongoing, two-way dialogue between *science-influenced human testimony* and *human-testimony-influenced science (Pathway #2)*, or, say, a two-way dialogue between *science-influenced ultimism* and *ultimism-influenced science (Pathway #1)*.

Some Closing Remarks

For some final, concluding remarks, so as to point out why humility is an important value in academic work, Susan Haack aptly remarks, "It can be hard, very hard, just to admit that you were wrong, that the investment of time, energy, and ego you have put into some question hasn't paid off. It can be hard, too, just to admit that you don't know; most of us like to have

---

85. Bartley, *The Retreat to Commitment*, 5.
86. Bartley, *The Retreat to Commitment*, 5.

What about the "Beyond"?   221

opinions, even on questions where we are in no position to know."[87] About the possibility that my conclusions are wrong—not a claim I support, but an accusation which is possible given some hypothetical objections to my work, and especially given the emotionally delicate nature of my topic, i.e., "religion"—I offer up the following suggestions: Even if you object to my conclusions, consider that at the very least what I propose is an alternative conception, a "facsimile," of contemporary religious life vis-à-vis modern science. While, yes, it would be possible for another scholar to sift through my work and change my assumptions (e.g., assume instead that CPS-agents are ontological realities) or adjust my arguments (e.g., conclude instead that wholly *a priori* religious experience be included in the source material for any experientialist epistemology), what the igmythicist approach provides is the possibility that, even if one does not adjust my assumptions or arguments to support traditional faith-based aims, one can still maintain the existential integrity of a religious life *contextualized in* the modern scientific cosmos. In this sense, values contained in religious life and pre-scientific myths *survive as* belief claims through an emotional and psychological framework. At the same time, knowledge claims set the exclusive epistemic benchmark for testing our human beliefs.

About alternative, twenty-first-century approaches to the philosophy of science and religion, other writers express sentiments embracing the possibility of new methods. Questioning whether theological realism is analogous to scientific realism, Willem Drees notes, "God might be totally different from the way God is believed to be, and beliefs about God might be untestable, while none the less the hope expressed in the beliefs might not be vain."[88] For Drees, then, "an attitude of existential trust,"[89] i.e., *belief in* (rather than non-tested beliefs expressed propositionally, i.e., *belief that*), becomes the order of the day. Also, as Mikael Stenmark puts it, "If science and religion are understood to be *multidimensional, social practices* then we must take into account that they change over time and look differently in different places."[90] Recall, too, that Schellenberg inspiringly asks, "How many more 'axial ages' may yet lie ahead?"[91]

So, although my project is different from Drees's, Stenmark's, or Schellenberg's own formulations (and different from projects of other writers considered), it seems that other science and religion scholars are at least

87. Haack, *Manifesto of a Passionate Moderate*, 11.
88. Drees, *Religion, Science and Naturalism*, 146.
89. Drees, *Religion, Science and Naturalism*, 146.
90. Stenmark, *How to Relate Science and Religion*, 268.
91. Schellenberg, *Evolutionary Religion*, 68.

prepared for new, alternative approaches to the science and religion question. To that end, it's three o'clock in the morning and I'm adding the final revisions to this book. As your writer, I don't want to belittle modern science; I don't wish to poke fun at contemporary religion either.

A part of my work concludes the scientific method is one's ideal epistemology. Another part of my work concludes I wouldn't understand a pure heart, or an honest heart, without some emotionally charged religiosity, too. In all honesty, then, what I'm really looking for is a belief in happy endings: I'll find my river yet. I trust you'll find yours, too.

Bibliography

Arnal, William E., and Russell T. McCutcheon. *The Sacred Is the Profane: The Political Nature of "Religion."* Oxford: Oxford University Press, 2013.
Asprem, Egil. "Parapsychology: Naturalising the Supernatural, Re-Enchanting Science." In *Handbook of Religion and the Authority of Science*, edited by Olav Hammer and James R. Lewis, 633–70. Brill Handbooks on Contemporary Religion 3. Leiden: Brill, 2011.
Ayer, Alfred Jules. *Language, Truth, and Logic.* 2nd ed. 1946. Reprint, New York: Dover, 1952. Kindle.
Barbour, Ian G. *Religion and Science: Historical and Contemporary Issues.* New York: HarperCollins, 1997.
Barrett, Justin L. *Why Would Anyone Believe in God?* Lanham, MD: AltaMira, 2004.
Bartley, William Warren, III. *The Retreat to Commitment.* 2nd ed. Chicago: Open Court, 1984.
Berger, Peter L. *A Rumor of Angels: Modern Society and the Rediscovery of the Supernatural.* Garden City, NY: Doubleday, 1970.
———. *The Sacred Canopy: Elements of a Sociological Theory of Religion.* Garden City, NY: Doubleday, 1967.
Berger, Peter L., and Thomas Luckmann. *The Social Construction of Reality: A Treatise in the Sociology of Knowledge.* Garden City, NY: Doubleday, 1966.
Blanton, Brad. *Radical Honesty: How to Transform Your Life By Telling the Truth.* Stanley, VA: Sparrowhawk, 2003.
Boyer, Pascal. *Religion Explained: The Evolutionary Origins of Religious Thought.* New York: Basic, 2001.
Brown, C. Mackenzie. "Vivekananda and the Scientific Legitimation of Advaita Vedānta." In *Handbook of Religion and the Authority of Science*, edited by Olav Hammer and James R. Lewis, 207–48. Brill Handbooks on Contemporary Religion 3. Leiden: Brill, 2011.
Capra, Fritjof. *The Tao of Physics: An Exploration of the Parallels Between Modern Physics and Eastern Mysticism.* 5th ed. Boston: Shambhala, 2010.
Cartwright, Nancy. *How the Laws of Physics Lie.* 1983. Reprint, Oxford: Oxford University Press, 2002.
Crisp, Oliver D. "On Analytic Theology." In *Analytic Theology: New Essays in the Philosophy of Theology*, edited by Oliver D. Crisp and Michael C. Rea, 33–53. Oxford: Oxford University Press, 2009.
Dewey, John. *Art as Experience.* 1934. Reprint, New York: Berkley, 2005.

Donald, Merlin. *Origins of the Modern Mind: Three Stages in the Evolution of Culture and Cognition.* Cambridge: Harvard University Press, 1991.

Downey, Jennifer, and Richard C. Friedman. "Neurobiology and Sexual Orientation: Current Relationships." *Journal of Neuropsychiatry & Clinical Neurosciences* 5/2 (1993) 131–53.

Draper, John William. *History of the Conflict between Religion and Science.* New York: Appleton, 1874.

Drees, Willem B. *Religion, Science and Naturalism.* 1996. Reprint, Cambridge: Cambridge University Press, 1998.

Dyrendal, Asbjørn. "'Oh No, It Isn't.' Sceptics and the Rhetorical Use of Science in Religion." In *Handbook of Religion and the Authority of Science,* edited by Olav Hammer and James R. Lewis, 879–900. Brill Handbooks on Contemporary Religion 3. Leiden: Brill, 2011.

Engler, Steven, and Michael Stausberg. "Introduction: Research Methods in the Study of Religion/s." In *The Routledge Handbook of Research Methods in the Study of Religion,* edited by Steven Engler and Michael Stausberg, 3–20. London: Routledge, 2011.

Evans, Gillian Rosemary. *Old Arts and New Theology: The Beginnings of Theology as an Academic Discipline.* Oxford: Oxford University Press, 1980.

Evans, Jonathan St. B. T. *Thinking Twice: Two Minds in One Brain.* Oxford: Oxford University Press, 2010.

Feyerabend, Paul. *Against Method.* 4th ed. London: Verso, 2010.

———. *The Tyranny of Science.* Cambridge: Polity, 2011.

Flanagan, Owen. *The Really Hard Problem: Meaning in a Material World.* Cambridge: MIT Press, 2007. Kindle.

Freud, Sigmund. "The Question of a Weltanschauung." In *The Standard Edition of the Complete Psychological Works of Sigmund Freud,* edited and translated by James Strachey, 22:158–82. London: Hogarth, 1932–36.

Friberg, Urban, et al. "Homosexuality as a Consequence of Epigenetically Canalized Sexual Development." *The Quarterly Review of Biology* 87/4 (2012) 343–68. Accessed March 2, 2015. http://www.jstor.org/stable/10.1086/668167/.

Gerrish, B. A. "'Assent' in Thomas Aquinas." In *Saving and Secular Faith: An Invitation to Systematic Theology,* 5–8. Minneapolis: Augsburg, 1999.

Gilson, Étienne. *Reason and Revelation in the Middle Ages.* New York: Scribner, 1938.

Goody, Jack. *The Domestication of the Savage Mind.* Themes in the Social Sciences. Cambridge: Cambridge University Press, 1977.

Gould, Stephen Jay. *Rocks of Ages: Science and Religion in the Fullness of Life.* New York: Ballantine, 1999.

Gutierrez, Cathy. "Spiritualism and Psychical Research." In *Handbook of Religion and the Authority of Science,* edited by Olav Hammer and James R. Lewis, 591–608. Brill Handbooks on Contemporary Religion 3. Leiden: Brill, 2011.

Haack, Susan. *Defending Science—Within Reason: Between Scientism and Cynicism.* 2003. Reprint, Amherst, NY: Prometheus, 2007.

———. *Evidence and Inquiry: A Pragmatist Reconstruction of Epistemology.* 2nd ed. Amherst, NY: Prometheus, 2009.

———. "Fallibilism and Faith, Naturalism and the Supernatural, Science and Religion." In *Putting Philosophy to Work: Inquiry and Its Place in Culture—Essays* on *Science, Religion, Law, Literature, and Life*, 199–208. Expanded ed. Amherst, NY: Prometheus, 2013.

———. *Manifesto of a Passionate Moderate*. Chicago: University of Chicago Press, 1998.

———. "Point of Honor: On Science and Religion." In *Defending Science—Within Reason: Between Scientism and Cynicism*, 265–97. 2003. Reprint, Amherst, NY: Prometheus, 2007.

Habermas, Jürgen. "Religion in the Public Sphere: Cognitive Presuppositions for the 'Public Use of Reason' by Religious and Secular Citizens." In *Between Naturalism and Religion*, 114–47. Translated by Ciaran Cronin. Cambridge: Polity, 2008.

Hacking, Ian. *The Social Construction of What?* Cambridge: Harvard University Press, 1999.

Hammer, Olav. *Claiming Knowledge: Strategies of Epistemology from Theosophy to the New Age*. Studies in the History of Religions 90. Leiden: Brill, 2004.

Hammer, Olav, and James R. Lewis. "Introduction." In *Handbook of Religion and the Authority of Science*, edited by Olav Hammer and James R. Lewis, 1–20. Brill Handbooks on Contemporary Religion 3. Leiden: Brill, 2011.

Hanson, Norwood Russell. *Patterns of Discovery: An Inquiry into the Conceptual Foundations of Science*. Cambridge: Cambridge University Press, 1958.

Hewitt, Marsha Aileen. *Freud on Religion*. Durham: Acumen, 2014.

Hick, John. "The Non-Absoluteness of Christianity." In *The Myth of Christian Uniqueness*, edited by John Hick and Paul F. Knitter, 16–36. London: SCM, 1988.

Hoodbhoy, Pervez. *Islam and Science: Religious Orthodoxy and the Battle for Rationality*. London: Zed, 1991.

Horkheimer, Max. "Traditional and Critical Theory." In *Critical Theory: Selected Essays*, 188–243. Translated by Matthew J. O'Connell. New York: Continuum, 1999.

Horton, Robin. "Tradition and Modernity Revisited." In *Rationality and Relativism*, edited by Martin Hollis and Steven Lukes, 201–60. Cambridge: MIT Press, 1982.

Huizinga, Johan. *Homo Ludens: A Study of the Play-Element in Culture*. Humanitas. Boston: Beacon, 1955.

Jensen, Jeppe Sinding. "Epistemology." In *The Routledge Handbook of Research Methods in the Study of Religion*, edited by Steven Engler and Michael Stausberg, 40–53. London: Routledge, 2011.

Kripal, Jeffrey J. *Authors of the Impossible: The Paranormal and the Sacred*. Chicago: University of Chicago Press, 2010. Kindle.

Kuhn, Thomas S. *The Essential Tension: Selected Studies in Scientific Tradition and Change*. Chicago: University of Chicago Press, 1977.

———. *The Structure of Scientific Revolutions*. 4th ed. Chicago: University of Chicago Press, 2012.

Kundt, Radek. "A Scientific Discipline: The Persistence of a Delusion?" In *Conversations and Controversies in the Scientific Study of Religion: Collaborative and Co-authored Essays by Luther H. Martin and Donald Wiebe*, edited by Luther H. Martin and Donald Wiebe, 256–59. Supplements to Method & Theory in the Study of Religion 4. Leiden: Brill, 2016.

Küng, Hans. *Theology for the Third Millennium*. Translated by Peter Heinegg. New York: Doubleday, 1988.

Kurtz, Paul. *The New Skepticism: Inquiry and Reliable Knowledge*. Buffalo: Prometheus, 1992.

Lakatos, Imre. *The Methodology of Scientific Research Programmes.* Edited by Gregory Currie and John Worrall. Philosophical Papers 1. Cambridge: Cambridge University Press, 1978.

Lange, Marc. "Laws of Nature." In *The Routledge Companion to Philosophy of Science,* edited by Martin Curd and Stathis Psillos, 235–43. 2nd ed. Routledge Philosophy Companions. London: Routledge, 2014. Kindle.

Laudan, Larry. *Science and Values: The Aims of Science and Their Role in Scientific Debate.* Berkeley: University of California Press, 1984.

Laughton, Charles, dir. 1955. *The Night of the Hunter.* Screenplay by James Agee. Featuring Robert Mitchum and Shelley Winters. MGM. iTunes, 2015.

Lewis, James R. "How Religions Appeal to the Authority of Science." In *Handbook of Religion and the Authority of Science,* edited by Olav Hammer and James R. Lewis, 23–40. Brill Handbooks on Contemporary Religion 3. Leiden: Brill, 2011.

Lopez, Donald S., Jr. *Buddhism and Science: A Guide for the Perplexed.* Chicago: University of Chicago Press, 2008.

Luscombe, Philip. *Groundwork of Science and Religion.* Peterborough, UK: Epworth, 2000.

Martin, Luther H., and Donald Wiebe. "Religious Studies as a Scientific Discipline: The Persistence of a Delusion." *Journal of the American Academy of Religion* 80 (2012) 587–97.

———. "Why the Possible Is not Impossible but Is Unlikely: A Response to Our Colleagues." In *Conversations and Controversies in the Scientific Study of Religion: Collaborative and Co-authored Essays by Luther H. Martin and Donald Wiebe,* 279–87. Edited by Luther H. Martin and Donald Wiebe. Leiden: Brill, 2016.

McCauley, Robert N. *Why Religion Is Natural and Science Is Not.* Oxford: Oxford University Press, 2011.

McCauley, Robert N., and E. Thomas Lawson. "Cognitive Constraints on Religious Ritual Form: A Theory of Participants' Competence with Ritual Systems." In *Bringing Ritual to Mind: Psychological Foundations of Cultural Forms,* 1–37. Cambridge: Cambridge University Press, 2002.

McCutcheon, Russell T. *Manufacturing Religion: The Discourse on Sui Generis Religion and the Politics of Nostalgia.* Oxford: Oxford University Press, 1997.

McMahan, David L. "Buddhism as the 'Religion of Science': From Colonial Ceylon to the Laboratories of Harvard." In *Handbook of Religion and the Authority of Science,* edited by Olav Hammer and James R. Lewis, 117–40. Brill Handbooks on Contemporary Religion 3. Leiden: Brill, 2011.

Mithen, Steven. *The Prehistory of the Mind: The Cognitive Origins of Art, Religion and Science.* London: Thames & Hudson, 1996.

Murphy, Nancey. *Theology in the Age of Scientific Reasoning.* Ithaca, NY: Cornell University Press, 1990.

Murray, Michael J. "Science and Religion in Constructive Engagement." In *Analytic Theology: New Essays in the Philosophy of Theology,* edited by Oliver D. Crisp and Michael C. Rea, 233–47. Oxford: Oxford University Press, 2009.

Nanda, Meera. "Madame Blavatsky's Children: Modern Hindu Encounters with Darwinism." In *Handbook of Religion and the Authority of Science,* edited by Olav Hammer and James R. Lewis, 279–344. Brill Handbooks on Contemporary Religion 3. Leiden: Brill, 2011.

Plantinga, Alvin. *Where the Conflict Really Lies: Science, Religion, and Naturalism.* Oxford: Oxford University Press, 2011.
Polanyi, Michael. *Personal Knowledge: Towards a Post-Critical Philosophy.* 1962. Reprint, Chicago: University of Chicago Press, 1974.
Polkinghorne, John C. *One World: The Interaction of Science and Theology.* Philadelphia: Templeton Foundation, 2007.
Popper, Karl R. "Back to the Presocratics." In *Conjectures and Refutations: The Growth of Scientific Knowledge*, 183–223. 1963. Reprint, London: Routledge, 2002.
———. *Conjectures and Refutations: The Growth of Scientific Knowledge.* 1963. Reprint, London: Routledge, 2002.
———. *The Logic of Scientific Discovery.* 1959. Reprint, London: Routledge, 1992.
Rayside, David. *Queer Inclusions, Continental Divisions: Public Recognition of Sexual Diversity in Canada and the United States.* Toronto: University of Toronto Press, 2008.
Rea, Michael C. "Introduction." In *Analytic Theology: New Essays in the Philosophy of Theology*, edited by Oliver D. Crisp and Michael C. Rea, 1–30. Oxford: Oxford University Press, 2009.
Riexinger, Martin. "Islamic Opposition to the Darwinian Theory of Evolution." In *Handbook of Religion and the Authority of Science*, edited by Olav Hammer and James R. Lewis, 483–510. Brill Handbooks on Contemporary Religion 3. Leiden: Brill, 2011.
Salam, Mohammed Abdus. Foreword to *Islam and Science: Religious Orthodoxy and the Battle for Rationality*, by Pervez Hoodbhoy, ix–xii. London: Zed, 1991.
Scharfstein, Sol. *Torah and Commentary: The Five Books of Moses: Translation, Rabbinic, and Contemporary Commentary.* Jersey City: Ktav, 2008.
Schellenberg, J. L. *Evolutionary Religion.* Oxford: Oxford University Press, 2013.
———. "Philosophy of Religion: A State of the Subject Report, Jay Newman Memorial Lecture in Philosophy of Religion." *Toronto Journal of Theology* 25/1 (2009) 95–110.
———. *The Will to Imagine: A Justification of Skeptical Religion.* Ithaca, NY: Cornell University Press, 2009. Kindle.
———. *The Wisdom to Doubt: A Justification of Religious Skepticism.* Ithaca, NY: Cornell University Press, 2007. Kindle.
Scherer, Jochen. "The 'Scientific' Presentation and Legitimation of the Teaching of Synchronicity in New Age Literature." In *Handbook of Religion and the Authority of Science*, edited by Olav Hammer and James R. Lewis, 673–86. Brill Handbooks on Contemporary Religion 3. Leiden: Brill, 2011.
Schröder, K. P., and Robert Connon Smith. "Distant Future of the Sun and Earth Revisited." *Monthly Notices of the Royal Astronomical Society* 386 (2008) 155–63.
Searle, John R. *The Construction of Social Reality.* New York: Free Press, 1995.
Slochower, Harry. *Mythopoesis: Mythic Patterns in the Literary Classics.* Detroit: Wayne State University Press, 1970.
Smart, Ninian. *The Science of Religion and the Sociology of Knowledge: Some Methodological Questions.* 1973. Reprint, Princeton: Princeton University Press, 2015.
———. *Worldviews: Crosscultural Explorations of Human Beliefs.* 3rd ed. Upper Saddle River, NJ: Prentice-Hall, 2000.
Sölle, Dorothee. *Thinking about God: An Introduction to Theology.* Translated by John Bowden. Harrisburg, PA: Trinity, 1990.

Spiro, Melford E. "Religion: Problems of Definition and Explanation." In *Anthropological Approaches to the Study of Religion*, edited by Michael Banton, 85–126. 1966. Reprint, London: Routledge, 2004.

Stenger, Victor J. *God and the Folly of Faith: The Incompatibility of Science and Religion*. Amherst, NY: Prometheus, 2012.

Stenmark, Mikael. *How to Relate Science and Religion: A Multidimensional Model*. Grand Rapids: Eerdmans, 2004.

———. *Rationality in Science, Religion, and Everyday Life: A Critical Evaluation of Four Models of Rationality*. Notre Dame: University of Notre Dame Press, 1995.

———. *Scientism: Science, Ethics and Religion*. Ashgate Science and Religion Series. Aldershot, UK: Ashgate, 2001.

Stokes, Geoffrey. *Popper: Philosophy, Politics and Scientific Method*. Cambridge: Polity, 1998.

Stove, David. *Scientific Irrationalism: Origins of a Postmodern Cult*. New Brunswick: Transaction, 2001.

Taylor, Charles. "Rationality." In *Rationality and Relativism*, 87–105. Edited by Martin Hollis and Steven Lukes. Cambridge: MIT Press, 1982.

Underhill, James W. *Humboldt, Worldview and Language*. Edinburgh: Edinburgh University Press, 2013.

Van Huyssteen, J. Wentzel. *Alone in the World? Human Uniqueness in Science and Theology*. Grand Rapids: Eerdmans, 2006.

———. *The Shaping of Rationality: Toward Interdisciplinarity in Theology and Science*. Grand Rapids: Eerdmans, 1999.

White, Andrew Dickson. *A History of the Warfare of Science with Theology in Christendom*. Vol. 1. 1896. Reprint, New York: Braziller, 1955.

Wiebe, Donald. *Beyond Legitimation: Essays on the Problem of Religious Knowledge*. New York: St. Martin's, 1994.

———. "Comprehensively Critical Rationalism and Commitment." In *Beyond Legitimation: Essays on the Problem of Religious Knowledge*, 1–16. New York: St. Martin's, 1994.

———. "Dissolving Rationality: The Anti-Science Phenomenon and its Implications for the Study of Religion." In *Rationality and the Study of Religion*, edited by Jeppe Sinding Jensen and Luther Martin, 167–83. 1997. Reprint, London: Routledge, 2003.

———. "Is Religious Belief Problematic?" In *Beyond Legitimation: Essays on the Problem of Religious Knowledge*, 17–28. New York: St. Martin's, 1994.

———. "Is Science Really an Implicit Religion?" In *Beyond Legitimation: Essays on the Problem of Religious Knowledge*, 87–99. New York: St. Martin's, 1994.

———. *Religion and Truth: Towards an Alternative Paradigm for the Study of Religion*. Religion and Reason 23. The Hague: Mouton, 1981.

———. "Religion, Science, and the Transformation of 'Knowledge.'" In *Beyond Legitimation: Essays on the Problem of Religious Knowledge*, 100–110. New York: St. Martin's, 1994.

———. "Science and Religion: Is Compatibility Possible?" In *Beyond Legitimation: Essays on the Problem of Religious Knowledge*, 57–73. New York: St. Martin's, 1994.

———. *The Irony of Theology and the Nature of Religious Thought*. McGill-Queen's Studies in the History of Ideas 15. Montreal: McGill-Queen's University Press, 1991.

Woodward, Andrew Ralls. *Adventure in Human Knowledges and Beliefs*. Lanham, MD: Hamilton, 2014.

Index

a priori religious concepts, 197, 219
alternative causal conceptions, 160
ancient *H. sapiens*, 11n.14
animism, 120, 153
anthropic principle, 43–44
application of meaning-enclaves in the world of natural human experience, 88, 156
apriorism, 133–34, 143–44, 171–72
argument from play, 193
arguments based on faith, 27, 128n.17
Arnal, William E., 35
as of yet unexplained, 47, 49
assumption, 12–18, 32, 52, 68–72, 107, 113, 125–26, 130–31, 139, 141, 163, 171, 181, 187, 190, 199, 210, 221; *a priori*, 64, 174; with initial plausibility, 7–8, 20–23, 166–67, 175; without initial plausibility, 155, 175
atheism. *See* methodological atheism
attempt to make religion "fit" science, 97, 169, 171
attempt to make science "fit" religion, 98, 169, 171
attitude of mind, 99, 118, 130, 138, 170
auxiliary hypotheses, 112
axial ages, 202, 221
Ayer, Alfred Jules, 89–91, 95

Barbour, Ian G., 43, 52, 108
Barrett, Justin L., 23, 153–57, 205

Bartley, William Warren, III, 58, 61–62, 64, 70, 123–32, 137, 152, 170–71, 202, 217, 219
bedrock foundation of tested, scientific beliefs, 204
belief(s): about a trans-empirical world, 37; background, 29, 112, 125, 143–44; basic, 57, 134–35, 142, 178; catechismic, 102; commonsense, 195; content of, 57, 62, 135; derived, 57, 64, 125, 132, 135; human-sourced, 195; non-tested yet faith-imbued, 4, 8, 28–29, 97–99, 179, 212; objects of, 5, 18, 22, 30–32, 38, 63–67, 90n.65, 117n.53, 123, 169, 175, 179, 206–7; propositional, 3–4, 7, 9, 22, 24, 122, 213–14; realize, identify, and explain, 63, 66, 174
belief in, 221
belief that, 221
belief-less form of evolutionary religion, 185
Berger, Peter L., 13–14, 37–38, 62, 66, 85–88, 163–64, 168, 181, 191–95, 199, 208
Blavatsky, Helena, 104n.117
Boyer, Pascal, 35–36, 41, 154–58
brute nature, 62–63, 86n.50, 117, 125, 143, 210

Cartwright, Nancy, 53
causality, 15, 33, 48, 113–14, 130, 177, 196
circularity, 35

claim: belief, 3–10, 13, 22–24, 28, 31–32, 34, 37, 57, 59–60, 62, 71, 79, 95, 122, 128, 133, 137–38, 153, 170–71, 174, 199, 212–15, 219–20; insurance, 5; knowledge, 3–10, 13, 24, 28, 30–32, 34, 57–60, 62, 104, 122, 128–29, 198–99, 211–15, 219–21
claimant: belief, 5–6, 212; insurance, 5; knowledge, 5–6, 211–12
cogency of belief about God, 154–56
cognitive: capacity, 17, 24, 101, 153–56; inference system, 24; state, 5–6, 18, 127, 211–12; values, 8–10, 50, 71, 108, 111, 127, 174, 210, 216; values peculiar to a scientific epistemology, 128n.16, 210
commitment, 23, 55, 57–59, 61, 96, 130–31, 152, 167; retreat to, 58, 125–26
community: belief, 38, 108, 170, 216; knowledge, 38, 108, 216; religious, 84, 127, 164, 202; scientific, 56, 112, 127
compatibility system, 7, 24–25, 51, 58, 60, 77, 79, 80–81, 84–85, 92–95, 99, 104, 106–7; between a scientific study of religion and a religious epistemology, 7, 24, 58, 60, 65, 156, 174, 177, 181, 209, 211–15, 217–18; demythologized, 119–21; faith-imbued, 155; neo-Tylorean, 113–15; post-Kuhnian, 108–13
conceptual and explanatory non-reductionism, 66–67
conceptualization, 18, 40, 171, 197, 219
"conflict" thesis, 78, 215
conflicting claims made by science and by religion, 25, 33, 145, 202, 214
conjecture, 4, 167
consensus, 36, 50, 110, 153
constitution of physical reality, 21, 32, 145, 178
constitutive reductionism, 66

constructive theology and cultural shaping of religiosity as social sciences, 204–5
contemporary religious life, 14, 24, 92, 135, 194, 200, 204–5, 208, 217, 221
contemporary scientific life, 97, 204, 208
conventionalist, 53
cosmos, 38, 80–81, 84–85, 93–94, 96–97, 107, 152, 164–65, 173, 180, 199, 202, 211–12, 215–17, 220–21
counterintuitive: human exercises, 203; radically, 16–17, 112, 218; representations of physical reality, 160, 218
Crisp, Oliver D., 15–16
critical: discussion, 101; rationalism, 47, 59 70; realist, 52; theory, 51n.67
criticizability, 129, 171
cultural: explosion of *H. sapiens sapiens*, 11; shaping of religiosity, 204–5; trappings, 42, 157 183, 198, 216
culturally postulated superhuman agent (CPS-agent), 10, 13, 15–16, 23, 32–33, 36, 42, 44, 61, 63, 83–84, 90, 96–98, 130, 136, 152–56, 168–69, 172, 179–81, 188, 194–98, 203, 206–7, 217–19, 221; -based, 33, 173, 179, 218; -talk, 91

deep time, 199–202
degree of testability, 59–60
deviant scientific ideas, 98
Donald, Merlin, 82
Drees, Willem B., 62, 66–68, 175, 221

emotional and psychological roles of testimonies, 167, 209
empirical: foundationalism, 134; theory, 3
epistemology: evolutionary, 141; experientialist, 133–34, 143, 145, 178, 221; modestly naturalistic,

20–21, 57, 89, 92, 124, 127, 134, 143, 165, 172, 177, 184, 189, 209–10
etymology of constructive theology, 173, 195
evidentialism, 99, 138
experience(s): background, 12; existentially oriented religious, 142; introspective and interpreted religious, 142–43; natural human, 63–64, 87–88, 125, 132–33, 156

fact(s): alleged mythological, 213; brute, 82–83, 86–88, 94–95, 114, 180, 187; institutional, 82–85, 91, 95, 152, 173, 181, 194, 212–13; social, 82–83
faith: inductive, 191–97, 200, 203, 206–9, 213–14, 216, 219, 220; operational, 186–87; postmetaphysical, 208–9, 213, 216; propositional, 186–87; struggle for, 163
falsifiability, 59–60
Feyerabend, Paul, 112
Flanagan, Owen, 93–94
Freud, Sigmund, 40, 48–49, 116

Gerrish, B. A., 28
Gilson, Étienne, 25–28
Goody, Jack, 100–101
Gould, Stephen Jay, 98–99, 100, 220
great disparity, 200

H. sapiens sapiens, 11, 216
Haack, Susan, 20–22, 30, 57–58, 62–68, 71, 107, 124–25, 133–34, 136, 139, 142–44, 152, 165, 171–73, 177–78, 180–81, 184, 189, 204–6, 209–10, 220
Habermas, Jürgen, 106–7, 174, 210
Hacking, Ian, 38, 82, 111–12
Hammer, Olav, 47, 49, 71
Hanson, Norwood Russell, 82
Hewitt, Marsha Aileen, 48
Hick, John, 42
honesty, 9, 214–15, 222

Hoodbhoy, Pervez, 43, 50, 116–19
Horton, Robin, 113–15
Huizinga, Johan, 193
human condition, 164, 181, 194, 203, 205, 209, 216
Humboldt, Wilhelm von, 39–40
Huxley, Julian, 40
Huxley, Thomas Henry, 77
hypersensitive agency detection device (HADD), 10, 23, 64, 153–55, 179, 181, 211, 219
hypothetico-deductive method, 31, 58

identity crises, 219–20
igmythicism, 87, 173, 184, 191, 194–95, 197, 204, 207–8, 210, 213–14; as a solution to the problem that science seems sociologically fragile, 218–19
igtheism, 89–90. *See also* methodological igtheism
incompatibility system: "will to power," 115–19
instrumentalism, 53, 61–62, 123–24
intentionality, 63, 83, 101; conscious, 103, 105, 115, 209; unconscious, 102, 105, 115
intersubjective, 13, 20, 22, 29, 30, 32, 49, 60, 70, 121, 133, 143–45, 167–68, 174–75, 189, 191, 206, 208, 210, 214
intrinsic impulse, 192

James, William, 151

knowledge: counter-, 69; *eros* to, 37; for the sake of knowledge, 118; local, 69; morality of, 219
Kuhn, Thomas S., 55–56, 108–11
Kundt, Radek, 218
Kurtz, Paul, 4, 89, 95, 173

Lakatos, Imre, 55
last chapter syndrome, 168
Laudan, Larry, 111
laws of nature, 52–53
legitimation strategy, 43–45, 71, 80, 119, 155

Lewis, James R., 49
Lopez, Donald S., Jr., 44, 120–21
Luckmann, Thomas, 37–38, 62

Martin, Luther H., 205–6
maturationally natural cognitive system, 17, 23, 159–60, 167, 172, 179, 181, 205, 207, 211
McCauley, Robert N., 112, 153, 159–61, 170, 196, 218
McCutcheon, Russell T., 35, 131
meme-transmission, 157
mentation, 103–5, 107, 109, 118–19, 121
methodological agnosticism, 88n.57
methodological atheism, 16, 19, 168–69, 192
"methodological atheism" about the truth of scientific statements, 19, 169
methodological igtheism, 88–89, 92
Mithen, Steven, 100
modern scientific enterprise. *See* science
modern research university, 8, 20, 58, 91, 124, 145, 165, 167, 173
"mystification" of norms and values, 94
myth(s): as informed by an inductive faith, 197; as informed by perceived signals of joy, order, and hope, 208; as mere delusions, 87, 197; human-sourced, 173–74, 208, 213
mythopoesis, 81–82

naturalism: meta-epistemological, 144; modest, 65, 133–34, 171, 184
neurotic compulsions, 116
new metaphysics for signals of transcendence, 194
"non-conflict" thesis, 78, 215
non-gnostic conception of understanding, 185n.10
non-overlapping magisteria (NOMA), 98–99, 220

pancritical rationalism, 58, 61, 64, 124, 126, 128–32, 152, 170, 175
panrationalism, 128
personal motivations for questions and problems pursued in the scientific study of religion, 209, 214
philosophical shifts in evolutionary religious thought: from involuntary belief to voluntary faith, 185; from theism to ultimism, 185
philosophy: -laden, 38; analytic, 3, 13; Aristotelian, 26; of criticism, 129; of interpretation, 143; of science and religion, 216, 220–21
place science and religion in separate "compartments," 98, 169, 171
Popper, Karl R., 51–54, 58–60, 68–70, 111, 127, 132–33, 152, 178
postmodernist challenge to the scientific study of religion, 136–37
practiced naturalness, 159
prefix *ig*, 89, 173
presumptionism, 138
proclivity toward detecting agency, 203, 217

rationality: axiological, 137; contextually based, 139–41; postfoundationalist, 139, 142, 176; postmodernist, 136, 141, 175; practical, 137; theoretical, 137; theory of, 7–9, 24, 34, 122, 125–26, 128, 130, 138–39, 176, 218; transversal, 139–41; universal, 140–41
Rea, Michael C., 16
realism: epistemic, 55; hypothetical, 140–41; innocent, 58, 62–66, 107, 124, 143, 152, 171, 173–77, 181, 208–10; naive, 47
reject the modern scientific enterprise, 96–97, 169, 171
reject the non-tested beliefs of religious life, 99, 169, 171
religion: as making "a jump," 37; cognitive science of, 13, 152–56, 159–60, 172, 179, 205; critical

theory of, 40; diachronic conception of, 184, 199–201, 204, 215; instrumentalist, 61; non-temporal status of, 202; synchronic conception of, 184, 201
religiosity, 10–11, 23–24, 35–36, 41–42, 55, 79, 118–19, 150–53, 157, 159–61, 170–71, 199, 201, 203–5, 211, 215, 218; emotionally charged, 203, 222
road map analogy to integrate natural sciences and social sciences, 206

Schellenberg, John L., 29–31, 65, 72, 95, 182–89, 199–202, 208, 215, 221
science: extraordinary, 110–11; history of, 113; instrumentalist, 61; normal, 56, 110–11; postmodernist challenge to, 136; as sociologically fragile, 160–61, 177, 217–18; for the sake of science, 118
scientism: 21–22, 66, 68–72
Searle, John R., 66, 82–83, 95, 194
Smart, Ninian, 25, 39, 41, 66, 79–82, 85–88, 92–93, 96, 98, 108, 176–77, 180, 182, 212–13, 215

Stenmark, Mikael, 4, 21–22, 69–72, 136–39, 142, 175, 221

theology: -laden, 38; academic, 15; analytic, 16; constructive, 173, 179–80, 182, 188, 191, 195–96, 199, 201–10, 216, 219, 220; experimental, 24, 152, 155, 157; faith-imbued, 27, 175; systematic, 96; temporally sensitive constructive, 210; the irony of, 209
traditional, *a priori* theism, 65, 95, 194
tu quoque argument, 109–10; immunity from, 126, 130, 137

ultimism: belief about, 185; disbelief about, 185; imaginative faith response to, 186, 189, 201
unnatural cognitive system, 159–60, 167

value maintenance, 93–94
van Huyssteen, J. Wentzel, 4, 136–37, 139–44, 176, 198

Wiebe, Donald, 5, 13, 15, 24, 37, 58–59, 81, 84, 99–103, 109, 137, 168, 175, 205–6, 219

www.ingramcontent.com/pod-product-compliance
Lightning Source LLC
Chambersburg PA
CBHW051055230426
43667CB00013B/2304